HERMAN REITH, C.S.C.

Department of Philosophy
University of Notre Dame

An Introduction
to
PHILOSOPHICAL
PSYCHOLOGY

Englewood Cliffs, N. J.
PRENTICE-HALL, INC.
1956

IMPRIMI POTEST

Reverend Theodore J. Mehling, C.S.C.
Provincial

✠ *IMPRIMATUR*

The Most Reverend Leo A. Pursley, D.D.
Apostolic Administrator,
Diocese of Fort Wayne, Indiana.
November 9, 1955

FOREWORD

I particularly enjoyed reading *An Introduction to Philosophical Psychology,* and I wish to congratulate the author wholeheartedly on this scholarly work.

As far as the methodological arrangement of the book and its practical educational value are concerned, I am delighted that it offers reading selections from Aristotle and Thomas Aquinas—particularly from the latter—because they are in themselves of outstanding interest and provide us with that genuine contact with the masters and that "pure reading of a pure text" which nothing can replace. Not only students but scholars as well (particularly psychologists and psychiatrists interested in philosophy) will be grateful for the inclusion of these selections.

But I am still more appreciative of the philosophical content of the book as a whole. I refer to that kind of introduction to Thomas Aquinas' psychology that constitutes Father Reith's own "text." It is of utmost importance, to my mind, to strive for a genuine *rapprochement* between Thomistic psychology and modern psychology, and to make available to scientists and psychologists the philosophical insights by virtue of which they can make more intelligible, on the plane of theoretical reason, many problems with which they are struggling on the plane of experience, clinical observation, or therapy.

An Introduction to Philosophical Psychology appears to me a remarkable step in this direction, and, at the same time, an impressive instance of the revival of interest in the writings of Thomas Aquinas.

JACQUES MARITAIN

PREFACE

In the prologue to his *Summa Theologiae, Thomas Aquinas* * wrote:

We have kept in mind the beginners in this study, realizing that they are often hindered by the diversity of things written on the subject: partly because of the number of useless questions, articles, and arguments; and partly because the things that are necessary to learn are not given in the proper order of learning, but according to the order required by certain books, or by the occasions that happened to arise for discussing such matters; finally, these beginners have been hindered by frequent repetition, which created in their minds both weariness and confusion.[1]

I have tried to make this statement of purpose my own in *An Introduction to Philosophical Psychology*. The book is intended to serve as an introduction to the perennial problems of philosophical psychology and to the principles and solutions as they are found in the writings of *Aristotle* * and St. Thomas.

The first philosophers, says St. Thomas, began to philosophize because of wonder.[2] We are all interested in and wonder about such problems as the existence of the soul, the nature of life, and the freedom of the

---

* Items followed by asterisks are proper names and technical terms that appear in the glossary at the end of the book.

[1] St. Thomas Aquinas: *Summa Theologiae,* Part I, Prologue.

[2] St. Thomas Aquinas: *Commentary on the Metaphysics,* Book I, Lesson 3, Number 54.

will.   Aristotle and St. Thomas always approached their philosophical teachings by way of problems, for in their view philosophy comes by a kind of illuminating discovery, when the mind is in the process of solving a problem.   Philosophy is not for them an *a priori* process of learning, such as is mathematics in the order of natural learning, or sacred theology in the order of revealed truths.   In my exposition and in the selection of reading material, I have tried to adhere to the strict philosophical method of Aristotle and St. Thomas, but the skeletal construction of this work does not always allow this method to appear, nor does the present work sufficiently expose the *dialectical* * processes by which these two philosophers arrived at the principles of their psychology.

An Introduction to Philosophical Psychology is made up of two kinds of material: the first, which I call the "text," is an exposition of the teaching of Aristotle and St. Thomas based upon reading selections; the second includes the actual selections from these two philosophers, taken from various contexts in which their psychology is treated.   I have attempted to adhere closely to the method outlined in Aristotle's treatise *On the Soul* and in St. Thomas' commentary on the same work. But I have supplemented the readings from these basic works with many others, such as the *Summa Theologiae* and the *Quaestiones Disputatae* [1] where St. Thomas is writing theological treatises *on man,* rather than a philosophical treatise *on the soul as the principle of operation in man.*   I have taken many of these readings out of their original context and put them into what appears to me to be the philosophical order outlined in the treatise *On the Soul.*

All of the reading selections from both Aristotle and St. Thomas have been re-translated in order to achieve uniformity of terminology and meaning.   I have made the translation of the passages from the work of *William of Moerbecke,* * the source used by St. Thomas for his commentaries on the works of Aristotle.   At all times in the reading selections I have included continuous readings, generally full lessons chapters, or articles, rather than selected paragraphs or shorter excerpts, which might have seemed more to the point.   Besides my primary purpose, which is to acquaint the reader with the original sources and method of inquiry of Aristotle and St. Thomas, my other purpose is

---

[1] Except for the *Summa Theologiae,* I have given the English equivalent for all Latin titles found in the text and in the readings. *Quaestiones Disputatae* will be called the *Disputed Questions.* For example, a passage may be cited as *Disputed Question on Truth.*

to make available, in compact form, scarce source materials that could otherwise be found only with difficulty.

Some readers may wonder why I have restricted myself to the works of Aristotle and St. Thomas and omitted many other valuable selections from both classical and contemporary philosophers that could throw much light on the questions discussed. One reason was the advantage of having a unified point of view and method of procedure, but the most important reason was the conviction that there is more to be gained from a continuous contact with Aristotle and St. Thomas and their strict philosophical method than from any other source. If this book had as its purpose only the transmission of psychological knowledge, it could be argued that some of the selections contained here might be deleted and other selections from great philosophers of the past and from contemporary writers on psychology be profitably included. For the purpose of this introduction, however, it is more important that one coherent point of view be presented and divergent views be omitted, except where they are useful for setting up a problem.

The book is divided into four parts: the first consists of an introduction to the method of philosophical psychology and a study of the general principles that belong to all natural living things; the second is a study of the sensory powers of the soul; the third is a study of the rational powers of the soul and of habits; the fourth is a study of the nature of the human soul and of the origin of man.

The reading selections are placed at the end of each of these four divisions of the book. The reader should be forewarned, however, that the text and reading selections do not fit hand-in-glove. Often the points of doctrine found in the text are scattered throughout the readings, or may have been conclusions reached without benefit of direct textual authority in Aristotle or St. Thomas. Whenever direct references are possible, however, within the limits of the selected readings, either cross-references to the sources are given after the sub-headings, or I have incorporated the sources into the text itself.

For the convenience of the reader, a bibliography is placed before the reading selections for each part. This bibliography is not exhaustive, but rather is typical of contemporary writing in the field. The views contained in these writings do not necessarily express my own point of view. Paragraph numbers have been added so that reference to particular paragraphs can be made easily.

At the end of the book is a glossary of terms and proper names. Only when the term appears for the first time, or when the psychologist or philosopher is first mentioned, is a reference made by means of an asterisk and by italicizing.

An Introduction to Philosophical Psychology should serve as an instrument for an intelligent reading and for a lively discussion of the selections from Aristotle and St. Thomas; but it should be remembered that, although familiarity with this text and with the reading selections will stimulate the philosophical appetite, it will never satisfy it.

I want to thank all who have taken part in the preparation of this work, especially my colleagues at Notre Dame, my students, the members of the staff of Prentice-Hall who have given me invaluable help, and finally, M. Jacques Maritain for his encouragement during the preparation of this book, and in particular for showing us by example what it means to be a Christian philosopher and teacher.

H.R.

TABLE OF CONTENTS

PART III.   THE RATIONAL POWERS
OF THE SOUL

A GENERAL STUDY OF THE SOUL AND ITS POWERS

SECTION A: THE NATURE AND METHOD OF PHILOSOPHICAL PSYCHOLOGY

The etymology of the word *psychology* (from the Greek Psyche, which means *soul,* and Logos, which means *science*) introduces us at once to the subject of our study. *Psychology is the science of the soul.* Inasmuch as the soul is the subject of this inquiry, we shall investigate its common definition, its various powers, and, finally, the specific nature and origin of the human soul. Psychology does not have as its entire subject man himself, although this view is commonly held. Man is the conclusion of this inquiry rather than its subject, for it is only by studying the operations of the soul that we can come to know what man is. For the same reason, we do not consider *person* to be the subject of psychology; the notion of *person* presupposes the study of psychology and is really defined by the *metaphysician.**

In the opinion of many contemporary psychologists, the existence of the soul is a theological archaism which makes no sense today. On the other hand, many people who believe in the existence of the soul think of it as some kind of ethereal substance floating about in our bodies. The meaning of soul has become so obscure that its very existence to some seems sheer nonsense, while to others it remains a mystery

---

* See the Glossary of words and proper names at the end of the book.

1

about which they can say nothing at all. Therefore, when we say that psychology, as part of the *philosophy of nature,** is the science of the soul, we must determine more clearly what we mean by *science* and by *soul,* so that we can determine how the soul is the subject of a scientific inquiry. Let us begin with a brief reference to the meaning of *science* and point out the distinctive scientific character of the philosophy of nature, of which philosophical psychology is a part. In the next section, we shall take up the definition of the soul.

Neither in Aristotle's nor in St. Thomas' view of nature was there an essential difference between the philosophy of nature and the science of nature. If there was any distinction at all, it concerned the difference of knowledge to be attained about the general principles and general causes of the subject and that to be attained about the phenomena through which the principles and causes were made manifest. The changeableness of phenomena was an obstacle to an understanding of the physical world, yet Aristotle saw that beneath appearances lay an intelligible set of principles which could become the framework of a science in the strict sense of that term. The principles and causes of the science, about which there could be certitude, could be *abstracted* * from the phenomena. The detailed explanations of the proximate causes, however, were more or less tentative and dialectical. Hence, there arose a distinction which, perhaps, was not always clear and definite to the early philosophers of nature, but which we, in retrospect, can more easily make. We can call the certain knowledge reached through *demonstration* * and derived from general principles and causes discovered in nature the *philosophy of nature*. The knowledge derived from nature through an *experimental* * method that results in a synthesis of facts by means of *hypothesis* * and provides the direction and structure for further experimentation and discovery is called the *knowledge of experimental science*. We should be aware of the *analogous* * character of the term *science* as it is applied to these two different kinds of knowledge, realizing that the term has, because of the methods peculiar to experimental science, undergone a change from the older meaning of the term as it is applied to philosophy, namely, *universal and certain knowledge through causes.*

The Philosophy of Nature

Science is formed by a movement of the mind from first principles to conclusions. There are as many different sciences as there are sets of first principles from which conclusions may be drawn. The philosophy of nature studies *mobile being* * and draws its scientific conclusions

from its first principles: from *matter,** which is the subject of *motion;* *
and from *form,** which is the end of motion. If philosophical psychology is studied in the ideal order of learning, it is preceded by a
general philosophy of nature, studying the first principles of mobile
being as they are found in the *Physics* of Aristotle. In such a setting,
the scope of psychology can be more clearly shown and the student's
grasp of such concepts as *matter, form, agent,** and *end,** can be
presupposed.

From a general study of the natural world of change as found in
the *Physics,* one can proceed to the study of various kinds of change:
local motion (like the flight of a baseball); change in quality (like
the reddening of an apple); change in size (as in the growth of a
child); and change in substance (as in death and decay). The study
of the various kinds of change takes place in the various parts of the
philosophy of nature. Psychology forms one of these parts. It is
not a distinct science because it has no set of first principles of its own;
its principles are subtypes of the general principles of mobile being like
matter, form, agent, and *end.* But the kind of motion or change
that psychology treats is vital motion or mobile being as animated.

The philosophical psychologist wants to learn the nature of living
things—of plants, animals and man. But that which they have in
common, and that which makes them living things, is the presence
of a soul. In his treatment of living things, then, Aristotle began with
a book called *On the Soul.* After treating of what all living things
have in common insofar as they differ from the nonliving world, he
proceeded to an analysis of the parts and functions of the various kinds
of soul.

Philosophical and Experimental Psychology

The distinction between the philosophy of nature and the experimental sciences, when applied to the field of psychology, does not of
itself give rise to an antagonism between the two types of scientific
knowledge. Nor should the impression be given that each is completely independent of the other. Philosophical psychology is in itself
not a distinct science but part of the philosophy of nature, differing from
other parts of the science because it studies living beings, whose principle of movement is the soul.

Philosophical psychology as differentiated from experimental psychology deals with the more general principles while the latter deals
with more particular considerations because it operates in the field of
phenomena where principles are applied. The data of experimental

psychology should serve, therefore, to bring out more clearly the truth of the first principles and causes of philosophical psychology. While the methods, the degree of certitude, and the proximate goals of these two areas of psychology differ ultimately, they both study the same kind of object, namely, animated being, and tend toward the same goal, namely, a fuller knowledge of man in his relationship to nature.

MUTUAL DEPENDENCE OF THE TWO PSYCHOLOGIES

Because of the composite nature of man, the two psychologies can render mutual service that will greatly benefit both types of investigation. Man is highest among all the bodily creatures and the lowest among the intellectual creatures. We cannot understand him unless we see him from the vantage points of both matter and spirit. The mutual aid of the two psychologies, however, cannot consist in dividing man into two areas of research, the bodily and the spiritual, assigning to experimental psychology the first and to philosophical psychology the second. The result of such a division would be a distortion of man's nature, for man is not made up of two independent substances that can be studied in isolation. Both the philosopher and the experimental psychologist see man correctly when they see him as composed of body and soul, which constitute one harmonious composite substance.

However, not every experimental psychologist need have a detailed philosophical knowledge of psychology, nor need every philosopher treating of psychology have a detailed knowledge of experimental psychology. Just as a bricklayer can work without knowing a carpenter's trade, and a plumber without knowing the electrician's trade, so the experimental psychologist can carry on scientific work without formal training in philosophical psychology. There should be, however, as an introduction to experimental psychology, a kind of scientific knowledge that would correspond to the role of the knowledge of an architect or engineer in the building trades. In the over-all picture, philosophical psychology investigates the universal principles which underlie experimental psychology, though in its own field of research and in its own *methodology*,* experimental psychology enjoys independence. Hence, it is unfortunate if the philosopher criticizes without good reason or simply neglects the work of the experimental psychologist. He runs the risk, as *Cajetan* * said, of talking in a vacuum.[1] And it is unfortunate if the experimental psychologist regards philosophy as useless speculation.

---

[1] See quotation, p. 6.

THE METHODS OF THE TWO PSYCHOLOGIES

We have said that the experimental psychologist is independent of formal philosophical psychology in his methodology; the approach, the immediate area of investigation, and the results of the two psychologies differ. Philosophical psychology is based more immediately upon the common experience of all men, while experimental psychology is based more immediately upon controlled experimentation in which mathematics often plays a major role. Moreover, much of the data of philosophical psychology is outside the scope of experimental psychology. How, for instance, can a judgment be measured? How can the nature of free choice be put down in mathematical terms? The very notion of life itself eludes the experimental psychologist, for it cannot be analyzed by instruments that are themselves without life. The special methods of experimental psychology, therefore, are not always applicable to the area of philosophical psychology, nor are they necessary to it. It is the task of philosophical psychology, among other things, to explore those areas which cannot be analyzed by the methods of experimental psychology. It is the role of the experimental scientist to make fruitful the general principles of the philosopher by examining the phenomena in which the principles are manifest. It is his role to show the intimate connection that the material part of man has with the spiritual, and thus to unfold, in conjunction with the philosopher, a more comprehensive view of man.

The First Principles of Philosophical Psychology

The *mind,** says Aristotle, in its original condition is like a tablet on which nothing is written. Its first concepts, judgments and reasoning processes are potential to further elaboration. In like manner in a science, which is a *habitus** of the mind, the initial stages are vague and potential. Therefore, the principles of philosophical psychology, the initial definitions of *soul* and of *life,* and, in general, the whole investigation of the living world, has the note of potentiality found in the imperfect possession of knowledge.

There are two important considerations, however, in regard to these first principles of psychology. The first is that the principles must be established scrupulously, with the initial steps leading from them made correctly, because a small error in the principles and methods of a scientific investigation will lead to great errors in its conclusions.

The second consideration is that though the first principles and definitions are in the area of generalities, the goal of psychological knowledge cannot consist in these generalities. If it is scientific, psychology cannot remain satisfied with generalities, for the perfection of science is the knowledge of the particulars in the light of universal principles. If, on the one hand, we should be convinced of the necessity of a careful analysis of universal principles, we should, on the other hand, realize that this knowledge, like the vital principles of life itself, must develop and become more perfect. Philosophical psychology must keep pace with all the truly scientific developments of experimental psychology, for the goal of all psychology is the knowledge of man as he is found in the concrete conditions of his existence. Cajetan, one of the earliest commentators on the writings of St. Thomas, wrote as follows of the need of applying the general principles of our philosophy.

> Just as the judgment of the practical intellect in the technical domain is imperfect if it cannot be applied to details, that is, to individuals, so speculative judgments are imperfect unless they apply to the existing things of nature as revealed through sense experience. For the purpose of philosophical speculation is surely not to have us talk in a vacuum, but to give us a knowledge of the realities apprehended in the universe.[2]

The First Datum of Philosophical Psychology: The Existence of the Soul

We suppose in philosophical psychology the existence of the soul and the nominal definition of it as *the principle of life*. Now it may seem paradoxical to begin our study with the existence and definition of the soul. Many people deny the existence of the soul. How can it be one of the self-evident truths that serves as the basis of our investigation? However, without an agreement on the existence of the soul and on the nominal (common) definition of the soul, it is impossible to begin a study of psychology. (All scientific inquiry is based finally on some indemonstrable knowledge that is immediately evident.) As Aristotle says in the *Posterior Analytics:* "All intellectual

---

[2] Cardinal Cajetan de Vio: *Commentary on the Posterior Analytics,* Book II, Chapter 13.

teaching and learning arises from something already known," and "this may be either 'the fact of the existence of something,' or 'a comprehension of the meaning of the term used.' " [3]

The Soul: The Common Bond of Living Beings

The reason given by St. Thomas for beginning psychology with a discussion of the soul is elemental: It is because the soul is precisely what all living things have in common. The soul is a datum that cannot be demonstrated because it is a first principle and the subject of the investigation. Furthermore, no demonstration is needed because there is sufficient evidence for the existence of the soul in each person's experience of living. By this we do not mean that we have a *Platonic* * or *Cartesian* * "intuition" * of the soul, but that we must start with the existence of the soul, at least in the indeterminate meaning of the word, as a *principle of life.* We all know that there is something within us, some kind of immanent principle, by which we move ourselves, and think and desire. This experience of life does not tell us specifically what the soul is, but only that there is a principle in which our activity as living beings originates.

We call this experience an "intuition" because it is knowledge that does not involve discourse or the mediation of any other scientific principles. Nothing is more evident to us than the fact that we are alive. Whether material or spiritual, the soul is the principle of life, the source of our living operations, and its existence is known to everyone with the utmost certainty. For us to live means, for example, to feel pleasure and pain, to imagine, to fear, to plan and to choose, and so on. Of all these experiences we are conscious. And we know that the activity that we experience comes from something within us. St. Thomas said of the existence of the soul:

> When a person actually knows, he realizes that he has a soul within him; thus, the soul is known through its activity. A person knows that he has a soul and is alive and exists because he is aware of his sensation and of his knowledge, and that he experiences other things of this kind. Hence the *Philosopher* * says in IX *Ethics:* "We perceive that we perceive and we understand that we understand; and because we perceive this particular thing, we know that we exist." No one sees that he understands except by understanding something, be-

---

[3] Aristotle: *Posterior Analytics*, Book I, Chapter 1, Lines 71a 1 and 71a 11.

cause a person must first understand something to know himself; and, therefore, the soul arrives at the actual knowledge of its existence because it understands or has sensations.[4]

The certitude and the immediacy of our knowledge of the soul impels us to begin our study of psychology by defining the soul from the evidence of our own experience rather than by means of an inference from some general definition of life that can be formulated by observing life in things around us. At the very beginning of our investigation we are certain of life only in ourselves, and upon that experience we base our general definition of life. We are certain of the existence of life in plants and animals because they have operations that, in some respects, are like our own. Hence, our general definition of life depends on the awareness that we have of existence of our own soul, which is manifested to us in our sensations, in our thinking, and so on.

DIFFICULTIES INVOLVED IN THE MEANING OF SOUL

The difficulty that some people have in accepting the existence of the soul may come partially from the way in which the soul is defined and partially from the intimate nature of this experience. Since the common experience of living does not immediately furnish men with clear and distinct evidence as to the nature of the soul, there may be as many different definitions of soul as men hold opinions on the cause of life. If one person defines soul as a spiritual substance but another person does not accept the existence of spiritual substances, the latter may deny the existence of the soul on the basis of the other person's definition. Nevertheless, the second person may be just as firmly convinced as the other that there is a specific cause within him to explain his vital activities, but he does not like the word *soul*. St. Thomas said: "No one is ever deceived in the awareness of living, for he knows what is going on in his soul . . . nevertheless, many persons err in the knowledge of the nature of the soul." [5]

A second difficulty concerning the soul's existence is the very obviousness of its existence. We may miss the truth because we expect something much more difficult. The knowledge of the soul is like the knowledge of the first principles of judgment which become more elusive the more we try to analyze them.

---

[4] St. Thomas Aquinas: *Disputed Question on Truth,* Question 10, Article 8, Body of the Article.

[5] *Ibid.,* Reply to Objection 2.

So much, then, for the soul as the subject of psychology. Now let us say something about the nature of the study.

The Dignity of Psychology (Readings: I, A, No. 1)

Psychology possesses a special dignity among sciences, says St. Thomas: first, because of the excellence of its subject; second, because of its utility for other sciences; and third, because of its certitude in the sphere of science. With regard to its certitude, the contrary might appear to be true, for we seem to have only a tenuous probability about the activity of our soul. Indeed the soul seems to be much more of a mystery than do chemical compounds, which act determinately according to their less complex principles. Yet in the study of the soul, man has an approach to knowledge that he does not have in the other sciences. This unique approach gives psychology its certitude. For man is indirectly conscious of his soul in the inner experience of living. On the other hand, he cannot get inside the very natures of the objects of sciences like chemistry, botany, physics and so on. Often he can only conjecture about them; he can interpret natures apart from himself only in terms of his own experience. He measures and judges them by the norms of his own senses and intelligence; and sees them, therefore, as a kind of reflection of himself. Thus, St. Thomas and Aristotle assign a special dignity to psychology, because it has a certainty greater than that of the other branches of the philosophy of nature.

Certitude and Clarity

A faulty principle inherited from Cartesian philosophy is the identification of certitude with clarity. *Descartes* * himself, in his work entitled *A Discourse on Method,* sets down clarity and distinctness as the criteria of certitude and truth in philosophical matters. However, when we attain certitude in psychology, it does not necessarily mean that we have clarity. Certitude is really opposed to uncertainty, doubt, or probability, while clarity and distinctness are opposed to vagueness, generality or confusion. Something can be very certain but still not clear and distinct. For example, a person can be certain of another's love but may not know it clearly and distinctly. There are for all men intuitions that leave no room for doubt, but which lack the kind of clarity found in mathematical propositions. Thus certitude in psychology is not incompatible with lack of clarity.

Conclusion

Our certitude about the existence of the soul does not at the same time give us clarity about the nature of the soul. Neither at the initial stage of our inquiry when we are analyzing its general definition, nor later when we arrive at a scientific proof of its properties do we actually achieve such clarity about the human soul. In the distinction between clarity and certitude, we can understand the words of warning Aristotle gives his students in one of the opening paragraphs of his work *On the Soul:* "To achieve indisputable knowledge of the soul is one of the most difficult of tasks." [6] The difficulty does not concern the fundamental facts of experience that preface the scientific study of the soul, but rather the clarity of our knowledge about its nature, because the soul is one of those objects in respect to which—to use the figure Aristotle employs—we are like owls that cannot see in broad daylight but only in the dimness of evening.

Failing to distinguish between the confused but certain knowledge that belongs to common experience, and the distinct knowledge that belongs to mathematical science, Descartes had attributed to the initial stage of psychological investigation the qualities of knowledge that could be achieved, if ever, only after a long painstaking investigation. But it was the view of Aristotle and St. Thomas that we do not achieve in the beginning a clear and distinct intuition of the *nature* of the soul. Indeed, our knowledge about its nature comes through an indirect process called abstraction, which always retains some obscurity. While the view of Descartes is very difficult to reconcile with the many divergent opinions of philosophers on the nature of the soul, that of Aristotle and St. Thomas can be more readily reconciled with this divergence if we understand the difficulty of arriving at the knowledge of the nature of the soul. It is with a feeling of restrained optimism, then, that we proceed to the definition of the soul, the subject of our philosophical inquiry.

SECTION B: DEFINITIONS OF THE SOUL AND OF LIFE

Definitions should be formed from the weight of evidence rather than from the weight of authority. But there is an advantage in examining the opinions of others when we are in the process of

---

[6] Aristotle: *On the Soul,* Book I, Chapter 1, Line 402a10.

formulating our own views. In arriving at his definition of the soul, Aristotle examined the opinions of previous thinkers on the subject to see what truth could be gathered from them. His method has the advantage of hindsight; it profits from the insights of others while avoiding their mistakes. Aristotle said of his method:

> While we should reasonably doubt the opinions of our predecessors when there is ground for doubt, nevertheless in our own investigation we should try to understand the point of view of those who had something to say about the soul, in order to profit from anything that is worth while, and to avoid what is erroneous in their opinions.[7]

Ancient and Modern Theories on the Life-Principle

Theories on the nature of the soul varied as greatly in antiquity as in our own times, and many of the views of the ancients find their parallel in modern theories. In the first book of *On the Soul,* Aristotle outlined the many different opinions of his predecessors. Some of the early philosophers began their analysis of the soul with the phenomenon of motion, others with the experience of knowing, and still others with both of these. There are some who identified the soul with particular kinds of elements, some who thought of it as a spatial magnitude, some who regarded it as a harmony added to the body, and some, finally, who held it to be a self-moving essence. It is not difficult to find the counterpart of all these opinions among contemporary psychological theories: in the *mechanism* * of *Freud* * or in the *structuralism* * of *Titchener;* * in the *mathematical psychologism* * of *Weber,* * *Fechner* * and *Wundt;* * in the *functionalism* * of *Brentano,* * *Külpe,* * *James* * and *Dewey;* * in the *parallelism* * of *Leibnitz;* * in the *entelechy* * of *Driesch;* * in the *gestaltism* * of *Köhler* * and *Koffka* * or in many other schools of thought in modern psychology.

It is dangerous, of course, to try to arrange opinions that vary so greatly under some convenient heading like *materialism* * or *mechanism,* or *dualism,* * because there is no common agreement on what these terms mean. Furthermore, modern experimental scientists who approach the study of living things differently and more restrictively than do the philosophers, cannot be classified as materialists in the same way, for example, that *Democritus* * in ancient times and *Karl Marx* * in modern times are called materialists.

The experimental scientist as such need not, in a sense cannot, recog-

---

[7] Aristotle: *On the Soul,* Book I, Chapter 2, Line 403b20.

nize the role of all four causes in nature, because if he is pursuing knowledge as an experimental scientist and not as a philosopher, his methodology will limit him more or less to the study of the material cause. On the other hand, when the scientist goes beyond the limits of his scientific methodology and speaks as a philosopher, we may classify him under one of several philosophical points of view.

It is difficult, in any event, to summarize the opinions about the nature of the soul, without labeling them in a way that becomes inevitably too neat and oversimplified. Hence, we should try to avoid the labels as far as possible and let the facts of the positions speak for themselves. Let us take one example from among the views of earlier philosophers to serve as a background for Aristotle's definition of the soul.

THE ANCIENT ATOMISTIC THEORY OF THE LIFE-PRINCIPLE

Among the ancient materialistic interpretations of the life-principle, that of the Greek *atomistic* * school is pedagogically valuable because its principles are typical of all materialistic approaches to the study of life, and because it points up the problem for Aristotle's teaching on the nature of the soul. *Leucippus* * was the founder of the atomistic school, but little of his teaching has come down to us directly. It is through his disciple, Democritus, whose doctrine is found throughout the writing of other early Greek philosophers, that we are able to reconstruct Leucippus' atomistic view. According to the Greek atomists, nature is constituted of three elements: atoms, void, and motion. | The atoms are tiny, invisible particles, indivisible as units, but capable of being joined in different combinations and shapes. The more proximate principles of nature—earth, air, fire and water—are composed of the atoms. Among the atoms, which differ in shape and mass, the most perfect type were the round, light atoms of which the soul is constituted. A second element in nature is the void, which makes it possible for atoms to arrange themselves in various combinations. The third element is the vortex motion of the universe by which the atoms are propelled until they fall into the different combinations. Since the movement of the vortex is irrational and has no mind to cause or direct its movement, the whole of nature is deterministic according to the invariable laws of matter and motion. The early atomists taught, however, that at some point in the eternal movement of the minute particles, intelligence was formed, and this intelligence in turn caused the combinations that have souls, such as plants, animals and men.

The Greek atomists explained life in terms of a soul that was made up of the light, round atoms which gave to the composite some of those characteristics associated with life: the power of local motion, bodily heat, breathing. The soul atom's mobility came from its being light and spherical; the bodily heat came from the principle of fire which is constituted from the more elemental atoms; and the breathing came from the incessant moving in and out of the atoms in the form of air. Life continued as long as the predominance of soul-atoms could be maintained by the breathing in of the highly mobile units in the form of air and fire.

Though the early atomists held what seems to us a crude materialistic view of life, their theory is worth investigating, because in its principles it is not far removed from some of the explanations of life that appear more than two thousand years later.

LATER MATERIALISTIC THEORIES OF THE LIFE-PRINCIPLE

Materialistic explanations of life reappear in all periods of the history of philosophy. Early in modern philosophy it appeared in the mechanistic view of Descartes who held that all natural life, except that of man, which he considered solely the life of spirit and of thought, is constituted of the two principles of which the whole of physical nature is made up, namely, extension and local motion. All differences within nature, excluding the soul of man, are accidental. Minerals, plants, animals and the bodies of men, in this view, are all essentially the same, the only difference coming from the greater complexity of the composite of extension and motion. Only man has a soul in the strict philosophical meaning of that term. Strictly speaking, man is soul, and his body, being an entirely different substance, does not belong to his essence.

Except for their newer terminology, contemporary and materialistic explanations of life differ very little from the atomism of Democritus and the mechanism of Descartes. While some materialistic philosophers have seen the need of bringing in some kind of unifying principle to explain the difference between an *aggregate* * and an *organism,* * the explanation remains one that is based primarily on material causality and local motion.

The Need of an Internal Principle of Unity

We can argue against the purely materialistic interpretation of life that every living body needs an inner unifying principle of activity. Life has a unity of action from within which indicates that it is not simply an aggregate.   Unity of action, the tendency of all our organic parts toward the well-being of the living *composite,** argues for the presence of a single life-principle distinct from the material parts. Nor can structure, taken simply as the assembly of the material parts into a pattern or configuration, explain life any more than the isolated material parts explain it, for structure itself is the product of an intrinsic unifying principle.   The truth of this statement is evident especially in the process of reproduction and growth.   Unlike the *coming to be* of a machine, which starts with a complexity of materials that are given an artificial unity from the outside, a living organism starts its process of *coming to be* from a single cell which develops into a complex organic structure through the agency of a principle that is within the cell itself.   This inner principle is what Aristotle calls the soul.   This principle, the substantial form, determines the nature and the operations of living beings, and is the cause of the concerted activity of the body's diverse parts for the welfare of the whole.

Since in a purely materialistic interpretation of life, living things would be reducible to aggregates, like machines or societies, in which each part would have its own substantial form and operate in its own way (the unity of the aggregate being imposed by an extrinsic principle), this interpretation cannot adequately explain the substantial unity of our person that we all know through our experience of living. There must be some inner principle that gives unity to the whole of our being.

In the last analysis that principle cannot be itself a body, for it is precisely the characteristic of body that all substances in the physical world have in common.   But some bodies are alive and some are not. What differentiates living things from nonliving cannot be the same characteristic that makes them bodies.   The specific difference cannot be the same as the common genus.   If a person says that there is a special quality in the kind of body which is found in living beings, the question can again be asked whether that special quality is itself a body or something different.   Thus, the discussion goes on *ad infinitum* without really explaining what differentiates bodies into living and nonliving.   Hence, the soul must be a principle that is distinct from the body as such.

We shall not go into detail about other opinions which Aristotle mentions in Book I, *On the Soul*.   We have given the atomistic view simply as an illustration of the type of definition that Aristotle examined before he gave his own definition of the life-principle, and to point out the similarity between the ancient views and contemporary views on the nature of this principle.

Aristotle's First Definition of the Soul (Readings: I, B, No. 1)

Aristotle begins his own explanation with this preface:

> We first spoke of what was handed down by our predecessors on the question of the soul. Now let us go back as if we were starting all over again, and try to determine what the soul is, and to see what its most general definition is.[8]

He then gives his first definition of soul: "The soul is the first act of a natural (physical) body which has life in potency." Let us examine the details of this definition.

THE SOUL IS A FIRST ACT

The soul is the first act of a natural body. It is called *first act* because it is through the soul that matter first exists as part of a living composite. The soul, like any substantial form, gives existence as well as essence to the matter which it informs. This does not mean that the matter which is now part of a living substance did not previously have existence under some other form; but it means that the matter *as living* achieves that state of existence because of the soul.

Second act, on the other hand, presupposes the existence of a substance. A second act is any kind of perfection of the accidental order, any one of the nine categories of being that depend upon substance. A second act can be a specification of a substance like shape, color, size, or it can be an activity such as the act of walking, thinking, imagining, and so on. It is evident that secondary acts presuppose the existence of a substance, that is, that they presuppose a first act. In living things, the soul is the first act. It follows, therefore, that the manifestations of life like walking, speaking, desiring, and the like, presuppose the existence of a first act, or what Aristotle calls soul.

Because it is first act, it follows that the soul is in the category of substance. Substance is that kind of being which can exist in virtue of itself and does not need another subject in which it has existence. For example, a man is a substance but whiteness is not. *Substance* is contrasted with *accident,* the former being that which primarily has existence and the latter that which has existence in and dependent upon substance. Now the soul is in the order of substance and

---

[8] For the full text of Aristotle, see Readings: I, B, No. 1.

not in the order of accident. However, neither the soul nor the body taken separately are complete substances, but together they constitute one substance.

The soul is the *form of the body*. Because it is form in the substantial and not in the accidental order, the soul is not to be regarded as a shape, configuration, or appearance for these specifications are incidental to the essence, or at least only indirectly connected with it. The soul is the intrinsic, substantial form which causes matter to exist as part of a living composite. Nevertheless, it is true that the outward appearance of the body indirectly reflects the essence of the living being and we should not think of the soul as having no influence whatsoever on the appearance of the body. As substantial form it affects the whole of the matter that it "informs," and thus has its effect upon outward appearances of a living being.

Matter and form do not exist in separate compartments. The union of water and a sponge is far different from the matter-form or body-soul union of natural substances. We shall have a difficulty in grasping the meaning of the body-soul relationship if we depend too heavily on our imagination. If we imagine body and soul, we must imagine them as two distinct bodies. Hence, we come to think of the soul as well as the body as having dimensions, the one contained within the other or juxtaposed with it, although such notions and images are misleading and even false. Matter and form, body and soul are not two things but two principles that make up one thing.

THE SOUL IS THE FORM OF A PHYSICAL BODY

Next the soul is called the act or form of a *natural* or *physical body*. The word *physical* derives from *physis,* which in Greek means *nature.* Now there are bodies other than natural ones. A typewriter, for instance, is not a natural but an artificial body. It has no inner principle of unity through which it comes into existence and by means of which it operates. Its principle of becoming and operation is an extrinsic agent. In addition to natural and artificial bodies there are accidental bodies which are in a sense natural but lack an inner principle of unity. A vegetable garden, for example, is natural but not a natural body; it is an aggregate made up of many natural bodies. Finally, there are mathematical bodies, such as spheres, cubes and so on. Evidently they are not natural bodies. Therefore, when we say the soul is the form of a natural or physical body, we mean that it is the substantial form of the kind of body that is the product of nature and is part of the substantial composite.

THE SOUL IS THE FORM OF AN ORGANIC BODY

The body which the soul informs is called an *organic* body. The bodies of plants, animals, and men are constituted of heterogeneous materials and of a variety of parts which are called *organs*. *Organ* means instrument. These physical parts are instruments for the various operations of the soul. A diversity of organs is demanded by the diversity of activities proper to each kind of soul. Thus, the more perfect soul will demand greater variety and complexity in the organs with which it operates. In emphasizing the diversity of the organs we should keep in mind that it is the soul that makes them parts of an organism by being the principle of their operation. It is a paradox that greater substantial unity will be found among living things in something that has greater diversity of materials and organs than in what is more homogeneous. Thus, man has greater organic unity than a worm. The explanation of this is that man has a more perfect principle of substantial unity than a worm.

THE SOUL IS THE FORM OF A BODY HAVING LIFE IN POTENCY

The body which is united to the soul is said to be one having life in potency. There are two possible meanings to the phrase *having life in potency*. The first is that the materials of the natural body must be prepared for their union with the soul, because in any union of matter and form the matter must be in proximate potency for the reception of the act, just as wood, for example, has to be seasoned before it can be used for making furniture. The second meaning is that the soul as first act is in potency together with the body with respect to life understood as second act. Life as second act means vital activity, like walking, speaking, growing, and so on. Thus, a natural body which has received a soul would be in proximate potency for the exercise of vital operations, which we call second acts. In his commentary on Aristotle's definition of the soul, St. Thomas points out that the word *organic* is the equivalent of the phrase, *having life in potency,* because a body which is organically constituted by the presence of soul is in potency with respect to the vital operations of the composite.

ANALOGIES TO EXPLAIN HOW THE SOUL DETERMINES
THE ESSENCE (READINGS: I, B, NO. 2)

As a kind of epilogue to his first definition, Aristotle compares the soul to artificial forms and to the powers of organs. He wants to illustrate how the definition of any living being depends upon the kind of soul it has, just as living things in general will be defined as natural bodies that have souls as their substantial forms. The soul is compared to that quality in an instrument which makes it an axe rather than a saw; and to that power in an organ which makes it an eye that has vision, rather than an artificial or depicted eye. Aristotle says that if an axe were a living natural body, the quality that makes it to be an axe, that is, what makes it capable of cutting, would be called its soul. Likewise, if the eye were a complete substance and not merely an organ, its power of vision would be its soul, because it is from the power of vision that it receives its name. So it is with all living bodies and organic parts: a body is called a man's body, a tooth called a dog's tooth, a paw called a cat's paw, and so on, because of the kind of soul that first of all makes them live.

Aristotle's Second Definition of the Soul (Readings: I, B, No. 3)

After defining the soul as the first act of a natural organic body, Aristotle gives a second definition by means of which he intends to prove his first definition. His method is to demonstrate that the soul is the substantial form of the body because it is the intrinsic principle that causes vital activity. Therefore, the soul is the first act of the natural body having life in potency. Though the soul must actually come before the exercise of vital activity, because it is the first act as a substantial form, it is only by seeing the soul as the intrinsic cause of the activity that we can establish its more fundamental character.

His second definition of the soul is as follows: "The soul is the primary principle by which we live, sense, move and understand." [9]

Let us say something first of all about how the two definitions are related. First of all, we should note that neither definition is merely descriptive. Both refer to the soul as to the fundamental principle in living beings, namely, that by which they are radically different from nonliving beings. The first definition, however, points out a different relationship of causality than the second: The first says that the soul is the substantial form of the organic body, thus defining the soul by reason of the matter-form relationship, or by reason of the relationship of the intrinsic causes of the substance. The second definition points to the relationship of efficient and final causality when it lays stress on the soul as the principle of the vital operation which it

---

[9] See Readings: I, B, No. 3.

naturally tends to produce. Thus, the two definitions complete each other in the sense that when taken together they consider all the four causes found in nature.

The two definitions complete each other also from the point of view of knowledge, because the second definition is the proof of the first definition. The first definition is, as it were, a statement of a fact, while the second definition gives the reason for the statement. It is not sufficient, as Aristotle says, that a definition should state a fact. It should also make evident the cause.[10] He employs the second definition as evidence for the first. The type of argument employed is the *a posteriori,** that is, from effects to cause. It is not possible to employ an *a priori** argument to prove the validity of the first definition, since this would be begging the question—it would presuppose an essential knowledge of the nature of the soul in which its character of substantial form of the body would be self evident. On the contrary, it is by seeing the effects of the soul that we can judge the nature of the source. Hence, the argument is based upon the axiom, *operatio sequitur esse:* A being acts according to its nature. Since in this case, operation is what is most evident to us, we proceed from the knowledge of vital operation to the knowledge of the existence of a substantial principle of vital operations, though in the order of actuality the substantial principle must be presupposed in order that the operations take place.

In his commentary on Aristotle's second definition, St. Thomas points out that our necessary point of departure in the argument is the fact (which is generally accepted) that living things differ from nonliving. Unless there is agreement on this point, there is no use pursuing the discussion, for the whole purpose of the discussion is precisely to point out what is the nature of the principle that differentiates the living from the nonliving.

St. Thomas sets up the argument in the following syllogistic form: "The first principle of life is the form of living beings. But the soul is the first principle of life in living beings. Therefore, it is the act and form of the living body."[11] The premises of the argument have to be made evident, and this he does by an examination of the vital operations and powers that we experience within ourselves. From this evidence we conclude to the necessity of an underlying substantial form that makes the operations possible.

---

[10] Aristotle: *On the Soul*, II, 2, 413a14.
[11] See Readings: I, B, No. 3, ¶ 1, 253.

We observe in ourselves vegetative functions, sensations, movement in space, and understanding. We know that these operations belong to us, and hence they come from some principle intrinsic to us. By analogy with our own vital operations we can arrive at the fact that other things in nature are alive, because they manifest activities like our own. Such are plants, animals, and other men. We also know that some things in nature are not alive because they do not give evidence of having the kind of operations that we have. Such are stones, water, earth, and the like.

When we ask ourselves whether it is possible that the different vital operations that we experience have their ultimate explanation in diverse but independent powers within ourselves, we are faced with the evidence that our vegetative powers, our powers of sensation, our power of locomotion, and our power of understanding are not really independent entities, but that they belong to us as persons. They belong to us as parts; we employ them at our discretion. We, as substances, are the subjects in which different powers and operations inhere.

The substance in which the different powers inhere is the composite, which is made up of matter and form. It is evident that the power of sight, for example, as a vital power, exists and operates as part of the body, and so, too, with the power of locomotion. Whether there is any power in me that can exist or operate independently of my body is not clear at this first point of inquiry.

Now if the subject of my powers is the composite, there is still a question as to whether it is primarily the material or formal principle of my substance that primarily accounts for the existence and operation of these powers. We can argue that it is to the formal rather than to the material element that we must finally go for an explanation of life's activities. In the question of whether health is predicated primarily by reason of the body or by reason of a quality in the soul we must answer that it is primarily by reason of the qualitative form; likewise, in the question of vital operations we say that it is predicated primarily of the substantial form, of the matter only because of the form. The form is related to the matter as the principle of its essence because it is the specific difference. While matter is the subject that is common to all material beings, form is what differentiates matter into specifically different substances. Since the soul is the substantial form, it follows that the soul determines what is formal and specific in the living being because the body as matter is what is common to natural beings. Whether they are living or nonliving, whether they are sensitive, vegetative, or human, what all natural beings have in common is a body, but what makes them different substances and hence what makes them operate differently is the presence of soul.

Therefore, the argument concludes to the fact that the soul is the primary principle which accounts for vital operations like vegetative operations, sensing, locomotion and understanding. The soul is, therefore, the first act or substantial form of the body. It is the act of an organic body because it has different parts and different functions. Finally, it is the act of a body, which has life in potency because the soul does not "inform" any and every body, but only such as are capable of receiving it and capable of forming with it a natural composite which will result in vital operations. Thus, the original definition of the soul is proved.

A General Definition of Living Beings

After proving that the soul is the substantial form of an organic body that has life in potency by showing that the soul is the primary principle of vital operations, it is possible to give a general definition of living beings. Living beings are those things in which a soul is present; and the proof that they have a soul is that they act from an intrinsic principle and are not simply moved by other things. Different kinds of living beings will have different kinds of souls within them and will move themselves in different ways by means of an intrinsic principle.

There are three distinct ways in which the principle of self-movement operates. In the lowest kinds of living things, namely plants, the agents act through their own form and are not moved by another; but this is self-movement only with respect to the carrying out of the motion. The form through which they act is determined in them by nature. There are other beings which move themselves both with respect to the form that is the principle of movement and the carrying out of the motion. For example, they receive through themselves the form which is the principle of their operation. For example, animals perceive the object that is the cause of the movement of the sense appetites proper to animals. These beings, however, do not determine the end to which their activity leads, for this is implanted in them by nature. Finally, there are beings which have self-movement not only with respect to the principle of activity, or the form which makes the principle operate, but also and with respect to the end toward which the operation tends, since this end is freely selected. Hence, there are three different kinds of soul, three different kinds of self-movement in nature, three different kinds of life—the vegetative, the sensitive and the rational. The passage from St. Thomas in which these distinctions are made runs as follows:

Since things are said to live that act by themselves and are not, as it were, moved by other things, the more perfectly this can be attributed to something, so much more perfectly is life found in it. In moving things and things moved, three things are found in this order. First of all, the end moves the agent. The principal agent is the one which acts through its own form. Sometimes it acts through some instrument, which acts not by its own power, but by that of the principal agent. To the instrument belongs only the carrying out of the action. Accordingly, there are some beings which move themselves, not in respect to a form or end which is in them by nature, but only in respect to the carrying out of motion.

The form through which they act is determined in them by nature. Plants are of this kind of being, moving themselves to growth and decrease by a form put in them by nature.

There are other beings, however, which move themselves not only with respect to the carrying out of movement, but also with respect to the form that is the principle of movement. This they acquire of themselves. Animals are of this kind, for the principle of their movement is a form which is not bestowed by nature, but which is received through the senses. The more perfect their sensation is, therefore, the more perfectly they move themselves. Those animals which have only a sense of touch move themselves only by a motion of expansion and contraction, such as oysters. These are but a little higher than the plants. Those animals, however, which have complete sensitive powers, not only recognize that things are connected to and touch themselves, but also recognize distances and move themselves to a distant place by a progressive motion.

Although animals of this kind receive through their senses a form which is the principle of their movement, they do not determine of themselves the end of their activity or of their movement. But it is implanted in them by nature, under whose impulse they are moved to do something by a form apprehended by sense. Beyond these animals there are the ones which move themselves even with respect to an end which they have set for themselves. This, however, is done through reason and intellect, which recognize the relation between the end and what is for an end, and (reason) ordains the one to the other. Therefore, the mode of life of those beings which have an intellect is more perfect, for they move themselves more perfectly.[12]

Immanent Activity

The question now arises whether life in general may be defined as *immanent activity,** for immanent activity is certainly self-movement. Let us see, first of all, how St. Thomas defines immanent activity, by contrasting it with transitive activity, the kind that is found even in nonliving beings:

> As we said in IX, *Metaphysics,* there is a twofold kind of activity: One which is transferred into external material, like heating and cutting, and another which remains in the agent, like understanding, sensing, and willing. There is this difference between them, that the first kind of activity is not the perfection of the agent which moves, but the perfection of the thing moved, while the second kind of activity is the perfection of the agent. Because motion is the act of a mobile being, the second kind of activity, insofar as it is the act of an agent, is called its motion. Employing this comparison, we see that just as motion is the act of a mobile being, so this kind of activity is the act of an agent cause. Although motion is the act of an imperfect being, that is, one existing in potency, this later type of activity is the act of a perfect being, that is, of one existing in act. In the way that understanding is called a movement, in the same way that being that understands itself is said to move itself.[13]

In mechanical motion, for example, the motion or the energy of one body is transferred to another, like water running from one pipe into another. This kind of activity is called *transitive.* Its effect takes place in a subject different from that in which it originates and its purpose is the perfection of the thing produced rather than the perfection of the power that is operating. The meaning of immanent activity can be seen more clearly in an example like the attainment of speculative knowledge, where the effect produced by the intellect is for the perfection of the intellect. But St. Thomas speaks of immanent activity in all the cognitive and appetitive powers, whether they are sensory or intellectual. Seeing, for example, is immanent activity, because the act of seeing is produced by the power

---

[12] St. Thomas: *Summa Theologiae,* Part I, Question 18, Article 3, Body of the Article.
[13] St. Thomas: *Summa Theologiae,* I, 18, 3, *ad.* 1.

of sight and is the perfection of the power of sight. However, the power of sight has a less perfect immanent activity than the intellect.

Plants, on the other hand, do not have immanent activity according to the strict meaning of the term. The effect of the vegetative powers does not take place primarily in and for the powers themselves. Nutrition and growth, for example, have as their primary effect the welfare of the organic body rather than the good of the power of growth and of nutrition. And the power of reproduction has as its purpose the continuity of the species rather than the perfection of the reproductive power. Nevertheless, plants do have self-movement, because they move themselves in different ways through an intrinsic principle, and in this respect they are different from stones and things of that kind.

Since a general definition of life must include all species of living beings, we cannot define life in general as immanent activity in the proper sense of that term. That definition would exclude plants. Therefore, we give a broader definition, namely, that life is self-movement, which includes all natural living beings from the least perfect of plants to the most perfect of animals, which is man.

From the general definitions of the soul and of life we proceed to a study of the specific powers of the soul, so that we can give a specific definition for each of the orders of living things and eventually arrive at a scientific knowledge of the nature of man.

SECTION C: THE POWERS OF THE SOUL IN GENERAL: THE VEGETATIVE POWERS IN PARTICULAR

The soul was defined as the first principle by which we live, sense, move and understand. It would seem that these specifically different operations require specifically distinct souls, or, at least, a division of the soul into specifically distinct parts.

On the one hand we have Plato's view that man possesses three distinct souls: the sensitive, the courageous, and the intellectual. To this we object that if the soul is the first act of the body, it is not possible for one body to have three souls, since it would mean in effect that man is three different substances.

Materialistic philosophers, on the other hand, ascribed the diversity of operations in man to a diversity of materials or to a diversity of structure of the body. But it is not possible that matter be the ultimate principle of vital operations, since matter is only potentially alive, and structure is an accidental modification of matter. The soul must account for vital operations, and the distinction among vital operations must lie within the soul itself.

Therefore, in opposition to both the Platonist view which posited a plurality of souls and to the materialist's view which posited no soul but only matter, we hold that there is within the soul itself a division into specifically different parts or powers which can account for the specifically different vital operations.

A difficulty remains, however, since substantial forms, like numbers, are not divisible. They are present totally in a subject or not at all. How can we ascribe parts to what is indivisible without destroying the unity of the soul as the substantial form of the body?

How Forms Can Be Present in a Subject (Readings: I, C, No. 1)

As a starting point in the solution to this difficulty we take the distinction made by St. Thomas with respect to the ways that forms can be present in a subject. He says that, in general, forms can be present in a subject in three ways: quantitatively, essentially, and potentially. As we shall see shortly, the word potentially is to be taken in an active or dynamic sense and not in the passive sense.

QUANTITATIVE PRESENCE

Forms have a quantitative presence when they are co-extensive with the extended parts of a body. A color, for example, can be present only where there is extension, since color needs a surface on which to exist. In this way, whiteness is present in a piece of paper. This kind of presence is not to be attributed to the soul, however, because the soul is not dependent on the accident of quantity for its existence as whiteness is. Rather the quantity of a living body presupposes the existence of soul, as we shall see, because the quantity results from growth, which is a vital process. Since the soul does not exist quantitatively in the body, properly speaking, it is not divisible into parts in the same way that accidents which do depend on quantity are divisible, as whiteness is divisible, for example, through the divisibility of the surfaces on which it is present.

The plant and animal soul is, nevertheless, indirectly divisible by reason of the division of the body in which the soul inheres. Thus, a plant can be divided and become several plants, as when shoots are cut off the parent-stock. This division causes indirectly the multiplication of the powers of the soul by multiplying the subject in which these powers exist. But the division of the body of the plant does not directly multiply the specific kinds of vegetative powers. But that is our problem: What is the basis of a division of the soul into specifically distinct parts or powers?

ESSENTIAL PRESENCE

Forms have an essential presence in a subject when the whole with its parts is given its essential definition by reason of the presence of the form. The whole and the parts of living beings are named after the soul which is present in them. This is, as we saw, the substantial form. But substantial forms are indivisible units; if they are present at all, they are totally present. Thus, the human soul is totally present in the hands, in the head, or in any other part of a man. In this respect the soul is indivisible and we cannot speak of it as having essentially distinct parts.

POTENTIAL PRESENCE

Forms are totally present by potential presence when they are capable of producing all the types of activity that are latent in the nature of the subject. In this respect, the soul is totally present in the whole organic body, but not in each and every part. The soul does not have, for example, the power of seeing in the hands nor the power of hearing in the tongue. If it is a question of an organic power, the power of the soul is present and operates in that part of the body which is specifically constructed for its exercise. It is in this way that we can speak of a division of the soul into its parts. The parts of the soul are its capacities for operation. The soul is divided into as many distinct parts as there are specifically different operations of which it is the primary principle. Thus, the question of the parts of the soul refers not to a division of the soul into quantitative or essential parts, but to a division into potential or dynamic parts.

Psychologists of the Aristotelian tradition call these parts *faculties,** *potencies,** or *powers.** In contemporary psychological literature the word *faculty* has a pejorative connotation. Those who are critical of this term have in mind, possibly, a caricature of the Aristotelian faculty theory as seen in the school of psychology of *Hutcheson* * and *Reid.** In this view, faculties of the mind were looked on as isolated units which operate independently of each other, almost as separate substances. The faculties were not thought to have an organic unity but to be like independent sets of muscles that could be trained for different types of work. Because of this unfortunate connotation, many contemporary Aristotelian psychologists avoid using the term *faculty*.

The Powers Are Properties of the Soul (Readings: I, C, No. 2)

By way of understanding more precisely the powers of the soul, let us recall the meaning of *property,** as a predicable in logic. A property is a characteristic that follows necessarily only and always from the essence of something. Although a property is inseparable from the essence, it is not identical with it. Thus, the ability to construct tools is a property of reason. The *powers* of the soul are *properties* in this sense.

To show how one and the same soul can have different powers in the sense of properties and at the same time keep its substantial unity, St. Thomas explains Aristotle's analogy from geometry.[14] The triangle, square and pentagon, he says, are three different geometrical figures, each with its own essence of definition. In the same way the vegetative powers, the sensory powers, the intellectual powers, and the powers of appetite and local motion, are essentially different types of powers. But just as the pentagon contains all the potentialities of the triangle, and square, so the one rational soul contains an addition to its own special powers all the powers of the vegetative and animal souls. Without being identified formally with the vegetative and animal souls, the rational soul because of its superiority as form, can carry out all the operations of the other two.

Basis of the Distinction of Powers

We must look within the soul itself for the reason of the diversity of powers. We must not imagine, however, that the soul has compartments within which diverse powers reside, as though sight, hearing, and imagination and other powers were localized in different parts of the soul. But the soul is the basis of diverse powers by reason of the capacity that it has to perform different operations; some by means of corporeal organs, and some, as we shall see later, without the aid of corporeal organs. But the various capacities of the soul are diversified by something even more fundamental, namely, by the objects to which the powers tend, for powers are not independent of objects. The eye, for example, is a power for seeing colored objects and the ear a power for hearing sounds. Powers of the soul, therefore, only have meaning when they are related to their objects taken in the sense of *formal object.** Several distinct powers of the soul may relate to the same *material object,** for the material objects do not

---

[14] St. Thomas: *Commentary on Aristotle's On the Soul,* Book II, Lesson 5, Numbers 296–298.

diversify powers. The sense of touch and the sense of taste may come in contact with the same piece of fruit, for example, but the diversity in these powers consists precisely in attending to different properties or objects within the same or diverse material objects. The doctrine of the distinction of powers according to formal objects is contained in a text from St. Thomas' *Commentary on the Soul* and is repeated almost *verbatim* in the *Summa Theologiae*. The following passage is taken from the *Commentary*.

When it is necessary to define a power of the soul, for example, the intellectual, sensory or vegetative, we must, first of all, speak of the acts, that is, define understanding and define sensing. This is because in the order of definition, activity and operation are prior to the powers. A power, insofar as it is a potency, implies a relationship to act: For power is the principle of acting or being acted upon. Therefore, it is necessary to put *act* into the definition of the powers. And if this is true of the relationship of act to potency, there is also something prior to the acts, namely, their objects.

Acts and operations are distinguished according to their relationship to the objects. Every operation of the soul is either the act of an active or of a passive power. The objects of the passive powers are related to the operations of passive powers as agent causes, because they make the potencies active. For example, a visible object causes seeing, and every sensible object causes sensation. The objects of the active powers are related to the operations of the active powers as ends, for the objects of the active powers are the effects produced by them. It is clear that in any active power effects are produced, over and above the operations, inasmuch as the effects are the ends of the activity, as is said in Book I of the *Ethics:* the house which is built is the end of the act of building. It is is clear, therefore, that every object is related to the activity of the soul as its agent cause or as its final cause. From each of these the activity is specified. Now it is clear that specifically different kinds of agent-causes have specifically different activities just as heating is caused by heat and freezing by cold. Likewise, activity is specified by the end or final cause, just as becoming well or becoming ill differs specifically because health and sickness differ. Thus, the objects are prior to the activities of the soul in the process of becoming.

Therefore, objects must be specified before acts for the same reason that acts must be specified before powers. The objects are like food in respect to a vegetative power, a sensible object to the sense, and an intelligible object to the intellect.

We must note, however, that acts and powers of the soul are diversified only by objects taken in the formal sense of object, such as visible or audible. For if the same formal notion of object is retained, no other kind of diversity will cause a diversity in the species of activity or of the power. The same power, for example, sees a man as colored and a stone as colored. This latter kind of diversity is incidental to the notion of object as object.[15]

The Soul Is Distinct from Its Operations and Its Powers

Some philosophers have identified the soul with the activity of its powers. We may recall Descartes' definition of man as substantial thought, or *Hegel's* * definition of man as self-consciousness, or William James' definition of life as a stream of consciousness. Identifying the soul with its activity may not seem at first to be radically opposed to St. Thomas' teaching. Did he not, after all, call the soul an immanent principle of self-movement? But it is a crucial point in Thomistic philosophy that the activities of the soul are really distinct from the substance of the soul, as act is distinct from potency.

Several difficulties follow, if activities of the soul are identified with the soul. First, it means that the being of the soul is its operation, and hence the soul exists only when it is in operation. Second, it follows that the activities themselves are identical: knowledge the same as free choice; sensation the same as thought; seeing the same as hearing. From this follows the identification of the powers themselves, for if several things are identical with another thing, they are identical with each other.

The Divisions of the Powers of the Soul (Readings: I, C, No. 3)

The first division of the powers of the soul is into the vegetative powers which are nutrition, growth, and reproduction. These powers are found wherever natural life is found, whether it is in plants, animals, or men. The vegetative powers are the substratum of the other powers of the soul. The sensory and intellectual powers presuppose the existence of the vegetative, since the purpose of the vegetative powers is the production and preservation of the natural life of the body. All the powers of the soul are related to each other like the stones of a pyramid: the vegetative powers form the base and support the sensory; the sensory powers support the rational; and the rational powers are the peak, the point at which all the other powers converge. Because they are the basic powers of life and are found in all living

---

[15] St. Thomas: *Commentary on Aristotle's On the Soul,* II, 6, 304–307.

beings, we take up the vegetative powers in this first part, which is a general study of life.

The Vegetative Powers of the Soul (Readings: I, C, No. 4)

The vegetative powers to some persons might seem to lie outside the scope of philosophy and to be unworthy of philosophical study. But they belong to philosophic psychology precisely because they are the basic powers of the soul; they are not unworthy to be studied, because we cannot neglect the powers which deal more immediately with the material part of man without failing in our knowledge of the spiritual. St. Thomas said of the Platonists that they spent so much time studying the soul that they neglected the study of the body, and as a result understood neither body nor soul. Actually, the purpose of the vegetative powers is not so much the welfare of the body as of the composite of body and soul. Hence, the taking of food, the development of the body, and the use of the sexual power pertain to the whole person, and share, therefore, in the dignity of the human person.

THE POWER OF NUTRITION

The food which is provided directly by nature as in the case of plants and animals, or selected and prepared by intelligence and art as in the case of man, must be chemically transformed so that it can be assimilated by the body. This is a good example of nature working for an end, since the transformation of the food is made in accordance with the specific needs of the body. In the preparation of food, science can aid nature, but it cannot substitute for it. It is unlikely that scientists of the future will ever supersede nature's digestive process.

After the food is digested, that is, chemically prepared according to the needs of the body, it is carried by an elaborate system of canals to different parts of the body where it is used either for the growth or restoration of cell life. This activity is called *metabolism.** Because of the delicate balance of cell structure, nature must provide carefully for the transportation of the proper amount and proper quality of digested food.

When the food has been carried to the part of the body where it is needed, the final step in the process of nutrition takes place; the food is actively assimilated by the living composite. Though it retains many of the natural qualities it had as food, the material now assumes a higher type of existence: It becomes capable of self-movement, because it has been vitally united to a living body. How this transformation takes place will probably always remain a mystery for us, though we may make some generalizations about what takes place.   It is certain, for example, that the substantial form that was previously in the food is replaced by the substantial form of the being that takes nourishment.   Two substantial forms cannot exist simultaneously in the same material subject.   Some characteristics of the original substance are contained in the living substance, analagous to the way that higher types of soul virtually contain the powers of inferior souls.

Part of the difficulty in understanding the transformation of food into a living substance comes from imagining that our bodies are containers for our souls, as bottles are containers for liquid.   Actually, it is closer to the truth to imagine the soul as the container and the parts of the body as contained in it, for the parts of the body are said to be alive only when they are substantially united to the soul. As long as they are under the dynamic influence of the soul they are living parts, but they cease to be living parts as soon as they are removed from its influence.   The soul, therefore, is the point of reference.   It is, in a way, the container that holds the parts of living things together.

THE POWER OF GROWTH

Though the effect of nutrition is the growth or preservation of the bodily structure, we should not think of growth and nutrition as one undifferentiated activity, coming from one and the same power. Growth, as a natural function, is not directed simply to the assimilation of food and an increase in quantity, but rather to the organic development required by the potentialities of a particular kind of soul. The power of nutrition is instrumental to growth.   Just as the mass of the organism is subordinate to its structure, so the structure is subordinate to its function.   Each kind of soul tends to be united to a body which is quantitatively and structurally most efficient for its powers.   While there is no absolutely critical point which we may call the terminus of natural growth, there is a relative maximum and minimum beyond which nature does not operate well.   Hence, it would be ridiculous to have the soul of an elephant in the body of a flea.

Because the growth of a living thing comes from an inner principle, it differs from the growth by accretion which is found in certain nonliving compounds, such as crystals.   Growth in nonliving things is simply an increase in mass, a homogenous addition, depending solely upon the agency of extrinsic substances such as the growth of crystals or pearls.   The growth of living things, however, is more than a mere juxtaposition of homogenous parts; it is an organic development of a variety of parts and organs, under the agency of an intrinsic principle that we have already identified as *soul*.

THE POWER OF REPRODUCTION

The last of the vegetative powers and the power to which nutrition and growth are subordinated is reproduction. The reproductive power is defined as a capacity of soul by which a living natural substance can reproduce another living substance of the same species.

The power of reproduction is not the same as the power of generation found in all natural substances, which consists in the production of a new substance through the corruption of the old. The specific kind of generation which is characteristic of living beings (reproduction) differs from the generic kind of generation in several respects. First, in the generation of nonliving substances, the original substantial form must be destroyed, as when coal is destroyed to make synthetic drugs. Second, in nonliving substances, the principle of generation is extrinsic, not only to the thing produced but also to the thing which produces the substantial change, since it is not a case of self-movement as it is the chemist who makes the synthetic drugs. Third, nonliving substances do not reproduce other substances of the same nature, for the coal does not produce new coal but something different.

The act of the power of reproduction, being the act of a vegetative power of the soul, does not have the same perfection of self-movement that is found in the higher powers of the soul like intellect and will. In these higher powers, the activity begins and ends in the powers themselves and the essential goal of the act is the perfection of those powers. Reproduction is, however, an image of what takes place in the understanding. It is an activity originating within the organism itself. In the act of reproduction, the substance of the new-living thing is taken from the substance of the parents. There is a likeness, therefore, not only because the new-living substance and the old belong to the same species, but also because they have the same original matter. The assimilation of the offspring to the parents in this respect is of great importance in the question of genetics. Because of the mutual causality of matter and form, the materials of the human body transmitted by the parents predetermine in many ways the biological and intellectual characteristics of the child. Without accepting the extreme view that geniuses are born and not made, we can agree that some predispositions to talents and personality traits are transmitted by parents.

Conditions required for reproduction

Among the conditions that are required for natural reproduction are physical maturity and integrity. Therefore, though the power of reproduction is found in all species, it is not found in every member of a species. Since the purpose of reproduction is the continuation of the species (a goal that can be attained even if only a certain number of individuals of a species reproduce), the power of reproduction is not developed or exercised in every member of a species. The laws of genetics as discovered in plants and animals, must be modified to fit man's rational nature when they are applied to human reproduction. Among human beings some are not capable of having children because of physical defects, but others are not desirous of having them for legitimate reasons; and many who are physically capable of having children are not psychologically fit. Thus, the whole question of eugenics for human beings rests on a different plane. The principles that apply to plants and animals cannot be applied universally to man, because man's spiritual nature must be taken into account along with his physical nature.

A natural tendency toward immortality

Let us make one final observation about the power of reproduction. All natural reproduction is, in the words of Aristotle, "a tendency of the perishable and imperfect to share insofar as that is possible in the imperishable and the immortal." Since individual natural substances are corruptible, being composed of matter and form, and since existence, on the other hand, is an absolute good, every living being tends to sustain life in the way that it can. This is accomplished by means of reproduction. While man's natural desire to be immortal is fulfilled to some extent by reproduction of others like himself, it is not fulfilled for him personally. However, a discussion of personal immortality is not relevant at this stage of our study. The question of unending existence as pertinent to philosophical psychology will be taken up when we study the properties of the human soul.

Conclusion

We have considered briefly each of the vegetative powers insofar as they are common to all natural living substances. These powers have an excellence that comes from the fact that they are the basic powers of life. It is for this reason that we treat them in philosophic psychology. As potencies are prior to actualities and subordinate to them, so the vegetative powers are prior to but subordinate to the other powers of the soul which we shall study in subsequent parts of this text. To elucidate this matter of the relative excellence of the powers of the soul, we again employ the analogy of the pyramidal structure of these powers: the powers of the sensory part of the soul rise upon the substructure of the vegetative powers; and the rational powers rise upon the substructure of the sensory powers in the order of excellence. The lower powers always serve as instruments and necessary presuppositions for the higher powers, without formally achieving the excellence of the superior powers, while the vegetative powers share in their excellence because of the substantial unity of all powers in the living composite.

Bibliography for Part I

Andrews, Thomas G.: *Methods of Psychology.*
  New York: John Wiley & Sons, Inc., 1948, Chapter 1.

Brennan, Robert E.: *History of Psychology.*
  New York: The Macmillan Co., 1945.

Donceel, J. F.: "What Kind of Science Is Psychology?"
  The New Scholasticism, Volume XIX, 1, 117-135.

Flugel, J. C.: *A Hundred Years of Psychology.*
  New York: The Macmillan Co., 1933.

Hart, Charles A.: *The Thomistic Concept of Mental Faculty.*
  Washington, D.C.: The Catholic University of America Press, 1930.

Maritain, Jacques: *Philosophy of Nature.**
  New York: I. C. Byrne, New York Philosophical Library, 1951.

Pegis, Anton Charles: *St. Thomas and the Problem of the Soul in the 13th
                Century.*
  Toronto: St. Michael's College Press, 1934.

Shute, Clarence: *The Psychology of Aristotle.*
  New York: Columbia University Press, 1941.

Spearman, Charles: *Psychology down the Ages.*
  London: The Macmillan Co., 1937, 2 volumes.

Thomas, Ivo: *Introduction to the Translation of St. Thomas' Commentary
                on the De Anima of Aristotle.*
  New Haven: Yale University Press, 1951.

---

* This work contains an essay: "Maritain's Philosophy of the Sciences" by Yves Simon.

READINGS FOR PART I

PART I. A GENERAL STUDY OF THE SOUL AND ITS POWERS

SECTION A: THE NATURE AND METHOD OF PHILOSOPHICAL PSYCHOLOGY

No. 1. *Evaluation of the Study of the Soul and the Order of Procedure*

Aristotle: *On the Soul,* Book I, Chapter 1, Lines 402a1–403a2

St. Thomas: *Commentary on Aristotle's On the Soul,* Book I, Lesson 1, Numbers 1–15

SECTION B: DEFINITIONS OF THE SOUL AND OF LIFE

No. 1. *The First Definition of the Soul*

Aristotle: *On the Soul,* Book II, Chapter 1, Lines 412a1–412b9

St. Thomas: *Commentary on Aristotle's On the Soul,* Book II, Lesson 1, Numbers 211–234

No. 2. *Further Explanation of the Soul as a Substantial Form*

Aristotle: *On the Soul,* Book II, Chapter 2, Lines 412b10–413a10

St. Thomas: *Commentary on Aristotle's On the Soul,* Book II, Lesson 2, Numbers 235–244

No. 3. *The Second Definition of the Soul*

Aristotle: *On the Soul,* Book II, Chapter 2, Lines 413a11–413b12, and 414a4–414a28

St. Thomas: *Commentary on Aristotle's On the Soul,* Book II, Lesson 3, Numbers 253–261; and Lesson 4, Numbers 271–278

SECTION C: THE POWERS OF THE SOUL IN GENERAL: THE VEGETATIVE POWERS IN PARTICULAR

No. 1. *How Forms Can Be Present in Different Ways in a Subject*

St. Thomas: *Disputed Question on Spiritual Creatures,* Article 4, Body of the Article

No. 2. *The Relationship of the Soul to Its Powers and Operations*

St. Thomas: *Summa Theologiae,* Part I, Question 7, Article 1
Is the essence of the soul its powers?

No. 3. *An Outline of the Powers of the Soul*

Aristotle: *On the Soul,* Book II, Chapter 3, Lines 414a28–414b32

St. Thomas: *Commentary on Aristotle's On the Soul,* Book II, Lesson 5, Numbers 279–298

No. 4. *The Vegetative Powers of the Soul*

Aristotle: *On the Soul,* Book II, Chapter 4, Lines 415a23–415b28

St. Thomas: *Commentary on Aristotle's On the Soul,* Book II, Lesson 7, Numbers 309–323

SECTION A: THE NATURE AND METHOD OF PHILOSOPHICAL PSYCHOLOGY
  No. 1. Evaluation of the Study of the Soul and the Order of Procedure
    Aristotle: *On the Soul,* Book I, Chapter 1, Lines 402a1–403a2
    St. Thomas: *Commentary on Aristotle's On the Soul,* Book I, Lesson 1, Numbers 1–15

ARISTOTLE:

[¶ 1.] We believe that knowledge is a good and honorable thing. One kind of knowledge, however, may be more so than another, either because of greater certitude, or because it deals with better and more wonderful things. It is reasonable, then, that we consider our inquiry about the soul of primary importance, since it has both the qualities mentioned above.

[¶ 2.] It seems that knowledge of the soul is a great help toward attaining all truth, especially in regard to the natural world, for it is, as it were, the principle of living things.

[¶ 3.] Our aim, then, is to consider and know, first its nature and its essence and then its accidental qualities. Some of these seem to be common and to be in animals because of the presence of the soul.

[¶ 4.] To achieve indisputable knowledge of the soul is one of the most difficult of tasks. Since this is a question that is common to many areas of knowledge—I mean knowledge in regard to its substance and essence—perhaps it will seem to someone that there is one definite method of procedure for learning the essential nature of all objects as there is for demonstrating the properties of accidents. We ought, then, to look for this method. If, however, there is no one general method for discovering what a thing is, it is very difficult to proceed, for then we shall have to find a method for each individual study.

[¶ 5.] But if it is clear that some kind of demonstration or division or some other method is to be used, there still are many doubts and errors from which one must begin. For the starting points of different things are different, as are, for example, the starting points of numbers and plain figures. Perhaps the first thing necessary is to put the thing to be defined into a genus and then show what it is; that is, show whether this particular thing is a substance, a quality, a quantity, or some other one of the categories. And further, whether it is something which is in potency, or whether it is act. This is very important. Also, we should consider whether it is divisible or indivisible, and whether or not every soul is of a similar species; and if they are not, whether they are different in species or genus. Now, those who discuss the soul and seek knowledge of it seem to treat only of the human soul. We must be careful not to pass over the question whether there is one definition of it, as there is of *animal,* or whether there is another definition of each kind, as there is, for example, of *horse,* of *dog,* of *man,* or of *God.* For animal as a universal either does not exist or it is posterior; similarly, if any other general thing is predicated.

[¶ 6.] Furthermore, if there are not many souls, but rather only parts of one soul, there is the question whether we should first consider the whole soul or its parts. It is difficult to determine what parts differ by nature from each other. Then, whether we should consider first the parts, or their operations, that is, the act of understanding or the intellect, the act of sensation or the sensitive part, and so with the others. But if we consider operations first, someone may wonder whether the objects of these operations should not be treated first, for example, the sensible object before the sensitive part, the intelligible object, before the intellect.

[¶ 7.] It seems that not only is knowledge of a thing's essence useful in order to know the causes of the accidents in substances—as in mathematics knowing what *straight* and *curved* and *line* and *surface* mean in order to know how many right angles the angles of a triangle are equal to—but the accidents also help a great deal in knowing the essence. When we have something to say about accidents—either some or all of them—according to outward appearance, then we have something very pertinent to say about its essence. The starting point of every demonstration is a definition. Wherefore, definitions from which it is not·possible to know the accidents, nor to conjecture about them easily, are clearly dialectical and even useless.

ST. THOMAS:

[¶ 1.] *1.* As the Philosopher teaches in Book XI, *On Animals,* in considering any genus of things, it is first of all necessary to consider what is common and then separately what is proper to each kind of that genus. Aristotle follows this method in *First Philosophy,* for in Book I, *Metaphysics,* he discusses and considers what is common to being merely as being, and then he takes up what is proper to a particular kind of being. Without such a procedure, the same thing would be frequently repeated. There is a genus of all living beings, and so in studying living beings we should first take up what is common to all of them. Then we should consider what is proper to any particular one. What all living things have in common is a soul; in this respect they are all alike. And so, to treat the science of living things, it is first of all necessary to treat the science of the soul as common to them.

Aristotle therefore starts with science of the soul. After that, he determines the properties of individual living things in later books.

[¶ 2.] *2.* In the treatise on the soul, which we are considering here, he begins with an introduction. In this he does three things which are necessary in any introduction, for someone writing an introduction has three things in mind. He wants first of all to make his reader well disposed; secondly, to make him want to learn; and finally, to get his attention. An author achieves the first aim by pointing out the usefulness of the science; the second, by outlining the plan and divisions of the treatise; and the third, by pointing out the difficulties involved. Aristotle does these three things in his introduction. He shows first the dignity of this science; next the plan of the treatise—what it is and how it will treat of the soul, where he says "we inquire into, *etc.*"; then he shows the difficulty of this science at the words, "it seems that, *etc.*" In regard to the first point he first shows the dignity of the science and secondly its value, where he says, "it seems that, *etc.*"

[¶ 3.] *3.* Regarding the dignity of the science, we should note that every science is good—and not only good, but also worthy of esteem. Still one science may excel another. That every science is good is evident, for the good of a thing is that which perfects it as a being—and this is what everything desires and seeks. Therefore, since science is a perfection of man as man, science is a good for man. Now some goods are valuable because they have use in view of a final end—we value a good horse because he runs well. Some, however, are even more worthy of esteem—those which exist for their own sake, for we give honor to ends rather than to means. Some sciences are *practical** and some *speculative.** They differ in that the practical sciences are directed to some work, while the speculative sciences are for their own sake. Of the two, the speculative sciences are both good and worthy of esteem; the practical ones are only valuable (as means). Therefore, every speculative science is both good and honorable.

[¶ 4.] *4.* In the speculative sciences, however, we find degrees of goodness and dignity. Every science is valued insofar as it is science in act, and every act is valued on two counts—for its object and for its quality or mode. Thus, building is better than bed-making because the object of building is better than a bed. If we consider the same thing with respect to itself, the quality itself makes a difference—the better the mode of building, so much better will the building itself be. Therefore, if we consider science or its act from the viewpoint of its object, it is evident that a science of better and nobler objects is more noble; if we look at it from the viewpoint of quality or mode, the nobler science is the one with more certitude. We say then that one science is nobler than another either because it has better and nobler objects or because of its greater certitude.

[¶ 5.] 5. But in some sciences these are different. Some sciences have more certitude than others, yet their objects are inferior. Others have nobler and better objects, yet are less certain. Still, the one which treats of better and nobler things is the higher science. As the Philosopher says in Book XI, *On Animals,* this is because we are more eager to know a little about things noble and exalted, even if our knowledge of them is vague and probable, than to have certain knowledge of less noble things. The first kind of knowledge derives its nobility from itself and its essence; the second only from its mode or quality.

[¶ 6.] 6. The science of the soul has both these advantages. It is certain, for everyone knows by his own experience that he has a soul and that it is the source of his life. It is a science that has nobility because the soul is a more noble thing among lower creatures. He refers to this when he says, "We believe that knowledge is a good and honorable thing," that is, speculative knowledge. But one science is better and nobler than another in two ways. Either because it has more certitude—and so he says "according to certitude," or because it treats of higher things, that is, of things good in themselves, and "more wonderful things," that is, things of which the cause is unknown. "For both these reasons," he goes on to say, the investigation of the soul holds a primary place. He said "investigation" because he discusses the soul in a general way and does not give a final treatment of all that is involved in it. This is the nature of an "investigation." If the phrase "a primary place" is taken to include all of natural science, he does not mean primary *in order* but *in dignity,* but if it refers to the science of living things only, then he means a primacy of order.

[¶ 7.] 7. Then when he says, "It seems that knowledge of the soul is a great help," he makes his reader well-disposed by pointing out the usefulness of this science. He says that knowledge of the soul seems to be of great help in relation to the truth attained in other sciences. It is, indeed, of great profit to all the branches of philosophy. In first philosophy, for example, we cannot reach a knowledge of the divine and highest causes except through those things which we know from the power of our possible intellect, for if the nature of the possible intellect were unknown to us we could not know the realm of separated substances—as the *Commentator* * says when writing on Book XI, *Metaphysics.* In moral philosophy, too, we cannot perfectly arrive at a moral science unless we know the powers of the soul, for it is on this basis that the Philosopher, in the *Ethics,* assigns various virtues to different powers of the soul. In natural science, the science of the soul is useful because a great number of the things of nature have a soul, and the soul is the source and principle of every movement in living things. The phrase "as it were" does not mean that the soul is "like" a principle of living things but is to be taken literally.

[¶ 8.] 8. Then, at "Our aim is to consider, *etc.*" he points out the order of the treatise. He says that first we intend "to consider" by outward signs, and "to know" by demonstration, what the soul is—its nature and its essence, and then its accidental qualities, that is, its modifications. There is a diversity in these modifications, for some seem to be modifications of the soul only, such as understanding and the power of speculation. Others seem to be common to all animals because of the soul—such as pleasure, sorrow, sensation, and imagination.

[¶ 9.] 9. Then, when he says "One of the most difficult of tasks, *etc.*" he points out the difficulty of the treatise—first, the difficulty of knowing the soul's essence, and second, of knowing the accidental qualities or changeable characteristics proper to it. There is a double difficulty in regard to the essence—how it should be defined, and what the definition should consist of. And so he says that although the science of the soul is useful, it is hard to know what the soul is. This difficulty comes up in everything, since this problem of essence and what a thing is, is pertinent not only to the soul but to many other things. Our first difficulty in this respect is that we do not know how to proceed to the definition; some say by demonstration, others say we do it by dividing, still others, by composition. Aristotle preferred the method of composition.

[¶ 10.] 10. The second difficulty concerns the elements of the definition. A definition makes the essence of a thing known, and we cannot know this without knowing the principles. But different things have different principles. Thus, it is hard to know from what the principles are taken. The things that raise a difficulty for one stating and seeking a definition can be reduced to three: first, the question of the essence of the soul; second, the question of its parts; third, the question of the aids necessary for definitions that start from knowing accidental qualities.

[¶ 11.] 11. In regard to the essence of the soul, there is a doubt about the *genus,* for in defining anything we first try to find its genus. And so we must ask into what genus the soul should be put. Is it in the genus of *substance or quantity or quality*? And we must give not only the supreme genus, but also the proximate one, for when we define *man,* for example, we do not take as a genus *substance,* but *animal.* If we should find that the soul is in the genus of *substance,* we will still have to find out whether it is potential or actual, since every genus can be regarded in two ways—as in potency or as in act. Also, since some substances are composite and some are simple, we must try to find which of these the soul is; and whether it is divisible or indivisible. Also there is the question whether every soul is of one species or not. If not, we must then ask whether they differ in genus. There is difficulty, too, as to what belongs in the definition. Some things are defined as genus, others as species. And, therefore, there seems to be a question whether the definition of soul is that of a genus or of an *ultimate species.**

[¶ 12.] *12.* Some of those who inquire about the soul seem to consider only the human soul. Among the ancient philosophers there were two opinions about the soul. The *Platonists** held the idea of separated universals—that is, that there are forms and ideas which are the causes of knowledge and being in individual things. They held that there is a universal, separate soul which is the cause and exemplar of individual souls and that everything found in them is derived from it. The natural philosophers, on the other hand, maintained that there are no universal substances but only particular ones, and that there are no universals in reality. This is why the question arises as to whether we should look for only one common definition of soul as the Platonists taught, or of each and every soul—of *horse,* of *man,* or of *God*—as the natural philosophers held. He says "of God" because they believed that the heavenly bodies were gods, and said they were alive.

[¶ 13.] *13.* Aristotle, however, wishes to find a definition of both—a common definition of the soul, and a definition proper to each species of soul. Concerning this he says that "animal" as universal does not exist or is secondary. We must realize that we can talk about "universal animal" in two ways— either as universal, that is, as one thing in many individuals or predicated of many individuals, or as animal, either according to the way it is in reality, or as it is in the intellect. Considered as it is in reality, Plato held that the universal animal was an existing thing and that it existed before the individual. The reason, as we have said, is that he posited separated universals and ideas. Aristotle, however, maintains that the universal as such does not exist in reality, and that if it is anything, it is posterior to the individual. But if we take the nature of animal not according as it falls under the intention of universality, then it is something real and is prior, as that which is in potency is prior to what is in act.

[¶ 14.] *14.* Then when he says, "Furthermore, if there are not many souls, *etc.*" he touches on the difficulties which arise in regard to the soul's potencies. For in a soul there are potential parts, namely, the intellectual, sensitive, and vegetative. The question is, then, whether these are different souls, as the Platonists were inclined to think and even held, or potential parts of the soul. If they are potential parts of the soul, then we may ask whether we should discuss its potencies before its acts, or acts before potencies—as the *act of understanding* before the *intellect,* and *sensing,* which is act, before the *sensitive part* which is a potency, and in the same way for the other potencies and acts. And if we should consider acts before potencies, there is still another question, whether we should consider the objects of these acts before the potencies—that is, the object of the sense before the sense faculty, or the thing to be understood before the intellect itself.

[¶ 15.] *15.* Then when he says "Now it seems, *etc.*" he states the difficulties about the accidental qualities which are of assistance to us in arriving at a definition of the soul. In a definition, not only essential principles, but also accidental qualities ought to be made known. If essential principles could be known and correctly defined, a definition would not need the accidents. But because the essential principles of things are not known to us, we have to use accidental differences as indications of what is essential. Thus, *two-footed* is not an essential quality, but it is used as an indication of the essential, and through the accidental differences we come to the definition of essences. But this is the difficulty: We should first know what the essence of the soul is in order to know the accidents more easily, just as in mathematics it is very useful to know beforehand what the definition of *straight line, curve,* and *surface* are in showing how many right angles the angles of a triangle are equal to. On the other hand, even accidents, if they are previously determined, aid greatly in knowing definitions, as was said. If, then, anyone gives a definition through which the knowledge of the accidents of the thing defined cannot be reached, it is not a real definition, but remote and dialectical. But that definition through which one can reach knowledge of the accidents is a real one and is from the properties and essential parts of the thing.

SECTION B: DEFINITIONS OF THE SOUL
   No. 1. The First Definition of the Soul
      Aristotle: *On the Soul,* Book II, Chapter 1, Lines 412a1–412b9
      St. Thomas: *Commentary on Aristotle's On the Soul,* Book II,
                 Lesson 1, Numbers 211–234

ARISTOTLE:

[¶ 1.] We first spoke of what was handed down by our predecessors on the question of the soul. But now let us go back as if making a fresh start and try to determine what the soul is, and what its most general definition is.

[¶ 2.] We hold that there is one kind of thing that exists which we call *substance.* In this category there is *matter,* which of itself is not a determinate existing thing. There is also *form* and *species,* according to which something is said to be a determinate existing thing. Finally, there is what is composed of these. Now matter is a potency, while form is act. And act is of two kinds: one that is like habitual knowledge; and another, like actual knowing.

[¶ 3.] Bodies, above all, appear to be substances, especially natural bodies, since they are the principles of other things. Some natural bodies are alive, others are not. We say that something is alive when of itself it takes food, grows, and decreases. For this reason every natural body that has life is a substance, but a composite substance. Since, however, the body is the kind we call living, its soul surely cannot be a body.

[¶ 4.] The body is not included in those things which exist in a subject. It *is* rather the subject and the matter. The soul then must necessarily be substance, since it is the form of a physical body having life in potency. Substance is act; therefore, it is the act of this kind of body. There are two kinds of act: one like habitual knowledge and another like actual knowing. It is clear that the soul is like habitual knowledge, for the soul is in the body whether one is asleep or awake. Now being awake is like the act of knowing; being asleep is like having knowledge but not using it. In the order of generation, habitual knowledge comes first. Hence, the soul is the first act of a natural (physical) body which has life in potency.

[¶ 5.] The body we spoke of is an organic one. The parts of plants are organs, although they are very simple. The leaf's purpose is to cover the part in which the fruit is formed, and the latter part is to protect the fruit. Roots are like a mouth, since both take in nourishment.

[¶ 6.] And so, if there is a common definition which must be said of any kind of the soul, it is that it is the first act of a physical or natural organic body. It is not necessary to ask whether soul and body are one, as it is not necessary to ask whether wax and its shape, or the matter of a thing and that of which it is the matter are one. Unity and being are predicated in many ways, but what is actual is properly speaking *being*.

ST. THOMAS:

[¶ 1.] *211*. After stating the opinion of others on the soul in the first book, Aristotle proceeds in the second book to consider the soul according to his own view, which is the correct one. He does two things at this point: first, he speaks of his purpose, relating it to what has gone before; second, he proceeds to carry out his intention when he says, "And so we say that, *etc*." He says that in the first book he treated the opinions on the soul given by earlier philosophers, but that we must now determine from the beginning what the truth is. Because of its difficulty, we should undertake this rather than presume to assurance of the truth that we must yet discover. In the introduction, the question was raised whether we should first define the *soul* or its *parts*. As if answering this question, he says that we should first say what the soul is. In doing this the essence of the soul is made known; then later he will define the parts or powers of the soul. As if giving a reason for this, he adds, "what its most general definition is." For in showing what the soul is, what is common to all souls is conveyed. But when each of its parts or powers is determined, what is specific about the soul is conveyed. This is the order in teaching, to go from what is general to what is less general. This the Philosopher shows at the beginning of the *Physics*.

[¶ 2.] *212*. When he says "We hold that, *etc*."; he proceeds with the purpose he had set forth. This is divided into two parts. In the first, he shows what the soul is and in the second he determines what its parts and powers are. This first division is itself divided into two parts. First, he gives a definition of the soul which is as though the conclusion of a demonstration. Second, he gives a definition of the soul which is as though the principle of demonstration. We should keep in mind, as was said in the first book of the *Posterior Analytics,* that every definition is either the *conclusion of a demonstration*—for example, that thunder is a continuous noise in the clouds; or the *principle of demonstration*—for example, that thunder is the extinction of a fire in a cloud; or it is a *demonstration differing in position,* that is, differing in order—for example, that thunder is a continuous sound in the clouds on account of extinction of a fire in a cloud. Here we have both the conclusion and principle of the demonstration, even though it is not according to syllogistic order. The first part is divided into two subdivisions. In the first, he gives the first definition of the soul. In the second, he makes the definition clear. The first of these is again divided into two parts. In the first, he lays down certain preliminary divisions from which there is a way of investigating the definition of the soul. In the second, he investigates the definition of the soul where he says, "For this reason every physical body, *etc.*"

[¶ 3.] *213.* We should note, as the Philosopher teaches us in VII, *Metaphysics,* that there is a difference between the definition of substance and that of accident: In the definition of substance nothing is posited that is outside the essence of what is being defined, for any substance is defined by its material or formal principles. On the other hand, in defining accident something is posited which is outside the essence of what is being defined, namely, the subject, since the subject must be put in a definition of accident. For example, we say, "snubness is curvature of the nose." And this is so because the definition signifies what a thing is. Substance is what is complete in its being and in its species. Accident does not have complete being; it is dependent on substance. Likewise, no form is a complete thing as to species, but the completion of species is in the composite substance. Therefore, composite substance is so defined that in its definition nothing is placed which is outside its essence. In every definition of form something is posited which is outside the essence of form, namely, its proper subject or matter. Therefore, since the soul is a form, we must in defining it posit its matter or subject.

[¶ 4.] *214.* Hence, in the first part he proposes two divisions. The first of these is necessary to find out what should be put in the definition of soul to express its essence. The other is necessary to find out what should be put in the definition of the soul to express its subject. In regard to the first point he alludes to three divisions, the first of which is the division of being into the ten categories. This he does by saying that substance is said to be one genus of beings.

[¶ 5.] *215.* The second division is that of substance into *matter, form,* and the *composite.* Matter is that which of itself is not a determinate thing but is only in potency to be a particular thing. Form is that by which it is already a particular thing in act. Substance is the composite, which is particular thing. Form is that by which it is already a particular thing in act. Substance is the composite, which is particular thing. It is said to be a *particular thing,* that is, something that is seen to be complete in being and species. This fits only a composite substance in the realm of material things, for separated substances, although they are not composed of matter and form are nevertheless particular things, since they subsist in act and are complete in their nature. The rational soul in one respect can be called a *particular thing* insofar as it can be a thing subsisting by itself. But because it is not a complete species, but is rather part of a species, it does not altogether meet the requirements of being a particular thing. There is, then, a difference between matter and form, because matter is being in potency, while form is entelechy, that is, *act*. Through it matter is actualized. The composite which results is being in act.

[¶ 6.] *216.* The third division is that of *act,* which is taken in two ways: in one way, as science (habitual knowledge) is act; in another, as actual knowing is act. The difference between these two can be seen from their potencies. Someone may be said to be a grammarian in potency before he actually acquires habitual knowledge of grammar, by learning or finding out. This potency is actualized when he has the habit of science. But then he is again in potency to the use of his habitual knowledge, when he is actually not using it. This potency is actualized when he is actually knowing. Therefore, science (habitual knowledge) is act, and so is actual knowing.

[¶ 7.] *217.* Then when he says, "Bodies, above all, seem to be substances, *etc.,*" he points out the divisions that are prerequisite for defining the soul from the viewpoint of its subject. He alludes to three divisions. The first is of substances which are corporeal and substances which are not. Corporeal substances are most evidently substances, for incorporeal substances, whatever they are, are not evident since they are beyond the senses and can be investigated only by reason. This is what he means when he says that "bodies, above all, seem to be substances."

[¶ 8.] *218.* The second division is of bodies that are physical or natural, and bodies that are not natural but artificial. A man, a piece of wood, and a stone are natural bodies; a house and a saw are artificial. Natural bodies seem more properly to be called substances, since they are the principles of artificial bodies. Art works on material which nature supplies. Moreover, the form which is imposed on matter by art is an accidental one, such as a shape or something of that kind. Artificial bodies are in the category of substance not because of their form but because of their matter, which is natural. They are substances, therefore, insofar as they are natural bodies. Natural bodies, therefore, are more properly substances than are artificial bodies, for they are substances not only because of their matter, but also because of their form.

[¶ 9.] *219.* The third division is that of natural bodies into living and non-living. *To live* means that a thing through its own power takes nourishment, grows, and decreases. We should note that this explanation is more by way of example than definition, for it is not only when something grows and decreases that it is alive, but also when it senses and understands and exercises other vital acts. There is life in separated substances because they have understanding and will, as is shown in XI, *Metaphysics,* even though they neither grow nor take food. But because in things that are generated and corrupted, the plant soul, to which belong growth and nutrition, is the principle of life, he explains "having life" by way of example, as that which takes nourishment and grows. But the essential notion of life consists in something being able to move itself, taking "movement" here in a broad sense, to include also the operation of the intellect as a sort of motion. We say things are not alive which can be moved only by an outside principle.

[¶ 10.] *220.* Then when he says, "For this reason every natural body, *etc.,*" he investigates the definition of the soul, supposing the preceding divisions. He does three things in this part: first, he investigates the parts of the definition; second, he gives his definition at, "And so if there is a common, *etc.*"; and third, by this definition he rules out an objection. In regard to his first step, he first takes up the parts of the definition which concern the essence of the soul, and then those which concern the essence of the subject at, "The body we spoke of, *etc.*" In regard to the first he does two things: In dealing with the parts that concern the essence, he takes up first the statement that the soul is *act;* and then that it is *first act,* when he says, "There are two kinds of act, *etc.*" Therefore, he first draws the conclusion, that since physical bodies are more evident examples of substance, and every living body is a physical body, we must say that every living body is substance. And since every living body is being in act, we must say that it is a composite substance. When I say *living body,* I am saying two things: that it is a *body,* and further that it is a body *of this particular kind,* that is, one that has life. But I cannot say that that part of a body having life, which is called *body,* is a soul. By *soul* we understand that by which a living thing lives, and so we must understand it as something existing in a subject. We are taking *subject* in a wide sense, not only as a subject is called being in act, in which way an accidental quality is said to be in a subject, but even as prime matter, which is being in potency, is called a subject. But a body which receives life is more like a subject and matter than like something existing in a subject.

[¶ 11.] *221.* Since there are three sorts of substance, the composite, the matter, and the form, and the soul is neither the composite (that is, the living body) nor matter (that is, the body which is the subject of life), then the only other possibility is that the soul is a substance as the *form* or *species* of a certain kind of body (that is, of a physical body which has life in potency).

[¶ 12.] 222. He says, "having life in potency," and not simply, "having life," for by a *living body* we understand a composite living substance, but the composite is not included in the definition of the form. The matter of a living body is related to life as potency is to act. The soul is the act by which the body lives. This is like saying that a shape is the act, not of a body that actually has a shape (that is, the composite of shape and body), but of a body that is the subject of shape which is related to the shape as potency to act.

[¶ 13.] 223. Should someone think that the soul is act like some accidental form, he adds that the soul is an act as substance is act, that is, as a form; and because every form is in determined matter, it follows that it is the form of a body of such a kind as has been stated.

[¶ 14.] 224. We should know the difference between substantial and accidental form. Accidental form does not simply make something *exist,* but makes it be of such a kind, or so much, for example, large, or white, or some such thing. Substantial form, on the other hand, simply makes something exist. Accidental form, then, is added to a subject that is already existing. A substantial form is not added to a subject actually existing but only to one existing only in potency, namely, prime matter. It is evident, then, that one thing cannot have many substantial forms. The first form would make a thing simply exist; all the others would be added to a subject already existing in act. For this reason they would be added accidentally to a subject already existing in act, and would not make it simply be, but be in some way.

[¶ 15.] 225. This refutes *Avicebron's* * position in the book called the *Fons Vitae*. He holds that parallel to the divisions into genera and species there are many substantial forms in one and the same thing. For example, in this individual man there is a form that makes him a substance, another that makes him a body, a third that makes him a living body, and so on. But according to what we have said previously, one and the same substantial form makes the individual a particular thing or substance, and makes it a body and a living body, and so on. For a more perfect form not only gives to matter whatever a less perfect form gives, but gives more. The soul, then, not only makes something a substance and a body (a stone's form does that), but makes it also a living body. We should not think that the soul is the act of a body and that the body is its matter and subject as if the body is constituted of one form which makes it to be a body, and that there is added to it a soul which makes it to be a living body. But the body both exists and lives because of the soul. Bodily being, which is more imperfect, is the material principle in respect to life.

[¶ 16.] *226.* Hence, when the soul leaves the body, the body does not remain the same in species. The eye and the flesh of a dead man are called "eye" and "flesh" only equivocally, as the Philosopher shows in VII, *Metaphysics.* When the soul departs, another substantial form fills its place and constitutes a new species, since there is never corruption of one thing without generation of another.

[¶ 17.] *227.* Then when he says, "There are two kinds of act, *etc.*," he considers the second part of the definition. He says that there are two kinds of *act,* one like science, the other like actual knowing, as was shown above. The soul is evidently an act like science because the soul is in an animal both in sleep and in wakefulness. Wakefulness is like actual knowing, for actual knowing is a use of knowledge, while sleep is like habitual knowledge, which someone is not using, for in sleep the powers of an animal are at rest.

[¶ 18.] *228.* Of the two kinds of act, science is first in the order of generation in the same thing, because actual knowing is compared to habitual knowledge as act to potency. Now act, as is said in IX, *Metaphysics,* is before potency by nature, for it is the end and completion of potency. But in the order of generation and time, act is, absolutely speaking, prior to potency, for that which is potential is brought into act by something already in act. But in one and the same thing potency is prior to act, for something is first in potency and afterwards in act. Therefore, he says that science (habitual knowledge) is prior to actual knowing in the order of generation, in one and the same thing.

[¶ 19.] *229.* He then concludes that, since the soul is an act like science (habitual knowledge), it is the first act of a physical body having life in potency. He says *first act* not only to distinguish the soul from the kind of act which is in operation, but also from the forms of the elements in the body which have their own activities unless they are hindered.

[¶ 20.] *230.* Then when he says "The body we spoke of, *etc.*," he takes up the part of the definition which concerns the subject. He had said that the soul is the act of a physical body having life in potency; he now says further that this applies to every organic body. An organic body is one which has a variety of organs, a variety made necessary in a living body by the various operations of the soul. Since the soul is the most perfect form among the forms of corporeal things, it is the principle of varied operations.

Thus, it needs a variety of organs for its own perfectibility. Since forms of inanimate things, because of their imperfection, are the principles of relatively few operations, they do not need a variety of organs for their perfection.

[¶ 21.] 231. Among souls the plant soul is found to be the least perfect. In plants, therefore, there is less diversity of organs than in animals. To show that every body which receives life is organic, he uses plants, in which there is less diversity of organs, as his example. He says that the parts of plants are different organs, but that these parts are very simple, that is, homogeneous. In them there is not so great a diversity as in animals. The foot of an animal, for example, is made up of different parts, of flesh, nerve, bone, and so on. But the organic parts of plants are not composed of such a great diversity of parts.

[¶ 22.] 232. He shows that parts of plants are organic by showing that they have different operations. The leaf is a covering for the part that bears fruit, that is, the part in which the fruit is produced. The fruit-bearing part in turn protects the fruit. The roots of plants correspond to the animal mouth, for both draw in nourishment.

[¶ 23.] 233. Then when he says, "And so, if there is a common, *etc.*," he puts together the definition of soul from all that has been said. He says that if there is a common definition which must be said of every kind of soul it is this: *The soul is the first act of a physical organic body.* It is not necessary to add "having life in potency," for in place of this is put the word *organic.*

[¶ 24.] 234. Then when he says, "It is not necessary to ask, *etc.*," by means of the definition that has been given, he refutes an objection. Many wondered how a unity could result from the body and soul. Some postulated some sort of a medium by which the soul is united to the body by a kind of bond. But this difficulty does not at present merit consideration since we have already shown that the soul is the form of the body. He says we need not ask whether the body and soul become one, for there is no doubt that wax and the shape given it are one, just as matter and the form which belongs to it are one. It has been shown in VIII, *Metaphysics* that form is directly united to matter as its act. Matter united to form is the same as matter existing in act. He also refers to this when he says that one and being are said in many ways, for example, of being in potency and of being in act. For just as being in potency is not being simply but only relatively, neither is it a unity simply but only relatively. Therefore, a thing is said to be a unity just as it is said to be a being. Since the body exists because of the soul, which is its form, it follows that it is united to the soul without any medium, but inasmuch as the soul is the mover of the body, we need not rule out an intermediary, since the soul moves one part by means of another.

No. 2. Further Explanation of the Soul as a Substantial Form
    Aristotle: *On the Soul,* Book II, Chapter 1, Lines 412b10–413a10
    St. Thomas: *Commentary on Aristotle's On the Soul,* Book II, Lesson
        2, Numbers 235–244

ARISTOTLE:

[¶ 1.] We have in a general way said what the soul is. It is substance in accordance with the definition. This means that it is the essence of the kind of body we have discussed. If any instrument, like an axe, were a physical body, what it is to be an axe would be its substance, and this would be its soul. Now if the soul were taken away, the thing would no longer be an axe, except equivocally. However, it is an axe. For soul is not the essence and definition of such a body, but of a physical body which has in it a principle of motion and rest.

[¶ 2.] We should next consider what has been said with reference to the parts of the body. If the eye were an animal, its soul would be sight, for this is the substance of the eye, that is, its essence. The eye is the matter of sight. When sight is lacking, there is no eye unless we speak equivocally, as when we call an eye of a stone or a painted figure an eye. Therefore, we ought to take what is applicable to a part of the body as applicable to the whole living body, for there is present in the relationship of part to part proportionally the same relationship that exists between the whole power of sensing and the whole sensitive body. Not by being deprived of a soul is a being in potency to live, but as having a soul. A seed and a fruit is a body with such a potency. Wakefulness, then, is act in the same sense as cutting and seeing. The soul is act like sight and the capacity of a tool. But the body is like a thing in potency. Just as the eye is made up of the pupil and the power of seeing, so the animal is made up of the body and the soul.

[¶ 3.] It is evident then that the soul is not separable from the body, or at least some parts of it are not (if it naturally has parts), since the acts of some parts are the acts of the parts as such. But some acts, however, may be separated because they are not the acts of a body. It is not yet clear whether the soul is the act of the body as a sailor of a ship. These definitions of the soul are figuratively given and are descriptions.

[¶ 1.] *235.* After giving the definition of the soul, the Philosopher explains it. To accomplish this, he does two things. He explains the definition, and from it he draws a conclusion, at the words, "It is evident, *etc.*" In regard to the explanation, he first explains the definition from the viewpoint of the soul itself; second, from the viewpoint of its subject, at the words "A being deprived of soul, *etc.*" With respect to the soul itself, he first explains the definition by comparison with artificial things, and then by means of the parts of the soul, at the words, "We should next consider, *etc.*" Since artificial forms are accidental forms, and are better known to us than substantial forms because they are closer to our senses, he wisely explains the definition of the soul, which is a substantial form, by comparison with accidental forms. Likewise, the parts or powers of the soul are more evident to us than the soul itself, for in knowing the soul, we go from objects to acts, and from acts to powers, and finally through these we come to know the soul itself. Therefore, the soul's nature is more easily shown by considering its parts.

[¶ 2.] *236.* First, he remarks that we have said what the soul is universally, since the definition given applies to every soul. He has said that the soul is a substance which is a form from which we get the definition of the thing. But there is a difference between a form which is a substance and one that is not. An accidental form which is not in the genus of substance does not pertain to the essence or "whatness" of a subject, for whiteness is not of the essence of a white body. But the substantial form is of the essence or "whatness" of the subject. The soul, then, is said to be a substantial form since it is of the essence or "whatness" of a living body. And he adds, "this means that it is" substance in accordance with the definition, "the essence of the kind of body we have discussed," that is, of a body made to be what it is by such a form. For form pertains to the essence of a thing, which is signified by the definition of what the thing is.

[¶ 3.] *237.* Because substantial forms, such as forms of natural bodies, are unknown to us, he clarifies the meaning by using the example of accidental forms in works of art. He says, "If any instrument" (that is, an artificial tool), like an axe, "were a physical body" (that is, a natural body), it would have its form in the way that has been explained. Therefore, he adds, "what it is to be an axe would be its substance," that is, the form of the axe, from which the definition of axe is taken. This he calls the "essence of the axe," since according to it an axe is said to be an axe, that is, this form is the substance of the axe. He says this because the forms of natural bodies are in the genus of substance. Furthermore, if the axe were not only a physical body, but also a living one, the form of the axe would be its soul, and if the soul were separated from it, it would be an axe only equivocally, just as when the soul leaves (the body) there is no longer eye nor flesh except equivocally. But since the axe is not a natural body, its form is not the essence of a natural body, and when the form is removed, the axe, that is, the substance of the axe, still remains. For the substance of artificial bodies is their matter which remains when the artificial form has been taken away, though the artificial body itself no longer actually exists.

[¶ 4.] 238. After saying that the axe is really different from what it would be if it were a living physical body, he gives the reason for this. The reason is that soul is not the essence and definition, that is, the form of an artificial body. Rather, it is the form of a physical body that is alive. In order to show what the physical body is, he adds, "which has in it a principle of motion and rest," for natural bodies are those which have in themselves a principle of motion and rest. Nature is said to be a principle of this kind, as he states in II, *Physics*.

[¶ 5.] 239. When he says, "We should next consider, *etc.*," he explains the definition of the soul from its parts. He says that what has been said of the soul as a whole and of the living body as a whole ought to be considered now in relation to the parts of each of these; for if the eye were an animal, sight would necessarily be its soul, because sight is the substantial form of the eye, and the eye is the matter of sight, just as the organic body is the matter of the soul. When sight is taken away, what remains is called an eye only equivocally, in the way that a stone eye or a painted eye is an eye only equivocally. Things are equivocal when they have the same name, but differ in definition. Therefore, if the form from which the eye receives its definition is taken away, there remains an eye only equivocally. What applies then to a part of a living body applies also to the whole body. Just as sight is the substantial form of the eye—and without it the name *eye* is applied only equivocally—so the soul is the substantial form of a living body, and when it is taken away, the name *living body* applies to it only equivocally. This is so because one part of the sensitive soul is related to one part of the sensitive body, as the whole of the sense power is related to the whole of the sensitive body.

[¶ 6.] 240. At the words, "A being not deprived of a soul, *etc.*" he explains what he means by defining the soul as "the act of a body having life in potency." A thing is in potency in two ways: in one way when a thing does not have a principle of acting; in another way when a thing has such a principle, but is not acting by it. Now the body, whose act is the soul, has life in potency, not in the first way, but in the second. When he says a body is "a being in potency to life," he does not mean that it is potentially alive because "it is deprived of soul," that is, as lacking a life principle; but rather because it has a principle of this kind. It is true, however, that a seed and the fruit in which the seed of the plant is contained is only potentially a living body with a soul. The seed does not yet have a soul. It is in potency, therefore, like something deprived of soul.

[¶ 7.] *241.* To illustrate how the body is potential to the life that comes from the soul, he says that wakefulness is the act of the sensitive soul, just as cutting is the act of a knife and seeing is the act of the eye, for each of these acts is the operation and use of a habitual principle. But the soul is first act, like the power of sight or the capacity of an instrument. Anything of this kind is a principle of operation. However, the body which is perfected by the soul is a potency, having first act but sometimes lacking second act. Just as the eye is made up of a pupil as its matter, and of sight as its form, so, too, an animal is made up of a soul as its form and of a body as its matter.

[¶ 8.] *242.* Then, at the words, "It is evident then, *etc.*" he deduces a truth from what has been said. Since he has shown that the soul is the act of the body as a whole, that its parts are the act of the body's parts, and further that act and form are not separable from the thing of which they are the act and form, it is clear that the soul, either as a whole or in any of its parts (if it naturally has parts), cannot be separated from the body. It is evident that some parts of the soul are really the acts of parts of the body, as sight has been shown to be the act of the eye. But there is no contradiction in saying that the soul can be separated with respect to certain parts, inasmuch as certain parts of the soul are not the act of the body. We shall prove this when we discuss the intellect.

[¶ 9.] *243.* Plato held that the soul is the act of the body as its mover, not as its form. Hence, he adds that it is not yet clear whether the soul is the act of the body as a sailor is the act of a ship, namely, as its mover only.

[¶ 10.] *244.* Then, in summary, he gathers together all that has been said, and remarks what he has determined and set down is a description of the soul, "an outline"—superficial, incomplete and somewhat extrinsic. It will be completed when he comes to the innermost details by which the nature of each power of the soul is determined.

No. 3. The Second Definition of the Soul

Aristotle: *On the Soul*, Book II, Chapter 2, Lines 413a11–413b12; and 414a4–414a28

St. Thomas: *Commentary on Aristotle's On the Soul*, Book II, Lesson 3, Numbers 253–261; and Lesson 4, Numbers 271–278

ARISTOTLE:

[¶ 1.] Since it is from what is less well established but more evident to us that certitude is achieved about what is more knowable according to reason, let us undertake once more to treat of this matter.

[¶ 2.] It is not enough that a definition should show that a thing is, as do many formulations, but it should also make evident the cause that is present. At the present time definitions of the terms are like conclusions, as when we answer the question "What is squaring"? by saying that it is constructing an equilateral rectangle equal to an oblong rectangle. Such a formulation has the nature of a conclusion. But a definition that says that squaring is finding the mean states the cause of the thing.

[¶ 3.] Let us say, therefore, beginning with the facts, that an animated being differs from an inanimate one by being alive. Though living is spoken of in many ways, we say a thing is alive even though only one is present, as understanding, or sensing, or movement and rest according to place. Finally, it may mean motion and rest with respect to nutrition, decay and growth.

[¶ 4.] Therefore, all vegetative beings are seen to be alive. They are seen to have within themselves a power and principle of the kind by which they increase or decrease in contrary directions. Thus, they do not grow up and not down, but grow alike in both directions. They are continuously nourished in all their parts and live as long as they are able to take nourishment.

[¶ 5.] It is possible to separate this kind (of life) from the others, but it is impossible for others to be separated from this kind, at least, among mortal beings. This is evidently true of plants, for there is no other power of soul in them. It is by this principle that all living things live.

[¶ 6.] An animal is said to live first of all because of sensation. Even those beings that do not move or have locomotion but do have sensation, are called animals and not merely living beings.

[¶ 7.] Of all the senses touch is the first that is present in all animals. Just as the vegetative power can be separated from touch and all the other senses, so touch can be separated from the other senses. We mean by the vegetative power that part of the soul in which plants participate. All animals, however, are seen to have the sense of touch.

[¶ 8.] We shall say later what the cause is of these two facts. At present let only this be said, that the soul is the principle of the operations we have mentioned and is characterized by the vegetative, the sensitive, the intellectual and the motive powers.

ST. THOMAS:

[¶ 1.] *253.* When he says "Let us say, therefore, *etc.*" he begins to demonstrate the definition of the soul given above, and he does it in the way mentioned, namely, from effects to cause. This is the demonstration that he uses. The first principle of life is the act and form of living bodies. But the soul is the first principle of life in living beings. Therefore, it is the act and form of the living body. However, it is clear that this is an *a posteriori* demonstration, because it is only because the soul is the form of a living body that it is the principle of vital operations, and not conversely. Hence, he does two things here. First, he shows that the soul is the principle of life, and second, he shows that the first principle of life is the form of a living body where he says, "Since that whereby we live and sense, *etc.*" With respect to the first point he does three things: first, he differentiates the modes of living beings; second, at the words "Therefore, all vegetative beings, *etc.*" he shows that the soul is the principle of life; third, at the words "We now ask whether each of these, *etc.*," he shows how the parts of the soul are interrelated and by means of them operates as the principle of life.

[¶ 2.] *254.* He says first of all that in order to carry out our intention of demonstrating the definition of the soul, we must take as our starting point the fact that animate things differ from inanimate by being alive. Animated things have life and inanimate things do not. Though there are various modes of life, if only one of them is present in a being, it is said to be alive and to be animated.

[¶ 3.] *255.* He gives four modes of life: the first is intellectual, the second is sensitive, the third is locomotive, and the fourth is nutritive, together with decay and growth. He points out only four modes of life, though he previously posited five genera of operations of the soul, because here he intends to differentiate the modes of life according to the grades of living beings, which are the four just mentioned. In some living beings, namely in plants, there is found only the nutritive, together with growth and decay. In others, however, there is found in addition, sensation without locomotion, as in imperfect animals such as oysters. But in others, as in perfect animals, there is in addition, locomotion for progression from place to place, as in oxen and horses. Finally, in some, namely in men, is found besides these, understanding. The appetitive power, however, which is over and beyond these four, does not constitute a diversity in the grades of living beings, for wherever there is sensation, there is also appetite.

[¶ 4.] *256.* At the words "Therefore, all vegetative beings, *etc.*," he shows that the soul is the principle of life according to all the aforesaid modes. Here he does three things: first, he shows how the soul is the principle of life in plants; second, at the words "Because of sensation, *etc.*" he shows it in animals; and third, at the words "We shall say later, *etc.*" he points out what has been said and what remains to be said. With the first point he does two things: first, he shows that the soul is the principle of life in plants, and remarks that it was said that only one of the four modes of life is present in some beings and they are said to live. Thus, all plants are alive, since they all have within themselves a kind of power and principle by which they grow and decay.

[¶ 5.] *257.* It is clear that this principle is not mere nature, but a soul. For nature does not move in contrary directions, but the movement of growth and decay is in contrary directions, for all plants grow not only up or down but in both directions. It is clear, therefore, that the principle of these movements is not nature but a soul.

ARISTOTLE:

[¶ 1.] Since *that by which we live and sense* can be taken in two ways, just as is *that by which we know,* for we are said to know in one respect because of knowledge and in another because of the soul, both of which enter in. Likewise *that by which* we are healthy is on the one hand health, on the other, it is either a part or the whole of the body. Of these, knowledge and health are forms, species, or essences, as act in respect to what is receptive— that is, knowledge in that which is capable of knowledge and health in that which is capable of health. The activity of agents is seen to be present in the recipient and in what is disposed. Now the soul is the primary principle by which we live, sense, move and understand. Therefore, the soul will be the defining principle or form and not as matter or as a subject. As we said before, substance is spoken of in three ways: as form, as matter, or as the combination of the two. Of these three, matter is potency; form is act; then what is made up of these is the living being, and the body is not the act of the soul, but the soul is the act of a certain kind of body.

[¶ 2.] For this reason those men judged correctly, to whom it seemed that the soul does not exist without the body, but that it is itself not a body, for the soul is not a body but it is something of the body.

[¶ 3.] Therefore, it is in a body, and in one of a particular kind, and not, as some earlier thinkers held, who related it to a body without specifying the nature and quality of that body, though it is evident that not every subject is capable of receiving any form whatever. That this is the case is reasonable, since the act of anything can exist only in that which is in potency to that act, that is, in appropriate matter properly and naturally disposed. From this it is clear that the soul is the act and the essential principle of a subject having a potency to have such a soul.

ST. THOMAS:

[¶ 4.] 271. When he says "Since that by which we live and sense, etc.," he concludes from the fact that the soul is the first principle of life, to the previously assigned definition of the soul. At this point he does two things: first, he demonstrates the definition, and second, at the words "For this reason, etc.," he draws some further conclusions from the demonstration. He demonstrates the definition in this way. Whenever there are two (principles) of being or operation, one of them, namely, the primary one, is as form and the other as matter. But the soul is the primary (principle) by which we live, though we live by reason of both soul and body. Therefore, the soul is the form of the living body. This is the definition that was given previously, namely, that the soul is the first act of a physical body having life in potency. It is clear that the middle term of this demonstration is the definition of the soul as the primary principle by which we have life.

[¶ 5.] 272. There are four parts to this demonstration. First, there is the major in which he says "that by which we live and sense" is taken in two ways, in one way as form, in another as matter. In the same way, that by which we know is said in two ways, the act of knowledge proceeding either from science or from the soul. Gaining health may be for a twofold reason, one of which is health itself, and the other is a part of the body or even the whole body. In both cases one principle is formal and the other is material, for science and health are forms and like act in respect to those things which are receptive—science the form of the scientific part, that is, of the part of the soul in which science exists; and health is the form of a body that can be healed. Therefore, he says "capable of health" and "capable of science" to show the capacity of the subject for such forms. For the acts of active beings, that is, forms produced in the matter by an agent, are in the subject and in what is disposed that is, in that which naturally receives the influence of such an agent and that which is disposed to attain the final end to which this is destined, namely, the form.

[¶ 6.] *273.* In the second place, at the words "Now the soul is, *etc.,*" he gives the minor premise, namely, that the soul is the primary principle by which we live, sense, move, and understand. These four operations refer to the four kinds of life which he had mentioned previously. *Living* refers to the vegetative principle because as he had already said, life is present in all (natural) living beings because of it. We should note that although it is by reason of both health and the body that we are said to be healthy, health is the primary principle by which we are healthy, since we are said to be healthy only because the body has health. Likewise, science is the primary principle that designates us as men of science, because as regards the soul, we are men of science only when the soul has science. In the same way, we are said to be alive in our bodies when they contain a soul. Therefore, it is stated here that the soul is the primary principle by which we live, sense, and so on.

[¶ 7.] *274.* In the third place, at the words "Therefore, the soul will be, *etc.,*" he gives the conclusion and connects it with the phrase "that by which we live." He concludes from his premises that the soul is related (to the body) as the defining principle and form, and not as the matter and subject.

[¶ 8.] *275.* In the fourth place, at the words "As we said before, substance is spoken of in three ways, *etc.*" he shows that the conclusion follows from the premises. At first it (life) did not seem to follow more from the soul by reason of its being form than it did from the body, for we are said to live because of both principles. Therefore, to complete the demonstration he adds that substance is spoken of in three ways, as was said, namely, of the matter, of the form, and of the composite of the two, of which the matter is in potency and the species or form of it is the act, and what is composed of both of these is the animated being. It is clear that the body is not the act of the soul, but rather the soul is the act of some body, since the body is in potency with respect to the soul. From the foregoing demonstration it was seen that either the soul or body is the form, and since the body, as was said, is not the form of the soul, it follows that the soul is the form of the body.

[¶ 9.] *276.* At the words "For this reason, *etc.*" he deduces certain conclusions from the premises: first, that those men judged correctly when it seemed to them that the soul does not exist without the body, but that it is not a body. It is not a body because it is not matter; but it is something of body, because it is the act of the body. Since every act is present in that of which it is the act, it follows then that "for this reason it is in the body."

[¶ 10.] *277.* He deduces as a second conclusion that the soul is in a body and in one of a particular kind, namely, a physical, organic one, but not present in it in the way that earlier philosophers of nature spoke of the union of soul and body who did not specify in what body or what kind of body the soul was present. The truth is, as we have said, that the soul is in a particular kind of body, since the soul does not unite with any kind of body that happens to be present, but with a definite kind. This is reasonable, since every act naturally comes into existence in its proper and determined matter. So, too, the soul must be received in an appropriate body.

[¶ 11.] *278.* In summing up, he concludes that the soul is the act and formal principle of what has being of this kind, namely, of what is potentially alive.

SECTION C: THE POWERS OF THE SOUL IN GENERAL: THE VEGETATIVE POWERS
    IN PARTICULAR
No. 1. How Forms Can Be Present in Different Ways in a Subject
    St. Thomas: *Disputed Questions on Spiritual Creatures,* Article 4, Body
      of the Article.

[¶ 1.] The truth of this question depends on what has already been said. It was previously pointed out that the soul is united to the body not as a mover, but as its form. Afterwards, it was shown that the soul does not presuppose in matter the existence of other substantial forms which would make the body and its parts actual, but the whole body and its parts are actualized, that is, have their substantial and specific being through the soul. And when the soul departs, just as "man" or "animal" or "living body" do not remain, so neither do "eye" nor "flesh" nor "bone," except in an equivocal sense, like a painted eye or one made of stone. Since every act belongs to that principle of which it is the act, it must be that the soul, which is the act of the whole body and all its parts, is in the whole body and in every one of its parts.

[¶ 2.] But the whole body is related in one way to the soul and in another way to its parts. The soul is the first and essential act of the whole body, but the act of the parts only because of their relation to the whole. In order to make this clear we should note that because matter is for the sake of the form, the matter must be of such a kind that it suits the form. Now in corruptible things, the more imperfect forms, those that are weaker, for example, have fewer activities. Therefore, variety in their parts is not necessary, as is clear in the case of inanimate bodies. But because the soul is a higher form with greater power, it is the principle of different activities, and for the carrying out of these, a variety of parts in the body is needed. Consequently, every soul requires a variety of organs in the parts of body of which it is the act. Greater diversity is required in proportion as the soul is more perfect. The lowest forms, therefore, perfect their matter in a more uniform way, while the soul does it in a non-uniform way. The result is that the whole body, of which the soul is the first and essential form, is made up of dissimilar parts.

[¶ 3.] We must still ask what it means to say that the whole soul is in the whole body and that the whole soul is in each part. In order to clarify this, we should note that there are three kinds of wholeness. The first and more obvious is wholeness according to quantity, since a whole is thought of as a quantity which is naturally divisible into quantitative parts. This kind of wholeness, however, cannot be attributed to forms, except in an accidental sense, that is, insofar as they are accidentally divisible because of the division of quantity. In this way, whiteness is divisible because of the divisibility of a surface. This kind of divisibility is characteristic only of those forms which are co-extensive with quantity. The reason why this characteristic belongs to some forms is that they have similar matter in their total being and in a part. Therefore, forms which require great diversity in the parts of the subject do not have this kind of extension and wholeness, as, for example, the souls of the more perfect animals. The second kind of wholeness is according to the perfection of essence; to this wholeness correspond the parts of the essence: physically, matter and form in composite beings; logically, genus and difference. This perfection is susceptible of degrees, that is, more and less, in the case of accidental forms, but not in the case of substantial forms.

[¶ 4.] The third kind of wholeness is according to power. If we could speak of a given form having extension in matter, for example, *whiteness,* we would say that whiteness is wholly in every part by a wholeness of essence and of power, but not by the first sort of wholeness, which belongs to it accidentally, just as the whole essence of the species *whiteness* is found in any part of the surface. But the total quantity which it has accidentally is not present in each part, but only part is present in a part.

No. 2. *The Relationship of the Soul to Its Powers and Operations*
St. Thomas: *Summa Theologiae,* Part I, Question 77, Article 1
Is the essence of the soul its powers?

[¶ 1.] *Objection 1.* Augustine (IX, *On the Trinity*) states that "mind, knowledge, and love are in the soul substantially, or, as he says, essentially"; he says further on (X, *Ibid.*) that "memory, intelligence and will are one life, one mind, one essence."

[¶ 2.] *Objection 2.* The soul is nobler than prime matter. Since prime matter is identified with its potency, even more so should the soul be identified with its potency.

[¶ 3.] *Objection 3.* Substantial form is simpler than accidental form; a sign of this is that substantial form can neither increase nor diminish but is indivisible. Since an accidental form is its own power, much more so should the soul, which is a substantial form, be its own power.

[¶ 4.] *Objection 4.* We sense by our sense power, and understand by our intellectual power. But according to the Philosopher (Book II, *On the Soul*), "the soul is that by which we primarily sense and understand." Therefore, the soul is identical with its power.

[¶ 5.] *Objection 5.* Anything which is not of the essence of a thing is an accident. If the power of the soul is not included in its essence, the power must be an accident. But this contrary to the opinion of Augustine (IX, *On the Trinity*) who declares that mind, knowledge and love "are not in the soul as in a subject, in the way that color or figure or some other quality or quantity are in a body. Such accidents do not surpass their subjects. The mind, however, is able to love and know other things."

[¶ 6.] *Objection 6.* "A simple form cannot be a subject." (Boetius, *On the Trinity,* Book I, Chapter 11.) The soul is a simple form since it is not composed of matter and form, as was said above. (*S.T.,* I, 75, 1.[16]) Therefore, the power of the soul does not inhere in the soul as in a subject.

[¶ 7.] *Objection 7.* Accident is not a principle of substantial difference. But "sensible" and "rational," which are substantial differences, are taken from sense and reason, which are powers of the soul. Therefore, the powers of the soul are not accidents and so it seems that the powers must be the essence of the soul.

[¶ 8.] *On the contrary,* Dionysius says (XI, *On the Celestial Hierarchy*) that "Heavenly spirits are differentiated into essence, power, and operation." Therefore, with more reason in the soul the essence is one thing, and the power or potency is another.

[¶ 9.] It is impossible to hold that the essence of the soul is its power, even though some have so asserted. This is satisfactorily shown for present purposes in two ways: (a) Since potency and act divide being and every genus of being, they must be referred to the same genus. Therefore, if act is not in the genus of substance, then the potency, which is related to that act, cannot be in the genus of substance. The activity of the soul is not in the

---

[16] *S.T.* is the abbreviation for the *Summa Theologiae.*

genus of substance, except in the case of God whose operation is His substance. Thus, God's power, which is the principle of His operation, is the same as His essence. This cannot be true of souls nor of other creatures; nor even of the angels as was said above. (*S.T.,* I, 54, 3.)   (b) This also is seen to be impossible in the soul, since the soul according to its essence is act. If the essence of the soul were an immediate principle of operation, anything which had a soul would always by that fact have vital operations in act, just as something, which has a soul in act, is always alive. The soul, considered as a form, is the final term of generation and not an act ordained to further act. Hence, the soul does not have a potency to further act by reason of its essence insofar as it is a form, but by reason of its potency. Since the soul is the substrate of its own powers, it is called "first act," which is ordained to subsequent act.

[¶ 10.] Thus, we see that things which have a soul are not always in act with respect to their vital operations. For this reason the soul is defined as "the act of a body which has life in potency"; this potency, however, "does not exclude the soul." We conclude that the essence of the soul is not its power, for nothing is in potency in respect to act insofar as it is act.

[¶ 11.] *Reply to Objection 1.* Augustine speaks of the mind insofar as it knows and loves itself. Knowledge and love when referred to the soul as known and loved, are in the soul substantially or essentially, because the soul's own substance, or essence, is known and loved. The words "one life, one mind, and one essence" should be interpreted in the same way. Or, according to the opinion of some, this statement is true in the same manner in which a potential whole is predicated of its parts; the potential whole lies midway between the universal whole and the integral whole. A universal whole is present in each part according to its own essence and power; as "animal" is present in man and horse; thus, the universal whole is properly predicated of each part. The integral whole is not in any part, neither according to its whole essence, nor according to its whole power; therefore, the integral whole is in no way predicable of its singular parts; however, it is predicated (although this is done improperly) of all the parts together, as when we say that the walls, roof, and foundations are a house.

[¶ 12.] The potential whole is present in individual parts according to the whole of its essence, but not according to its whole power, hence, in a certain way it can be predicated of each part, but not as properly as the universal whole. This is the sense in which Augustine says that memory, intelligence, and will are one essence of the soul.

[¶ 13.] *Reply to Objection 2.* The act to which prime matter is in potency is the substantial form; thus, the potency of matter is nothing else than its essence.

[¶ 14.] *Reply to Objection 3.* Action as well as being belongs to the composite, for action is found only in an existing thing. The composite has being substantially in virtue of its substantial form, while it operates in virtue of the power which results from substantial form. Thus, an active accidental form is related to the substantial form of the agent (for instance, heat related to fire) as the power of the soul is related to the soul.

[¶ 15.] *Reply to Objection 4.* An accidental form is a principle of action derived from substantial form. The substantial form is the primary principle of action but not the proximate principle. It is as a primary principle that the Philosopher says that "the soul is that by which we understand and sense."

[¶ 16.] *Reply to Objection 5.* If by "accident" we mean something which is divided against *substance,* there cannot be an intermediate between substance and accident, because they are divided according to affirmation and negation, namely, as existing in a subject and not existing in a subject. Since, then, the power of the soul is not its essence, the power must be an accident and in the second division (species) of quality. If by "accident" we mean one of the five predicables, there is something midway between substances and accident, for anything essential to an object belongs to its substance. However, not everything that is outside the essence can be called an accident, but only what is not caused by essential principles of the species. A "property" is not of the essence of a thing, but is caused by essential principles of the species; hence, a property is midway between essence and accident. In this way the powers of the soul are said to be midway between substance and accident, since they are, in a sense, natural properties of the soul. When Augustine says that knowledge and love are not in the soul as accidents in a subject, we must interpret him in the sense mentioned above (*S.T.,* I, 77, 1, *ad* 1); namely, insofar as they are related to the soul, not as to a lover or a knower, but insofar as they are the loved and the known. His argument for this is as follows: If love existed in the soul which is loved, as in a subject, it would imply that an accident could transcend its subject, since other things are also loved through the soul.

[¶ 17.] *Reply to Objection 6.* Although the soul is not a composite of matter and form, it has a certain admixture of potentiality, as was mentioned above (*S.T.,* I, 75, 5); and thus it can be the subject of accidents. The proposition which was employed by Boethius is verified in God, Who is Pure Act, which is the context in which he uses it.

[¶ 18.] *Reply to Objection 7.* The specific differences, *rational* and *sensible* are not derived from the powers of sense and reason but from the sensitive and rational soul. Because substantial forms, which are of themselves unknowable, are known by their accidents, we can, at times, substitute accidents in place of substantial differences.

No. 3. An Outline of the Powers of the Soul
     Aristotle: *On the Soul,* Book II, Chapter 3, Lines 414a28–414b32
     St. Thomas: *Commentary on Aristotle's On the Soul,* Book II, Lesson 5, Numbers 279–298

ARISTOTLE:

[¶ 1.] Of the powers of the soul which have been mentioned, all are in some beings, while only certain ones are in others, and in some beings there is only the one. We are referring to the vegetative, sensitive, appetitive, locomotive, and intellectual powers.

[¶ 2.] In plants, only the vegetative power is present. In other things, both this power and the power of sensation are present. And if there is sensation, there is also appetite. Appetite is desire, anger, and will. All animals have one sense at least, the sense of touch. Wherever this sense is present, there is also joy and sorrow, the sensation of what is pleasant and what is disagreeable; and wherever these latter are present there also is *concupiscence,** which is desire for a thing that is pleasant.

[¶ 3.] They furthermore have a sense for food, for touch is the sense for food. All living things are nourished by what is dry, moist, hot and cold. The sense that perceives these is touch. They are nourished only accidentally by other sensible qualities. For neither sound, nor color, nor smell contribute anything to nutrition. Flavors, however, are found in objects of touch. Hunger and thirst are appetites: hunger for the hot and dry, thirst for the cold and moist. Taste is the delight that comes from these. We shall make certain about these things later on. For the present, let us say that animals that have touch have also appetite. The case of the imagination is not clear and must be discussed later on.

[¶ 4.] In some animals, in addition, there is a locomotive power. In others there is the intellectual power and intellect, as in man, and in any other beings of this kind, or even superior to him, if there are such.

[¶ 5.] It is clear, therefore, that the definition of the soul is one in the same way as the definition of figure is one. For neither is there figure apart from triangle and the figures consequent to it; nor is there any other soul apart from the aforementioned ones. In the case of figures, a common definition can be given which will fit all of them, but will be proper to none, and likewise in the case of the souls just mentioned. It is ridiculous, therefore, either to look for a common definition, in these things and in others, which will be the proper definition of none of those things that exist, or to look for a definition according to proper and individual species but omit a common definition. In a parallel way, that which is figured is related to the common definition of figure as those things which are according to the soul are related to the common definition of soul. For always, in that which is consequent, there is in potency that which is prior, in both figures and living things; as the triangle is contained in the square, the vegetative power in the sensitive power.

ST. THOMAS:

[¶ 6.] 279. After the common definition of the soul, Aristotle now proceeds to determine its "parts." The soul does not have parts unless its powers are considered *parts,* as many powers which are related to singulars can be called parts. To determine its parts, then, is to determine its various powers. This section has two divisions. In the first, he determines the soul's powers in general, by distinguishing them from each other. In the second, he determines the individual powers. He does this at the words, "We must speak first of food and reproduction, *etc."* The first section is subdivided into two parts. In the first, he distinguishes the powers of the soul from each other. In the second, he shows what powers of the soul he will take up and indicates how and in what order he will determine them. In the first division, he does two things. First, he distinguishes the powers of the soul from each other. Second, he shows how the common definition of soul is related to its parts, at the words, "It is clear therefore that the definition of the soul, *etc."* He does two things in relation to this. First, he enumerates the powers of the soul. Secondly, he shows how they are related to each other at the words, "In plants, *etc."* He says first, therefore, that all of the powers of the soul mentioned above are in some things, as in man; some powers are in some, as in animals; and finally, there is only one power in some things, as in plants. Since he has not previously called them *powers,* but rather *parts* of the soul, he shows that he means by powers what heretofore he called parts. Of these there are five kinds: vegetative, sensitive, appetitive, locomotive and intellectual.

[¶ 7.] *280.* Two things should be noted about this division: first, why five kinds of powers of the soul are enumerated, when it has usually been said that there are three kinds of soul—vegetative, sensitive, and intellectual; second, why he here mentions five powers when previously he posited only four.

[¶ 8.] *281.* Regarding the first point, it must be noted that just as every potency is defined by the act proper to it, so an operative potency is defined in relation to the act which is its operation. The soul's powers are operative powers because such is the potency of form. Therefore, the diversity of powers necessarily follows from the diversity of operations of the soul. Now the operation of the soul is the operation of a living thing. Since, therefore, everything has an operation proper to it insofar as it has being, because everything acts insofar as it is being, we must consider the operations of the soul as they are found in living things.

[¶ 9.] *282.* Lower living things, whose act is the soul (which we are here discussing), have a twofold kind of being: one, material, by which they are like other material things; another, immaterial, by which they have something in common with higher substances.

[¶ 10.] *283.* There is a difference between these two kinds of being. According to material being which is limited by matter, each thing is only what it is, as this stone, for example, is a stone and nothing else. But according to immaterial being, which is broader and in some way infinite since it is not limited by matter, a thing is not only that which it is, but also, somehow, other things. In higher immaterial substances, therefore, all things are in some way present, as in universal causes.

[¶ 11.] *284.* In lower beings this immateriality has two grades. There is complete immateriality, as in intelligible being, for things in the intellect exist without matter, and without individuating material conditions, and even apart from a bodily organ. Then there is a halfway state of immateriality in sensory beings. Sensible being is a mean between both, for in sensation a thing exists without matter, yet not apart from individuating material conditions, nor independently of a bodily organ. The sense deals with individuals, but the intellect with universals. With respect to this twofold being, then, the Philosopher says in Book III that the soul is in some way all things.

[¶ 12.] *285.* The operations which belong to a living thing according to its material existence are those which are attributed to the vegetative soul. They are ordained to the same end to which actions in inanimate things are ordained, that is, to achieve and preserve existence, although in living things this is done in a higher and nobler way. Nonliving bodies come into existence and are preserved in existence by an extrinsic principle of motion. Living things, on the other hand, come into existence by an intrinsic principle which is in the semen; and they are kept in existence by an intrinsic principle of nutrition. It seems to be characteristic of living things that their activity originates from within. The completely immaterial activities attributed to living things pertain to the intellectual part of the soul, but those of a half-way kind of being pertain to the sensitive part of the soul. According to this threefold kind of existence, three kinds of souls are commonly distinguished: the vegetative, sensitive, and rational.

[¶ 13.] *286.* Since every existence is according to some form, sensitive being must exist according to sensible form, and intelligible being according to intelligible form. From any form there follows a certain tendency, and from this tendency, an operation. From the natural form of fire, for example, there is a tendency to a higher place, giving to fire its lightness. From this tendency follows its operation—that is, its upward motion. The tendencies that follow upon sensible and intelligible form are called *sensible appetite* and *intellectual appetite* respectively, just as a tendency that follows upon a natural form is called natural appetite. From this tendency activity follows, and this is local motion. This is the reason there are five kinds of powers of the soul—which was the first question asked.

[¶ 14.] *287.* Regarding the second point, we should note that in setting out to show that the soul is the life-principle in all living things, Aristotle distinguishes life according to the grades of living things, and not according to the activities of life, by which powers are classified. Beings with appetite do not constitute a different grade in living things, since everything which has sensation also has appetite; and so there remain only four grades of living things, as was shown above.

[¶ 15.] *288.* Then when he says, "In plants, only the vegetative power is present, *etc.,*" he shows how the aforementioned powers are related to each other, thus making clear what was said above, namely, that all powers of the soul are in some things, certain ones in other things, and finally only one in some things. At this point, we should note that the perfection of the universe demands that there be no gaps in the degrees of perfection, but that, step by step, nature proceed from the imperfect to the perfect. For this reason, Aristotle, in VIII, *Metaphysics,* compares species to numbers which gradually increase in size. Hence, among living things, some (the plants) have only one of the above-mentioned powers, for in them only the vegetative potentiality is present. This power is necessary in all living material beings, because to this power are attributed all the operations which pertain to material being. Other living things (animals, for instance) have both vegetative and sensitive powers. And wherever the power of sensation is present, there is necessarily present a third power, called *appetite*. This appetite is divided in three: desire, which is from the concupiscible power; anger, which is from the irascible power. These two appetites have to do with the sensitive part, for they follow apprehension by the sense power. Finally, there is the will, which is the appetite of the intellect, following upon apprehension by the intellect.

[¶ 16.] *289.* He proves in two ways that the appetitive power is in all animals. He shows first that all animals have at least one sense, namely, touch. But in anything in which there is sensation, there is joy and sorrow, pleasure and pain. Joy and sorrow seem to follow upon an inner apprehension, while pleasure and pain follow upon an apprehension by a sense, particularly the sense of touch. And if there is joy and sorrow, there must also be something either disagreeable or sweet, that is, something painful or pleasant. For everything which is sensed by touch is necessarily either agreeable, and thus pleasurable, or harmful, and thus painful. So wherever there is anything pleasurable or disagreeable, there you will find concupiscence, which is an appetite for the pleasurable. From first to last, therefore, in all animals in which the sense of touch is present, there is found appetite.

[¶ 17.] *290.* He gives the second reason to prove this when he says, "They furthermore have a sense for food, *etc.*" All animals have a sense by which they know their own food, namely, the sense of touch which is the sense of food. Since it is necessary for all animals to use food, as was said above, it is therefore necessary that they all have a sense of touch by which they sense the food that suits them. That touch is the sense dealing with food is clear from the fact that living bodies are made up of hot, moist, cold, and dry elements and are likewise nourished by such things. Touch is the sense which differentiates these. "But by other sensible qualities," that is, by other sensible objects, living things are nourished only accidentally, insofar as other objects are jointed to what can be touched. Sound and smell and color contribute nothing to nourishment as such, except when things which are hot, cold, moist, and dry happen to be colored, odorous, or happen to emit sound. Wetness, however (that is, savor), is a kind of tangible quality, just as taste is a kind of touch. It is evident, therefore, that all animals have a sense for recognizing food.

[¶ 18.] *291.* Wherever there is this sense for food, there is found hunger and thirst, both of which are a desire for nourishment. Hunger is a desire for the hot and dry, that is, for food; thirst is a desire for the cold and wet, that is, for drink. Savor is a certain delight in these things. A delightful taste indicates that there is correct proportion of the hot and cold, moist and dry elements in the food. For this reason it is connected more with the pleasure of eating than with the necessity. It follows then that wherever there is a sense of touch, there is also an appetite.

[¶ 19.] 292. How the imagination is related to appetite and the sense powers will be discussed later.

[¶ 20.] 293. In some animals, there is in addition to these three powers (the vegetative, sensitive, and appetitive) a power of locomotion. In others, there is, besides these four, an intellectual power and the intellect itself. This is found in man and in any other kind of being like man or superior to him. There are beings higher than man which have an intellect, namely, the separated substances and the heavenly bodies, if the latter are alive. Among living mortal things, however, there is no genus of living things having intellectual power except the human species.

[¶ 21.] 294. Since the intellect does not have a bodily organ, those beings having an intellect cannot be differentiated by reason of organic structure in the way species of sensory beings are differentiated in structure. It is by this difference in structure that sensory beings are related in various ways to the operations of sense.

[¶ 22.] 295. Then when he says, "It is clear therefore, *etc.*," he shows how the definition of the soul is related to the parts that have been enumerated. To understand this, we should note that Plato posited universals as separated beings, yet he did not say that those things which follow each other consecutively, as do numbers and figures, have one common idea. He did not posit one universal idea of number distinct from all numbers as he posited one idea of man apart from all men, for the reason that the species of numbers are related consecutively in the natural order. Thus, the first of these (duality) is the cause of all that follows. Hence, it is not necessary to posit a common idea of number to cause the species of numbers. The same is true of geometrical figures. Their species are related like those of numbers; the triangle comes before the quadrangle, and the quadrangle before the pentagon.

[¶ 23.] 296. He says, therefore, that it is clear that there is one idea of the soul in the same way as there is one idea of figure. For just as among figures there is no figure outside of triangle and the other species which follow it, as a common idea of all figures, so neither is there some soul existing separately, as it were, besides all the aforementioned parts.

[¶ 24.] 297. Although there is not, even for the Platonists who posit common separated species, one separated figure existing apart from all figures, there is nevertheless one common idea which fits all figures, and yet is not proper to any one of them.   The same is true of animals.   So it is ridiculous for anyone to look for a common idea, either in animals or in other things, which does not fit any particular kind of animal actually existing in nature. Nor is it reasonable for anyone to seek a definition of the soul which is peculiar to each species of the soul and yet ignore a common definition for all.   Therefore, we must neither omit the common definition of the soul, nor assign a common definition of soul which does not fit each soul.

[¶ 25.] *298.* After saying that the idea of the soul and the idea of figure are related in the same way, he goes on to what the likeness is.   He says that figures and souls are related in the same way to each other, for in both, that which is prior is in potency in that which follows.   Clearly, in figures, the triangle, which is prior, is potentially in the quadrangle, for a quadrangle can be divided into two triangles.   Likewise, in a sensory soul, the vegetative power is a certain power of it and is, as though it were, a soul in itself. The same is true of other figures and the other parts of the soul.

No. 4. The Vegetative Powers of the Soul
    Aristotle: *On the Soul,* Book II, Chapter 4, Lines 415a23–415b28
    St. Thomas: *Commentary on Aristotle's On the Soul,* Book II, Lesson
            7, Numbers 309–323

ARISTOTLE:

[¶ 1.] We must first speak of food and reproduction.   For the vegetative soul is present in all other living things and is the basic kind of soul.   For it is the most general power of the soul, by which life is present in all things, and whose operations are to reproduce and to take food.

[¶ 2.] The activity most natural to living things (if they are mature, not defective, and not spontaneously generated), is to produce others like themselves.   An animal produces an animal, and a plant produces a plant.   In this respect, they share as far as they can in divine and immortal being.   All things desire this; for the sake of this they do all things, whatever they do, according to nature.   But "that for the sake of which" something is done may be taken in two ways: that "for the sake of which," and that "by which." Therefore, since they cannot share in the divine by continuous being (because nothing corruptible can remain numerically one and the same), each being shares in this in proportion to its capacity, one thing more, another less.   And thus it endures, not really the same being, but the same in a way; not indeed numerically the same, but the same in species.

[¶ 3.] The soul is the cause and principle of a living body. Cause and principle, however, are said in many ways. The soul is called a *cause* in three definite ways: the soul is the source of motion; it is "that for the sake of which"; and it is a cause as the substance of animate bodies.

[¶ 4.] That it is a cause as substance is evident, for in everything the substance is the cause of its being. In living things, *living* is *being*. The cause and principle of this is the soul.

[¶ 5.] Furthermore, the reason for whatever is in potency is act. It is clear also that the soul is a cause "for the sake of which." Just as the intellect does things for the sake of something, so also does nature, and this is its end. In animals this end is the soul according to nature. For all physical bodies are instruments of the soul. They exist for the sake of the soul, whether they are of animals or of plants. The phrase, "for the sake of which," may be taken in two ways: that "for the sake of which," and that "by which."

[¶ 6.] The soul is also the principle from which comes local motion, but this power is not in all living things. Alteration and growth, too, are from the soul. Sensations appear to be a kind of alteration, and nothing senses unless it has a soul. The same may be said of growth and decrease, for nothing grows or diminishes physically unless it takes nourishment, but nothing takes nourishment which does not share in life.

ST. THOMAS:

[¶ 1.] *309.* After the Philosopher has distinguished the powers of the soul and shown what they are and in what order they must be discussed, he treats of them according to the order just mentioned. He divides this treatment into two parts: in the first, he determines what each individual part of the soul is; in the second, he gives the reason why they follow each other as they do at the words, "Every living being must have, *etc.*" He takes this up in the second chapter from the end of Book III. His first part has four subdivisions. In the first, he treats of the vegetative powers; in the second, of the sensitive powers, at the words, "After determining these things, let us speak of sensation in general, *etc.*"; and in the third, of the intellectual powers, at the words, "Concerning the power of the soul by which it knows, *etc.*"; and in the fourth, of local motion, at the words, "On motion which is perhaps from the soul, *etc.*" He does not give a special treatment of the appetitive powers, since these do not constitute a special grade of living beings, and also because he will discuss these along with the power of motion in the third section. The first of the four sections is divided into two parts. In the first, he prefaces his thought with some remarks that are necessary to understand the vegetative part. In the second, he treats of the vegetative part itself at the words, "Since the same potency of the soul is vegetative and reproductive, *etc.*" The first of these divisions is again divided into two parts. In the first, he speaks of his intention, and in the second, he points out what is necessary before there can be an understanding of the vegetative powers at the words, "The activity most natural, *etc.*"

[¶ 2.] *310.* He concludes first of all from what has already been said that we must treat of objects and of acts first, before we treat of potencies; and that we must treat first of the primary potency before that which follows. Thus, we must speak first of food, which is the object of the vegetative soul, and of generation which is its act. We must speak first of the object and the act of this part rather than of others, since this one is first among the parts of the soul, in subjects in which it is found in conjunction with other parts. It is, in a way, the foundation of the others; just as natural existence to which its operations pertain is the foundation of sensitive and intelligible existence. Another reason for its priority is the fact that it is common to all living things. For it can exist separately from the others, but others cannot exist separately from it, and we should first discuss what is common to all. The operations of this power are reproduction and the use of food, and so we should first speak of these.

[¶ 3.] *311.* Then when he says, "The activity most natural, *etc.*" he discusses those things which are necessary in advance for an understanding of the vegetative power. This is divided into two parts. In the first, he shows that to reproduce belongs to the vegetative power. This was necessary since he has not previously attributed reproduction to this power, but only growth and decrease. In the second, he shows that the operations of the vegetative power originate in the soul. This was necessary because of the kind of active or passive qualities used in these activities, for it might seem to some that the operations are from nature rather than from the soul. This is especially true because life in plants is hidden and concealed. He does this at the words, "The soul is the cause and principle of a living body, *etc.*"

[¶ 4.] *312.* His first argument is as follows. Every operation which is natural to all living beings belongs to the vegetative power, by which life is first present in all living things, as was said before. But to reproduce is natural to all living things; therefore, it pertains to the vegetative power. He says, therefore, that to reproduce is a work of the vegetative soul, because of all activities it is most natural to all living things. It is most natural, because in this respect it is like nonliving things, which have generation— although in another way. Inanimate beings have generation from an extrinsic source, while living things have it from an intrinsic principle, inasmuch as they are generated from a seed which develops into a living thing.

[¶ 5.] *313.* Among living things there are three cases in which the general rule does not hold. First, those things are excluded that are immature—children, for example, do not reproduce—for in any species that which produces another thing like himself is mature. Second, he excludes those which have some defect in this natural principle, such as the impotent and the eunuchs. Third, he excludes those animals and plants which are generated without seed, from putrefying matter. Because of their imperfection, a universal agent, namely, the power of the heavenly body, and disposed matter, is sufficient to produce these things—the spontaneously generated. In more perfect animals, many principles are required; a universal agent is not enough; a proper univocal agent is needed.

[¶ 6.] *314.* He says, therefore, that living things that can produce another like themselves are "mature" (to exclude children); "not defective" (to exclude eunuchs and those with similar defects); and "not spontaneously generated" (to exclude those things generated from putrefying matter, which are, as it were, born spontaneously, because they are brought forth from the earth without any seed, in the way we say someone does something spontaneously, when he is not compelled by any external force). When he says that a living thing produces another like itself, he means that an animal produces an animal and a plant produces a plant. Furthermore, that according to its species, a particular kind of animal produces another of that kind in the same way that man reproduces man and an olive tree reproduces an olive tree. Therefore, it is natural to living things to produce another like themselves, so that they may always participate insofar as they can, in the divine and immortal, that is, that they may be as like the divine as possible.

[¶ 7.] *315.* We must take into consideration that just as there are varying degrees of perfection in some one thing that goes from potency to act, so also there are varying degrees of perfection in different beings. The more perfect a thing is, the more it is like superior beings. Therefore, just as anything which passes from potency to act, when it is in potency is ordained to act and naturally desires act, and when it is less perfectly in act desires a more perfect act, so whatever is of a lower grade of nature desires, insofar as it can, to be like higher things. This is why he adds, "All things desire this," that is, to be united to divine and immortal being, and, "for the sake of this they do everything that they do by nature."

[¶ 8.] *316.* We must note that "that for the sake of which a thing is done" can mean two things: first, that for which a thing is done directly, as a physician acts for the sake of health; second, that by which a thing is done. This, also, can be taken in two ways. First, we may understand by it not only the end but also the subject having that for which something is done. We can say that the end of medicine is not only health, but also the body having health. Second, we can say that the end is not only what is principally intended, but also that by which we obtain it, for example, when we say that the end of medicine is warming the body, because by means of warmth there is achieved an organic balance in which health consists. Thus, when we say that perpetual being is that for the sake of which something is done, we may mean either something having perpetuity, which natural things tend to imitate by reproduction, or we may mean the reproduction itself, by which perpetuity is attained.

[¶ 9.] *317*. Inferior living things cannot communicate with eternal and divine being through a continuous existence; that is, they cannot remain numerically the same, for the reason that nothing corruptible can remain always one and the same numerically. And since the necessity of corruption is absolute, inasmuch as it comes from matter and not from the end, it follows that each thing shares in perpetuity as best it can; more so, if it has a longer duration; less, if its duration is shorter. However, by the process of reproduction a being does not always remain the same absolutely, but "the same in a way," by enduring in one that is similar in species. In explaining what he has said, he adds that it does not remain numerically the same, which is the same absolutely, but remains the same in kind, because each thing reproduces something like itself according to species.

[¶ 10.] *318*. When he says, "The soul is the cause and principle, *etc.*" he shows that the operations attributed to the vegetative power come from the soul. At this point he does two things. First, he shows the truth of the matter. Second, he refutes an error at "Empedocles, *etc.*" Regarding the first point, he again does two things. First, he points out his aim. He says that the soul is the principle and cause of a living body. And since principle and cause may be taken in many senses, the soul is called a principle and a cause of a living body in three ways. In one way, as it is the principle of motion; in another, as "that for the sake of which," that is, as the end; and thirdly, as substance, that is, as the form of animate bodies.

[¶ 11.] *319*. Second, at the words, "That it is a cause as substance, *etc.*" he proves what he had supposed. First, he proves that the soul is the cause of a living body as its form. This is true for two reasons, of which the first is this: that it is the cause of something as substance (that is, as form) which is the cause of being. For each thing is in act through form. But the soul in living things is the cause of being, for things live through the soul, and living itself is their being. Therefore, the soul is the cause of a living body, as form.

[¶ 12.] *320.* He gives the second reason at the words "Furthermore, the reason for, *etc.*" It runs as follows: that which is the act of something is the *reason for* and the *form* of that which is in potency. But the soul is the act of a living body, as is evident from what has already been said. Therefore, the soul is the reason for and the form of a living body.

[¶ 13.] *321.* Second, at the words, "It is clear also that the soul is a cause, *etc.*" he shows that the soul is the cause in the sense of end. That the soul is cause as end of living bodies, he shows in the following way. Just as the intellect operates for an end, so also does nature, a point which was proved in II, *Physics.* But the intellect in works of art ordains and disposes matter in view of form, and so also does nature. Since, therefore, the soul is the form of a living body, it follows that it is its end.

[¶ 14.] *322.* Furthermore, not only is the soul the end of living bodies, but it is also the end of all natural bodies among lower beings. He proves this as follows. We see that all natural bodies are in a way instruments of the soul, not only in animals, but also in plants. For we see that man uses animals and nonliving things for his own purposes. Animals use plants and nonliving things, and plants use nonliving things as nourishment and receive aid from them. In nature, the way a thing is acted upon is the way that it was made to be acted upon. We see, therefore, that all non-living bodies are instruments of living things and exist for them, and less perfect living things exist for more perfect living things. Following this, he distinguishes "that for the sake of which" as above.

[¶ 15.] *323.* Third, at the words "The soul is also the principle, *etc.*" he shows that the soul is the principle of a moving body as its source of motion. He uses this argument. Every form of a natural body is the principle of the motion proper to that body, as the form of fire is the principle of its motion. But certain motions are proper to living things, namely, locomotion, by which animals move themselves in a progressive motion according to place. This, however, is not present in all living things. Likewise, sensing is a sort of alteration which is only found in things having a soul. Also the movement of growth and decrease is present only in those things that take nourishment, and nothing takes nourishment unless it has a soul; therefore, the soul must be the principle of all these motions.

Part II

THE SENSORY POWERS OF THE SOUL

Introduction to the Problem of Knowledge

To try to explain the act of knowing analytically, in terms simpler than the experience itself, is like trying to tell a child what colors are by explaining to him how a spectograph works. Knowing, like the most obvious things, resists definition. To say that knowing means having ideas, or thinking, is to substitute synonyms which in turn need definition. A child has had enough experience in knowing to realize what knowing is, though he is not able to define it. The student, the craftsman, the artist, the philosopher, the theologian are all said *to know*. Even cats and dogs and birds *know*. But obviously knowing does not mean exactly the same thing for each. Though these kinds of knowing differ widely, there is, perhaps, some general definition of knowing that fits all of them and that is what we want to discover.

When I try to analyze the common elements in all different kinds of knowing, I must begin by asking what to know means for me. That is the kind of knowing I know best. One of the first things that comes to mind is that I, the knower, am different from what I know. Knowledge, then, means a dualism. This dualism of knower and known is present even when the thing that I know is myself. It is as though in knowing myself I were actually two beings: myself as the knower, and myself as the known.

The Union of Knower and Known

A second general characteristic that I can discover from my own experience is that when I know, I am joined in some way to the nature of things that exist apart from me as a knower. When I say that the knower is united with the things that surround him, I mean more than a physical union, for stones are joined to stones, and plants to plants, yet they do not have, apparently, the kind of union that is proper to knowledge.

We may be able to understand better the kind of union that is proper to knowledge if we consider first what is contrary to knowing. Not to know is to be isolated from other things. For example, even though surrounded by a thousand other beings, cabbages and stones exist in isolation, for they cannot become one through knowledge with the world around them. Each stone and cabbage is itself and nothing more. Perhaps in a negative way we can better conceive this special kind of communion with our surroundings, by imagining ourselves as blind, or deaf, or without the sense of touch in our hands. Without sensory powers we would be isolated from the beautiful things in nature that other people experience and enjoy. Without an intellectual power we would be isolated from the thoughts of other men.

The union of knowledge is more, therefore, than the contact of one body with another, like a tire on a rim, because in physical contact one body must always remain outside another. But in knowing we become identified in some way with something outside of us: it becomes absorbed into us and we into it. The union of the knower and the known is not like that of a horse and a carrot which the horse eats. When a chemical compound is formed by the union of two physical bodies, the elements of the combination must be altered in order that a union may take place. But in knowledge neither the knower nor the known is altered in the strict sense of that term. The person who sees a sunset, for example, does not suffer a loss of any kind, nor is the sunset destroyed, for it remains the same for each person who sees it. This is what St. Thomas means when he says that *to know means to become the form of another as other*. For if the object were physically assimilated by the knower, it would be destroyed by being known, and would not be the form of the other as other. We could have no knowledge of what exists outside of us, because in the act of knowing nothing would remain to be grasped by our powers of knowledge.

Knowledge as an Intentional Union

The union achieved in knowing is possible because forms can exist in two ways: first, in a way that is proper to things in their physical existence outside our powers of knowledge and this is called *entitative* * existence; and second, in a way that is proper to cognitive beings, and this is called *intentional* * existence. Music, for example, that comes from an orchestra and resounds in a hall is music in its entitative existence. Music in this mode of existence, as produced by members of the orchestra, has physical qualities of intensity, volume, or pitch, which create physical vibrations. But music can also exist in the form of knowledge, namely, as a musical form in the mind of the composer, or in the minds of the musicians, or the members of the audience. The music as intentional form is in some way different and in some way the same as the music that exists as a combination of real sounds. They differ in their mode of existence.

In the *Disputed Question on Truth*, St. Thomas prefaces his treatise on knowledge by differentiating these two modes of existence.

> We should note that a thing can be perfect in two ways. In one way, with respect to the perfection of its being, which belongs to it according to its species. Since the particular kind of being of one thing is distinct from that of another, it follows that in any created being there is a lack of perfection insofar as there is more perfection in other kinds of being. And the perfection of each thing considered in itself is incomplete because it is simply a part of the total perfection of the universe, which is made up of the individual parts taken together.
>
> As a remedy to this defect, there is perfection in created things in another way, according as the perfection which belongs to one thing is found in another. This is the perfection of a knower specifically as a knower, because in this way something is known and is in the knower in some way. In Book III, *On the Soul,* therefore, it is stated that the soul is in some way all things, since it is made to know all things.[1]

Modes of Existence of the Form

The intentional form, however, does not differ from the entitative as form but only in its manner of existing; the intentional form exists without the material characteristics that limit and isolate forms in their entitative existence. The colors, sounds, and shapes, for example,

---

[1] St. Thomas Aquinas: *Disputed Question on Truth,* Question II, Article 2, Body of the Article.

that exist in bodies are limited in their existence because they do not get beyond the limits of the physical bodies in which they are found. The cause of their individuality is the quantitative nature of the subject in which these forms have entitative existence. Quantity isolates things because the parts of quantity in which sensory forms exist are mutually exclusive, for we define quantity as that which has parts extended outside of parts. Sensory qualities, by their very nature, however, are not isolated and restricted, since colors, for example, are limited only by the subject in which they inhere physically. That is why in intentional existence, forms can be reproduced without limit, and why there is no limit to the number of times that a form as form can be known. What is true of the sensory forms of things is *a fortiori* true of their intelligible forms.

Immateriality—the Basis of Knowledge

Intentional existence requires immateriality. In the context of knowing, immateriality is not to be identified with *spirituality*.* Spirituality is a characteristic of form that can exist without matter, but immateriality here refers to the manner of receiving forms or to the manner in which intentional forms exist in the knower. When matter receives a form, the form is limited and restricted in such a way that it is incommunicable. In knowing, however, the form of the thing known, though received by the knower, still remains the form of another thing. This is why the knower in knowing can receive the form of another without destroying it or without losing anything of his own perfection.

This communicability of the thing known with the knower requires a certain freedom from the limitation of matter. In all knowing, some immateriality is the basis of knowledge and only immaterial beings can receive the forms of other things as other. In sharp contrast, beings without knowledge have only their own form, because they can receive forms only in a material way.

In the *Disputed Question on Truth,* St. Thomas points out that the perfection of knowledge is in proportion to the immateriality of the knower.

> The perfection of one thing cannot be in another according to the determinate being which it has in that thing, and hence in order that it be in another, it is necessary to consider it without those characteristics which determine it in its natural existence. Since forms and perfections of (natural) things are determined by matter, it follows that a thing will be knowable insofar as it is separated from matter. Hence,

that in which the perfection of such a thing is received must also be immaterial. If it were material, the perfection received would be in it by a determined mode of being and not insofar as it is knowable, that is, be in another while still existing as a perfection in itself. And, therefore, those ancient philosophers were in error when they said that like is known by like, because they thought that the soul, which knows all things, would naturally be composed of all things. Earth would know earth and water would know water, and so on. They thought that the perfection of the thing known has the same mode of being in the knower that it has in its own particular nature.

But that is not the way that form is received in the knower. And so the Commentator says, treating of Book III, *On the Soul,* that the mode of reception of the form is not the same in the intellect as it is in prime matter. It is necessary that it be received immaterially in the knowing intellect. Therefore, we see that the nature of knowledge in each thing is in proportion to the immateriality in each thing. Plants, and things below plants, can receive nothing immaterially, and, therefore, are without all knowledge, as is clear from Book II, *On the Soul.* The sense receives forms without matter, but with material conditions. The intellect receives forms purified even of the material conditions.[2]

In the chapters that follow we shall study the various kinds of powers of knowledge according to their levels of immateriality. We begin with the external sense powers. Though these are the least perfect of the knowing powers, it is essential to the problem of knowledge that we begin here, for paradoxically their very proximity with matter gives them an advantage that no other human kind of knowing can supplant.

SECTION A: THE POWERS OF EXTERNAL SENSATION
(Readings: II, A, No. 1)

The first thing to be noted about sensation, Aristotle says, is that it results from a movement; it is some sort of change of quality caused by the action of an external object upon the sense organ.

It is clear that what is sensitive is so only in potency, not in act. Hence, it does not sense of itself, just as a combustible object does not burn spontaneously but needs something to ignite it. If it would burn spontaneously, it would not need actual fire.[3]

---

[2] St. Thomas: *Disputed Question on Truth,* II, 2, Body of the Article.
[3] Aristotle: *On the Soul,* II, 5, 417a7.

The change and the movement found in the act of sensation [4] differ from the ordinary change and movement of the physical universe.

But the expression, "to be acted upon," has more than one meaning. In one way it is the destruction by a contrary, but in another way it is the perfection of what is in potency by the mediation of what is in act. It is acted upon by something like it, but this likeness is the kind that is found in the relationship of potency to act.

One having science becomes an actual knower, which either is not an alteration (it is an addition in him and in act) or it is an alteration in a completely different sense. Therefore, it is not correct to say that a wise man is altered when he uses his wisdom, just as you do not say that a builder is altered when he builds. [5]

The Different Modes of Passivity

There are different ways in which a being can be acted upon or be passive. In every physical change in the world, two contrary forms are involved, the first of which is destroyed in the process of change. When a piece of wood is given a shape by a carpenter, the previous shape of the wood is destroyed; or when a piece of fruit matures on a tree, it loses the color, hardness, and size that it had originally. But in the change that takes place in sensation, there is a fulfilling of potency without the loss of a previous form, for the new form is the effect of an agent that is already in some way like what is acted upon. Sensation then is more like the completion of what already exists than the destruction of an existing form. Aristotle says of this change:

A potential knower, learning and receiving knowledge from one who is a knower in act and teaches, either ought not to be acted upon (as has been said), or there must be two kinds of alteration: that change which is in *privative** dispositions, and that which is in habit and nature. [6]

The Power of Receiving Sensible Forms Without Matter (Readings: II, B, No. 2)

The difference in the two types of change is brought about by the difference in the manner of receiving forms into the subject at the

---

[4] Sensation is not the same as perception. The term *perception* should be limited to the activity of the internal senses, for it is not merely sensation but the recognition of sensation. It is sense awareness and is superior to the simple grasping of sensory qualities.

[5] Aristotle: *On the Soul*, II, 5, 417b2.

[6] Aristotle: *On the Soul*, II, 5, 417b15.

term of the two kinds of activity. For the sense power, unlike inert things of stone and wood, "has the power of receiving into itself the sensible forms of things without matter." To illustrate how a form is received without matter, Aristotle uses the analogy of a signet ring which impresses a form on soft wax and leaves nothing of the material of the ring in the wax. The material nature of the ring—gold, silver, or iron—is unimportant, because the only part of the ring that remains in the wax is the form.

Though this analogy is open to false interpretation, Aristotle's thought is evident. His purpose is to use an example that conveys the idea of a form that is transmitted without the material subject in which it inheres. Actually, the impression which the ring makes upon the wax is an alteration in the strict sense of the term, entailing the destruction of a previous form in the wax.

The capacity for a nonsubjective or immaterial reception of a form is, Aristotle says, the essential difference between plants and animals and the explanation of why plants do not have sensation.

> This also explains why plants do not sense, even though they have something like the power of touch in them and are capable of being affected by tangible objects (for they become both hot and cold). The explanation is that they have no medium, and so no principle in them capable of receiving sensible forms, but must be acted upon with matter.[7]

Evidently stones and plants, as well as animals, can receive sensible forms in a physical way, as when they are heated by a fire or colored by paints. The difference between this and sensation lies in the mode of the receptivity. Stones and plants and other nonsensory beings receive sensory forms in the way that prime matter in its own order receives substantial form, that is, in a way that limits the subject to the particular form that it has at that moment. In order to receive a new form, the previous form must be destroyed. But because in sensation the qualities that exist naturally in a material subject are received into the power of sense without the material subject, neither the form which is sensed nor the power which receives the form undergoes an alteration. Without differing as to quality, the sensible form in the act of sensation has a new immaterial mode of existence.

---

[7] Aristotle: *On the Soul,* II, 12, 424a33.

The Atomistic Theory of Sensation

How is the sensory form joined to the power of sensation if not as physical form? One of the earliest solutions was the microscopic image theory of the atomist philosophers, of whom Leucippus and Democritus among the Greeks, and *Lucretius* * and *Epicurus* * among the Romans, were the outstanding exponents. Though this was basically a materialistic explanation of knowledge, the atomists recognized the need of some kind of form which differed from the grossly material forms that exist in natural bodies. Common sense taught them what Aristotle was later to say of sight: "The stone is not in the eye, but the image of the stone." The sensible images which were thought to cause sensation were described as images which rose from the surface of bodies and were so minute they could not be seen as they passed through a medium. The microscopic images were called *eidola* * (appearances) by the Greek atomists. This word always has the connotation of knowledge. According to some, the particles themselves entered into the sense organ, while others held that it was the print or impression which the particle made upon a sense medium that made contact with the sense organ. While Democritus held the latter view, Lucretius and Epicurus taught the more mechanistic view. Lucretius wrote:

> Pictures of things and their shapes are emitted from things, off their surfaces, to which an image serves as a kind of film; or name it, if you like, a rind, because such images bear an appearance and form like the thing, whatever it is, from whose body it is shed. Therefore, the cause of seeing, it is plain, lies in images and nothing can be perceived without them.[8]

The Impressed Species of Sensation

Though some historians of philosophy want to identify Aristotle's doctrine of the *impressed species* * with that of the *eidolon* of the atomists, the difference is fundamental. While the impressed species is the form of the object, it is the intentional mode of the form, that is, the form exists in a power of knowledge and without the subjective conditions of matter. But the eidolon is a form in its entitative mode of existence.

The impressed species can be called a "representation" of the ex-

---

[8] Lucretius: *On the Nature of Things,* Book IV, Number 100.

ternal object, if we take this word in its basic meaning, that is, it *makes present again* to the knower what is present in the object. It would be incorrect to say that the impressed species is a representation as a painting or photograph is. A photograph is an entitative being, and it has not an identity with but only a similarity to the thing it represents. But the impressed species is the same form as that in the physical world—the same color, shape, hardness or heat—but differing in its immaterial mode of existence. The impressed species, however, is not formal knowledge of the thing, but a principle for acquiring knowledge of the thing which it represents. It is called a "virtual likeness."

The impressed species is not the kind of thing that can be imagined, since it does not belong to the order of things that exist in sensible matter. We have to reason to its existence. As St. Thomas says, "we come to the conclusion" that there are two different kinds of being, one whose primary perfection is to exist as part of nature, and another whose primary perfection is to represent.

THE IMPRESSED SPECIES IS A MEANS, NOT AN OBJECT, OF SENSE KNOWLEDGE

It is essential to a *realistic epistemology* * that the impressed species be understood as instrumental to knowledge rather than as the object of knowledge. When we see something, for example, we do not see the impressed species but the object itself. This conclusion is paradoxical, since we hold that the form is present in the knower not in its mode of physical existence but in its intentional existence; yet we hold that we know objective reality. On the explanation of this difficulty hinges the only satisfactory solution to the problem of knowledge. For if we say that through the senses we know an image and not reality, we shall have no certitude that our sensations correspond with reality.

It is not enough to say that we know the external world through an application of the universal principle that causes produce similar effects. Nor can we solve the problem on the basis of faith in our powers of knowledge or in the veracity of God Who made them. An application of the principle of causality is not enough, for even though every effect is like its cause, this need not be a formal likeness. Furthermore, the principle of causality itself cannot be known unless we have a prior certitude about our sense knowledge. And the same necessity holds for any kind of act of faith. The view that our sense powers must be reliable because God could not deceive us when He gave us these powers suffers from the fallacy of *circular argumenta-tion,** since God's existence is known through the use that reason makes of our sensory powers.

The sensible form has a twofold mode of existence which we can compare to the two sides of a tapestry. In a tapestry it is the very same stitching which is on the front and the back. The same thread and the same color are present on both sides. The back of the tapestry is comparable to the sensible form that exists in a physical way and the front of the tapestry to sensible form existing in an intentional way (the impressed species). Just as the form appears only on the front of the tapestry, so sensation takes place only in the union of the sense with an intentional form.

It is most important to stress the identity of the physical sensible form and the intentional form. Actually they are one and the same in a twofold perspective, the one material and the other immaterial. And the same is true of the sense organ as a body and the sense organ as a power of sensation. Thus in many places St. Thomas says that sensation is the act of an organ.

The sense organ is passive in two ways: as a physical organ and as a psychical power. The sensible qualities are physically present in and act upon the sense organ, and the sense organ receives these sensible qualities physically. But the sensible qualities also act upon the sense organ insofar as it is a psychical power where the sensible qualities are received intentionally.

The Activity of the Sense

Up to this point we have considered the relation of the sensible object to the sense power and have spoken of the activity of the sensible object upon the power. But sensation is not pure passivity. It is a vital process; it is immanent activity. To the action of the sensible object there comes a reaction on the part of the sense organ. This reaction in a vital way takes place again in a twofold way: in a physical reaction and in a psychical or intentional reaction.

This reaction will be in direct proportion to the nature and degree of the stimulus which acts upon the sense organ. We know that the condition of the sense organ plays an important role in the sensation. For example, a hand that is 30 degrees cooler than a heated object placed in it will be acted upon with greater intensity and will react with greater intensity than a hand whose temperature differential is two degrees. In sensation there is a reaction to a stimulus. On the one hand there is a reaction in the organ as physical, and on the other hand there is a reaction in the organ as a power of sensing, and this is psychical. The second is of the essence of sensation; it is here that the sense power becomes the sensible object in an intentional way.

The question might be asked: How does the sense power go out to its object? There is no going out because the object is actually present. There is simply a reaction to the presence of a sensible quality in the sense organ.

Hence, there is no intermediary in external sensation. It is not a reflective knowledge, as though it were reflected in a mirror. It is not knowledge by means of signs, as is the knowledge of fire through seeing smoke. It is not a knowledge by representation, as when a person knows someone else by seeing a picture, for the very sensible object that acts upon the organ is that to which the organ responds in both a physical and in a psychical way. In that response sensation consists.

Some of the difficulty with respect to sensation comes from a confusion of the type of knowing proper to the senses and that proper to the intellect. Knowing in the order of external sensation does not mean understanding the nature of the sensible quality. It does not even mean being aware of the sensation, since the property of awareness in the sense order is not found in the external senses but, as we shall see, in some higher power. Sensation consists in receiving the sensible qualities of things by means of an external sense organ and becoming those qualities in an intentional or immaterial way. It is the first stage in the psychical process which culminates in self-consciousness in the intellectual order.

We say that the object of knowledge is not the impressed species but the sensible form. Here we make a distinction between the species as an intentional form and the species as an entitative form. As an intentional form the species is the sensible form that is present in a physical way in the organ. The sensible form is the object of knowledge. But we do not sense the species in its entitative existence, as an accidental quality inhering in a power of sensation. What we sense is the form of the object that acts upon us.

The Entitative Aspect of the Species

Besides being an intentional or representative form, the impressed species is also an accidental form existing subjectively in the power of knowledge. It belongs to the category of quality, as a *disposition* * that modifies the power.[9] All immanent acts, concepts and impressed

---

[9] St. Thomas: *Summa Theologiae*, I–II, Q. 50, 16, Body of the Article.

species belong in the first species of quality as dispositions, because they dispose the power well or ill in respect to its object. Since it is an accidental quality, the sensory species must inhere in a subject; however, this union is not the essence of knowledge but concomitant with it. The intentional form by which the knower is identified with the object known does not belong to any particular category insofar as it is representational, for it is identical with whatever category or mode of being it represents. It is this psychological entitative existence of the species that puts us in contact with the intentional existence in which knowledge consists.

In concluding the comparison of the two modes of existence, we should say that the intentional and the entitative existence of the impressed species, while inseparable in the knower, must be sharply differentiated if knowledge is really a nonsubjective union of the knower and the thing known.

No Expressed Species in External Sensation

In some acts of cognitive powers there is produced an *expressed species*,* which, like the impressed species, is the form existing intentionally in the knower. But the expressed species differs from the impressed species in several respects: it is produced by the knowing power itself; it does not come before the act of knowing as a principle; and it is a *formal sign* * of the object.

The expressed species is necessary in those powers in which the object is not immediately present, as in the internal senses and in the intellect. In these powers of knowledge the expressed species serves as a term of the act of knowing, for the powers whose objects are not immediately present need an intentional form as a substitute in the very act of knowing. It is a medium in which the object is seen. Further explanation of the expressed species will be given in the study of the rational powers of the soul where we take up concepts, which are expressed species of the intellectual order.[10]

No expressed species is produced in the external senses because the conditions which demand this terminative species are not present in external sensation. The object is immediately present to the senses, and hence there is no need to substitute a sign for the reality. If external sensation would terminate in knowledge in a representation, we could never be sure of our contact with the real as it exists outside of the powers of knowledge, for we would have no way of knowing that the representation corresponds with reality. Unless we first have

---

[10] *Cf.* Part III, Section A.

knowledge of reality we cannot make a comparison between it and what represents it. Therefore, the kind of knowledge that gives final assurance of the real existence of things is the kind that grasps the object directly. This is the kind found in external sensation.

This characteristic of immediacy is not found in internal sensation and intellection, as we shall see; hence, they depend on external sensation. The immediacy of external sensation requires the presence of the object. External sensation cannot take place without it. Even if a sensible form could be presented to the sense power in some other way than by the activity of the external object upon the organ of sensation, the resulting knowledge would not be external sensation, according to the view of St. Thomas:

> If the form of heat were caused by any other agent (than fire), even if by our touch, we would feel heat, we would not feel the heat of fire nor would we feel that fire is hot.[11]

The word *presence,* in reference to external sensation, includes the notion both of time and of space. An object is present in time when it exists simultaneously with the knower at the moment of sensation. It is present in space when that object in some way makes physical contact with the organs of sensation. The notion of presence, however, remains a very difficult one. The answer to the difficulties about the objectivity of sensory knowledge depends upon what we consider the objects of sensation to be.

Therefore, let us briefly outline the different kinds of objects known by the senses.

The Objects of Sense (Readings: II, A, No. 3)

The *proper objects* are those which belong to only one sense. Each proper object is sensed only by that particular sense and specifies, therefore, the nature of that sense. Color, for example, can be grasped only by the sense of sight; odor only by the sense of smell; sound only by the sense of hearing; savor only by the sense of taste; and tangible qualities only by the sense of touch. The *common objects* are those which can be grasped by several or by all of the senses, inasmuch as these objects belong to the category of quantity which underlies all the sensory qualities which are the subject matter of the proper sensibles. The common sensibles are five: motion, rest, figure, size, and number.

---

[11] St. Thomas Aquinas: *Disputed Question on the Power of God,* Question III, Article 7, Body of the Article.

The proper objects and the common objects mutually depend on each other. The proper objects depend upon the common insofar that qualities depend upon quantity as their immediate subject. Colors, for example, could not exist at all were it not for extended surfaces. On the other hand, the common sensible object can be grasped in conjunction with the proper object. The shape, size and movement of a physical body can be recognized along with the contrast between light and shadow or the colors in the object which are the proper objects of the eye; or with the tactile impressions of pressure or hardness and so on, which are the proper objects of touch.

In addition to these two kinds of objects, there are accidental objects of sensation, of which there are two kinds: first, there are objects which are known directly by the intellect and only indirectly or accidentally by the senses. Such objects are essences. The sense powers cannot perform the act of abstraction, which is needed for an understanding of essences. Therefore, essences are properly the objects of the intellect and accidentally the objects of the senses. Second, there are objects proper to one sense and accidental to another. For example, color is proper to sight and savor proper to taste. Yet we can say that we smell something sweet, that we see something soft. Thus the proper objects of taste can be the accidental object of sight and the proper object of touch the accidental object of sight.

The Objectivity of Sensory Qualities

After describing the different kinds of sensible objects, we can now return to the question of the objectivity of sense knowledge. Perhaps it is best to limit our investigation of the objectivity of sensible qualities to what St. Thomas says about them. Nowhere do we find in St. Thomas a discussion of the objectivity of the proper sensory qualities as we find it in modern works in epistemology. However, there is no doubt that St. Thomas held the objective existence of proper sensibles. But he spoke of them as sensible objects only in the formal sense of object, namely, in respect to those powers that can grasp such qualities.

> Then when he [Aristotle] says "Some will wonder, if something which cannot have smell, *etc.*" he poses a certain problem about being acted upon by sensible objects. Since he had said that plants are acted upon by certain sensible objects, he first poses a problem as to whether something which does not have sense is able to be affected by any sensible objects. For example, can a being which does not have a sense

of smell be affected by odor, or that which does not have sight be affected by color, or that which does not have hearing be affected by sound?

At the words, "What is smelling, *etc.*" he answers the question posed above, saying that if something which does not smell is affected by an odor, what does it mean to smell, besides being acted upon by an odor? And he answers, that smelling occurs when an odor affects something that is capable of sensing that odor. However, air is not so affected that it senses, because it does not have the power of sense.[12]

Thus, St. Thomas gives his view on that well-worn question of whether sound is made in the forest by the falling of timber when no one is present to hear it. If there is no power of hearing, then neither is there sound, because sound is that which is capable of being heard. But whether a hearer is actually present in the forest or not (as long as there is such a power as hearing) then the falling of timber is capable of being heard, though it is not actually heard. Therefore, in his view, sensible qualities have an objective existence independently of their actually being sensed.

Errors of the Senses

Though we hold the objectivity of proper objects of sensation there is still a question of whether our senses grasp objects as they really are. From earliest times many outstanding philosophers have doubted the validity of sense knowledge. Both *Parmenides* * and *Heraclitus,* * for example, said that sense knowledge has only the appearance of truth. Plato held that only intellectual knowledge possessed certitude. Among Christian philosophers, *St. Augustine* * expressed a hesitancy about following the evidence of the senses. Among modern philosophers, *Spinoza* * and *Kant* * doubted that the senses could give us a real basis for universal and necessary knowledge. Apparently, all these philosophers felt that the senses are prone to error. The mistrust comes from the fact that the senses deal with the kind of object which cannot generate certitude, because the objects of sense are in a state of flux, and because the act of sensation is conditioned so much by the status of the organ of sensation.

The saying that there should be no arguing over tastes is applied by some philosophers to the whole order of sense knowledge and ultimately to intellectual knowledge itself. Now it is true that the temperature of one's hand, for example, influences the sensation of

---

[12] St. Thomas: *Commentary on Aristotle's On the Soul,* II, 24, 558 and 563.

touch when the heat of another body acts upon it, just as the condition of the tongue predisposes a person's sense of taste. It is not amazing, then, that some philosophers have distrusted the evidence of the senses, either because of the fluidity of sense objects or because of the differences in sensations due to the conditioning of the sense organ. Let us examine this question of the errors of the senses so as to see to what extent, if any, we can have confidence in the judgments based upon their evidence.

Error in the strict sense cannot be attributed to the external senses, for error properly occurs only in a faulty *judgment.** Error in the formal sense is due to a faulty judgment in which the person reflects upon his act of judgment and gives assent to it, just as formal truth consists in the judgment we make about the conformity of our mind with reality. Strictly speaking, therefore, there is no formal error in *simple apprehension** or in *reasoning,** though they both can be fallacious, that is, capable of causing a false judgment. In the *Disputed Question on Truth,* St. Thomas says that both truth and error depend upon an intellectual comparison, thus showing that it is found in judgment.

> Just as truth is present in the intellect before it is present in things, so it is present first of all in the act of the intellect which composes and divides rather than in the act of the intellect which forms the essence of things.
>
> The notion of truth consists in the conformity of the intellect with reality. Now, a thing cannot conform to itself, since conformity or equality is predicated of different things. Therefore, truth is found first of all in the intellect when it begins to possess something proper to itself, something which does not exist outside the soul, but which corresponds to what is outside, so that evidence is given of the conformity.
>
> The intellect has only the likeness of the thing existing outside the mind when it forms the essences of things, just as the senses have when they receive the forms of sensible things. But when it begins to judge about what is apprehended, then the judgment is something that belongs uniquely to the intellect and is not found outside it in nature. When the intellect conforms to what is outside in nature, it is said to have a true judgment.[13]

The senses have neither formal truth nor formal error, because they

---

[13] St. Thomas: *Disputed Question on Truth,* I, 3, Body of the Article.

have no judgment in the strict sense. The senses, however, can differentiate various objects within the order of sense experience, either among the proper or among the common objects of sensation. This power belongs essentially to the order of sense experience. If we can speak of error in the senses at all, it can mean only that the senses do not furnish the intellect with evidence upon which a judgment can be made. Therefore, the senses can be only the accidental causes of error. Let us see, then, how the senses can be the indirect causes of error, by not grasping sensible objects.

In regard to their proper objects, the senses do not err. If we understand the relationship that exists between a power and its proper object, we can see that an essential defectibility in the sense powers would entail a contradiction in nature. A power is a capacity for attaining a certain kind of object or producing a certain kind of effect. A power that cannot attain its proper object is not a power at all. We can take it as a universal principle of nature, that nature acts for an end, and in general attains its end (except where chance enters in); and, therefore, nature does not produce powers of knowledge that do not attain their proper objects. Defectibility is not ruled out absolutely, because the very definition of nature includes the possibility of defect, though nature attains its goal in the majority of cases. Defectibility in sense knowledge can arise, for example, from the defectibility of the sense organs. A defective organ will not accurately grasp sensible objects. But this does not mean that the senses are naturally defective.

Differences and inaccuracies in sensing proper sensibles do occur, but this is very different from saying that the senses are in error in regard to their proper object. Error is a mistaken judgment about what is. Thus, if an object is white and we see it as black, or if a surface is rough and we feel it as smooth, the sense power would be operating contrary to its natural tendency. But no sense power will be essentially disorientated about objects that are proper to it, and the intellect can depend upon the evidence of the senses for making a true judgment. This interpretation leaves the way open for errors that arise from a defect in the organ as well as for the differences and inaccuracies that arise from the varied conditions under which even what we call a normal sensory apparatus operates. The possibilities of accidental differences and inaccuracies in sensation are incalculable. They are not the sign of an essential defectibility.

The senses are not by definition directed to the common sensibles, but only indirectly by means of the proper sensibles. The senses are subject to inaccuracies in respect to them. Neither the eye nor the hand, for example, can always and everywhere grasp the common sensibles accurately, like the size, the shape, or movement of physical bodies. Many of the "illusions" of the senses belong to this category of object. This defectibility causes errors in perspective, in the recognition of shapes, size, and so on, or finally in the judgment of distance, motion, speed or rest.

Finally, in regard to the accidental sensible objects which are directly intellectual and indirectly sensible, such as essences, the senses can be the indirect cause of error by not furnishing sufficient evidence to the intellect. Since it is not within the scope of the senses to grasp essences, we cannot assign the cause of the error to the senses. The senses may be the accidental cause inasmuch as the intellect makes a judgment based upon insufficient sensory evidence. In that case, however, the error belongs principally in the judgment, since the intellect goes beyond the evidence furnished by the senses and makes comparisons without the further evidence that is needed. If a noise from an upstairs room, for example, is interpreted to mean the presence of a burglar, the evidence of the senses for such a judgment is of itself insufficient, and the senses are not the cause of the judgment.

Certitude Through the Senses

While all the senses are trustworthy in regard to their proper objects, though somewhat inaccurate in regard to the common objects, there are differences among the various external senses as to the degree of certitude they can furnish the judgment. The most certain of the senses, from the viewpoint of evidence about the existence of a sensible object, is the sense of touch. The reason for this is that the sense of touch is more directly in contact with the object in its physical presence; the hands, for example, become, as it were, a *continuum* with the external object. A sign of this certain evidence is the habit we have of touching something if we want to make sure that we are not deceived by an illusion. Of all the external senses, however, sight is closest to the power of intelligence, because being the most immaterial of the senses, it conforms most objectively to sensible forms. Of all the senses, its range of objects is also the most extensive; its grasp of the object is least distorted by subjective dispositions that frequently modify sensations in other powers, as in the sense of touch or taste, for example.

Divisions of the External Senses (Readings: II, A, No. 4)

We shall not investigate in detail the activities of each of the external senses. Many of these details are very interesting, but they are beyond the scope of an introductory text in philosophical psychology. Concerning these details, help must be sought from the experimental psychologists, for the solution of many problems in this area calls for extensive training in experimental methods. In an introductory course it suffices to understand in general the nature of external sense knowledge. Whether there are only five or many more avenues of sense experience, however, is of secondary importance because the multiplication of external sensory organs constitutes only a quantitative and not an essential diversity in the kind of knowledge received.

To hold that there is no essential difference in the mode by which the various external senses grasp their external objects is not the same, however, as to hold that there are no formal differences among the various external senses. There may be formal differences in the way that the senses grasp their objects without essential differences in the degree of immateriality of the different objects. Since all these powers grasp an object which is physically present to the sense organs, they all have radically the same kind of intentional union. In a way, all the external senses are forms of the sense of touch. Touch is the first and most elementary kind of sensation, and without it there cannot be animal life; sight, hearing, taste and smell are the perfections of the sense of touch, needed by the greater perfection of soul in the higher animals.

Because the formal objects of the various senses remain distinct, the powers themselves are formally distinct. Color, therefore, is perceived only by an animal with sight, sound by an animal with hearing, and so on with all the proper objects of the senses. The formal differences cannot be reduced to the category of quantity, that is, colors cannot be reduced to mere wave lengths; for example, the proper sensibles are not accidental variations that can be measured as distances are measured. When we reduce the qualitative differences of the senses to a common basis of quantity, we are no longer dealing with the sensible objects as such but with a mathematized conception of them. The mathematization of nature may be justifiable according to the method of the physicist, but not according to the method of the philosopher of nature.

If it were possible to reduce the different objects of sense to quantity, people blind from birth would not necessarily lack knowledge of color, for if colors are reducible to quantity, a blind person could come to know color, because he can know quantity through his sense of touch. Even an outstanding mathematician like Bertrand Russell, who is generally critical of traditional philosophical distinctions, upholds the formal distinctions among the various senses.

It is sometimes said that "light is a form of wave-motion," but this is misleading, for the light which we immediately see, which we know directly by means of our senses, is not a form of wave-motion, but something quite different something which we all know if we are not blind, though we cannot describe it so as to convey our knowledge to a man who is blind. A wave-motion, on the contrary, could quite well be described to a blind man, since he can acquire a knowledge of space by the sense of touch, and he can experience a wave-motion by a sea-voyage almost as well as we can. But this, which a blind man can understand, is not what we mean by light; we mean by light just that which a blind man can never understand, and which we can never describe to him.[14]

Conclusion

As a conclusion to this section on external sensation, let us again emphasize the importance of understanding well this initial phase of our knowledge, which is the basis of the rest of human knowledge. There is no internal sense knowledge and intellectual knowledge except what is rooted in some way in external sensory experience. Without sense knowledge, our intellect would remain in its native state of potentiality, which Aristotle compares to "a tablet upon which nothing is written." And without the assurance that comes from the physical presence of an object directly grasped by the senses, we should despair of ever reaching certitude in judgment. Thus, both the content and the certitude of our intellectual knowledge depends on the content and certitude of our external sense knowledge. Here we find a parallel to the relationship of the vegetative and the sensory powers: Just as the vegetative powers are the support of our sensory life, so, too, the external senses are the support of our intellectual life.

---

[14] Bertrand Russell, *The Problem of Philosophy*. Thornton, Butterworth, Ltd., London, 1912, 44.

SECTION B: THE POWERS OF INTERNAL SENSATION

Besides the act of external sensation which requires the physical presence of an object we can experience another kind of sensation which takes place even when objects are absent. We can recall, for example, a frightening experience of the distant past, perhaps the experience of falling from a boat into deep water. Or we may use our imagination to construct visual images of things that we have never actually seen. Another example might be the sensing of some object as harmful, without really knowing why, and without ever having had precisely that kind of sensation before. These experiences belong respectively to the *sense memory,** to the *imagination,** and to the *cogitative power.** They are examples of powers of sensation that operate without a physically present object.

Comparison With External Sensation and Intellection

We differentiate internal and the external sensation not so much by the position of the object, or of the sense organs, as by the kind of object that is grasped and the subsequent activity of the sense power. The object of internal sensation is more immaterial, since it is independent of the necessity of physical presence. Therefore, the internal senses are more immanent in their operations; their operations rise more from the dynamism of sense power itself than do the operations of the external senses. Indeed the activities of the internal senses so resemble the activities of reason in their immateriality that some psychologists and philosophers have not made a sharp distinction between these two types of cognitive activity. Without going into a strictly philosophical analysis of what intellectual activity is, it can be shown by an example from common experience that it differs from internal sensation. The sense memory of a childhood fear of deep water differs radically from the memory of an explanation why a person may drown in water. The difference between the two lies primarily in the type of object remembered. In sense memory, it is an object in which time and place, and fear, play an integral part, since we cannot separate from a sense experience the material conditions in which it took place; in the intellectual memory, the object remembered has no direct bearing upon a particular time and place and our personal reaction; the solution to the problem applies indifferently to any time or place, or person.

Divisions of the Internal Senses (Readings: II, B, No. 1)

When we look at the kind of thing perceived by the internal senses, we find two broad divisions of object: first, objects which had originally come through the external senses, such as colors, sounds, odors, shapes, and the like; and second, objects which originate only indirectly in the external senses, as an object recognized as harmful or useful. This latter kind of object, though not sensed externally, still possesses, however, the qualities of sensory objects, namely, the individuating conditions of time and place, and belongs essentially to the sense order.

St. Thomas calls the first division the *intentiones sensatae* (sensed intentions); and the second he calls *intentiones insensatae* (unsensed intentions). The words *sensed* and *unsensed* refer to the act of external sensation. When St. Thomas employs the word *sensation* and does not modify it, he is referring to external sensation. The distinction made by St. Thomas points out that some internal sense objects have a direct bearing on external sensation, and some do not. In the first division there are two powers, namely, the *central sense* * (*sensus communis*) and the *imagination;* and in the second division, there are two, namely, the *estimative* * power (called the *cogitative sense* in man) and the *sense memory* (named *recall* * or *reminiscence* * in man). Thus, there are four different kinds of internal sensory powers which are found in all kinds of higher animals. While these four powers are generically the same, they are specifically distinct from each other because they have distinct formal objects.

The Unity of All Powers in Man

Before we take up specific differences among the powers of internal sensation, let us say something about their unity. There is danger of regarding these formal distinctions too absolutely, in the manner that upholders of the strict *faculty theory* * have done. To avoid this danger, we must point out again the substantial unity of all the powers of the soul, inasmuch as they all originate in the soul and are for the perfection of the same substance. In man, internal sensations are not isolated psychic experiences, just as external sensations are not atomized sense experiences. This has been forcefully argued by the gestalt psychologists. There is, beyond the unity of the external and internal sense powers among themselves, a higher unity in which the sensory powers of the soul join with the powers of reason to give man a unified human experience. While the different powers of the soul may be differentiated with respect to their formal objects, they have a substantial continuity within the same subject and they are best understood when they are seen in their mutual causal relationships.

The Central Sense

We might imagine the external senses as series of telephone lines coming in from different geographical areas to one central receiving station. The external senses, operating singly, cannot co-ordinate the information they carry, no more than electric wires can co-ordinate messages. With only the external senses to serve him, man's experience of the external world would consist entirely of unrelated sense impressions. We know, however, that man does receive co-ordinated sense impressions in which the objects of several of the external senses are combined. We are aware, for example, that whiteness, sweetness, odor, and shape all belong to one object, food.

Consequently, man has a power which connects and correlates the objects that differ among themselves, joining them in a psychical unity which corresponds to the physical unity that things have in nature. Evidently it cannot be a question here of a kind of discourse, which belongs only to the power of reason. Even in the sense order man knows things as wholes. A unified sensible object is the object known by the central sense. By its detailed study of sensory experience, gestalt psychology has given us empirical evidence of the operation of such a power, and has, in this respect, reiterated a very important conclusion of Aristotelian and Thomistic psychology. Gestalt psychology has shown that our sense-knowing entails a synthesis of specifically diverse sensations.

The sense which performs this function of synthesis for the objects of the external senses we have called the *central sense.* We employ this name instead of *common sense,* which is frequently used. *Common sense* has connotations like *majority opinion* or *commonplace prudence,* which do not belong to this internal sensory power. It is better to adopt terminology that avoids these nonphilosophical overtones and points out at the same time the function of the power. Some authors employ the term *synthetic sense,* which is better than *common sense,* but does not make allowance for a function of this power equally as important as that of combining different external sensations, namely, the function of discriminating among the various objects of the external senses.

Though the ability to discriminate among various external sensory objects is the contrary of the power to co-ordinate, both acts belong to the same power. They belong to the same sense power because they involve the same genus of activity, namely, both are functions of a kind of sensory judgment.[15]   Any kind of judgment presupposes a unified power of knowledge which can recognize sameness and differences.   The central sense makes a sensory judgment about the objects and activities of the external senses.

Because of the close association in name between common sensible objects and the *Central sense (sensus communis)*, it was thought by some that the five common sensibles (movement, rest, number, figure, and magnitude) are properly the objects of this power.   It is true that the central sense perceives the common sensibles, but only because it perceives all the objects of the external senses.   Since the common sensibles are properties of objects as they exist in nature, if they are known at all, it is by means of the external senses.   Extension is not perceived by the central sense unless it is first sensed by the external senses.   For if the eye or the hand, for example, did not grasp the extension of a body, it would be impossible for the central sense to perceive extension.   Hence, the common sensibles are not properly the objects of the central sense.

Sensory Awareness

The root of the "judgment" of the central sense lies in the fact that the central sense is the physical and psychical prolongation of the external sensory powers.   This is why it can co-ordinate and discriminate the objects of the external senses, and why it can judge and direct the activities of these powers.   For it is not enough that the central sense *perceive the objects* of the external senses; it must also *perceive their activities* and constantly direct them.   The external senses do not make contact with the external world by a solitary act from which one can immediately have complete sense knowledge of the object.   They must be constantly redirected to their objects.   Thus, in hearing and seeing and other sensory activities there is a kind of continuity because of a permanent subject, the soul, and because of a constant back and forth movement between the senses and the external world.   The central sense exercises this role of liaison between the external world and the self.

The control which is exercised presupposes a sensory awareness.

---

[15] The term "judgment" is applicable to the central sense only in a derived usage. *Cf.* the notes on intellectual judgment in Section A of Part III.

Here is the first trace of a very important psychological phenomenon that we call *consciousness*.* Sensory awareness is the least perfect kind of consciousness, and not to be put on the same plane as the reflexive consciousness that belongs to the power of intelligence. The central sense does not have, for example, the kind of consciousness that the intellect has when it reflects on its own thoughts. No sense power can have this kind of complete reflection, because the activities of all the senses, external, and internal, are exercised by means of a physical organ. Since an organ is composed of matter which has its parts extended outside of each other, there can be no perfect reflection upon itself by the power of such an organ. At most, one part can reflect upon another that is joined to it. That is what the central sense does in respect to the activities of the external senses.

THE NECESSITY OF SENSORY AWARENESS

A sensory power of awareness is necessary. Without it, animals could not react in a fitting way to the stimuli which affect their external senses. External sensation alone is not enough to safeguard the life of the animal, for unless the various external senses are brought to bear upon objects through the inner experience of animals and related by means of the internal senses to the welfare of the animal, animal life could not long survive. But in man, the central sense plays a higher role, since it is an instrument in the life of reason, both in the practical and in the speculative order. The central sense plays a very important role, for example, in solving the problem of the objectivity of our knowledge. It is the bridge by which objects can pass from the external world through our external senses into our consciousness. Thus, the central sense gives us the final assurance of the existence of an external world. It is through the awareness we have of objects acting upon our external senses that we have a final guarantee of the existence of objects really distinct from us.

The central sense is operative also in preparing the mind for the abstraction of a universal nature from the phenomena gained through external sensation. The nature manifests itself through the phenomena. But the abstracted nature has a unity which somehow must appear already on the sensory plane. Thus, the central sense gives a pre-intellectual synthesis which corresponds analogously to the intellectual synthesis that takes place when the mind grasps the universal nature that underlies sense phenomena.

Finally, we can see the relationship of the central sense in judgments that involve individuals belonging to the world of sense. By a kind of reflection on the origins of its acts in sense experience, the intellect can judge of these individuals. The central sense plays no little part in making this judgment possible.

The Imagination

The second of the internal senses is called imagination. It has a twofold function: to retain images of past external sense experience and to compose new images from the experience of the past. Because it retains the species of objects grasped by the external senses, the imagination can reproduce them. It does not actually *recreate the external sensation,* for that would require the physical presence of an object, but it forms an image which corresponds to the original sensation. When we employ the word *image,* we should not think that the imagination retains and reproduces only the visual experiences of the past. This is only one type of imaginative object, the one with which we are most familiar. The imagination can retain and reproduce the sensory forms of all the external senses. But in most people the use of the power of imagination is very restricted, and it normally functions well only with visual objects. How inept most of us are in the use of this power can be shown easily if we try to reproduce in our imagination the forms of anything more than the most simple odors, sounds and tastes.

CREATIVE ROLE OF THE IMAGINATION

The imagination has a "creative" function which consists in making composite sensory images from various details of past experiences retained in the imagination. The details of the product of the imagination must have been received by the external senses at some time or other, but the arrangement is the work of the imagination. It is this power to combine various experiences that makes the imagination so valuable an instrument for the *mind.**

There is strong experimental evidence for the close relationship of this creative ability and acuteness of intelligence. Some intellectual habits more than others depend upon the imagination. The imagination is in a sense a more important instrument to the artist than his external senses, for while he must have acute powers of observation, it is more important for him to have a sharp imagination by which he can make use of his observations. For a work of fine art is not merely a repetition of what is found in nature but a *creation.** St. Thomas points out the importance of the imagination for the mathematician when he says that mathematical concepts, which employ *signate matter,** are ultimately resolved in the imagination. The intellect which directly knows only universals must employ a sensory power when it deals, for example, with the divisions of quantity from which numbers originate. For if these divisions were not grasped as distinct by means of the imagination, they could not be thought of as distinct. Like the mathematician, the physical scientist, who employs hypotheses in searching out the secrets of nature, makes continuous use of the imagination. Hence, we can say that the broad use to which the imagination can be put in the service of the intellect shows that it is a power that everyone should set high value upon and try to develop.

ORDERING OF THE IMAGINATION

Though the imagination is an invaluable instrument for the intellect, it needs control. It is a widely ranging power and very elusive; it is important that we keep careful check on it. With too free an imagination, a scientist may become too much of a dreamer, and an artist or moralist, too much of a visionary. Imagination is like a tool shop for the mind; it must be kept in order, clean, and uncluttered. A shop that lacks order, even though it contains the finest tools, can be a dangerous place to work in. The intellect must operate with a controlled imagination.

DREAMS

The most familiar example of the product of the imagination is the ordinary dream. A dream is the product of the imagination at such a time when the natural controls of the senses, or of the intellect, are not operating. The highest type of control is in the power of intellectual judgment; the other is in the central sense. There are times when control is lacking because of a disturbed physical condition of the body due to exhaustion or drugs. Lack of control may also be due simply to the effects of natural sleep. While the immediate and positive cause of dreams is the power of imagination, the indirect cause is the lack of control over the imagination. Physical stimuli like drugs, irritation, or pressure on the body, and psychological stimuli like fear or desire, disturbed states of mind, and so on, influence the imagination when control is lacking. These extrinsic factors which act upon the central nervous system, are not themselves the causes of dreams, for dreams are frequently not experienced when these conditions are present; they are, however, the occasions. That dreams can be occasioned not merely by physical causes but by our states of mind (by desires, for example, consciously or unconsciously repressed during our periods of wakefulness) is the view of many psychiatrists. It is a well founded opinion and it would be a mistake to disregard the contributions of men like Freud and *Jung* * and *Adler* * in this area of psychological research. But the view that dreams are always the symbols of latent sexual instincts or of deep seated conflicts seems to be an opinion as exaggerated as that which denies any such basis, since other physical explanations are possible.

The Estimative Power

The third of the internal sensory powers is called the *estimative power* or, as it exists in man, the *cogitative power*. It is a power of knowledge whose function is to provide for the physical welfare of an individual or of a species by judging the harm or benefit to be found in objects of the sensory order. The ultimate goal of this power is the preservation of animal existence itself. Other sense powers are subordinate to this one: the estimative power employs the particular acts and objects of the other sense powers in view of this common goal—the development and preservation of animal existence.

Since it is by the estimative power that an animal recognizes among sense objects what is beneficial or harmful to itself or to its species, this power is akin to prudence in man. It is the teaching of St. Thomas that in the universe the more perfect species of a lower order participate in some way in the perfections of the superior order, as though there were a shading over from one to the other. Hence, inanimate things would share in the perfection of living beings, plants in the perfection of animals, animals in the perfection of man, and man in the perfection of angels. But animal "prudence" is more of a "reflection" of prudence than the virtue itself, because an animal does not have reason, which belongs essentially to any prudential act. Human prudence, which is a virtue by which man correctly selects various means to an end in the contingent practical circumstances of life, operates through intelligence and free choice. But animal "prudence," though it is the effect of an intelligence that produced nature, does not operate as a free intelligent principle, but according to necessity.

There is no spontaneity in the operation of the estimative sense in irrational animals, because the end, the means, and the pattern of action have already been determined for each kind of animal by the intelligence that governs nature. Thus, birds of the same species build their nests in a uniform way and animals of the same kind procure their food or defend themselves in a uniform way. Within the same species of animals the kind of activity is the same for all individuals, with accidental degrees of difference among them. Though these activities are not learned from experience or instruction, they may be accidentally perfected through exercise. They are not haphazard, for they are intelligently directed to the goal which is the welfare of animal life. They are as invariable as the species, because they are *teleologically* * directed to a specific kind of animal life.

The material object of the estimative sense is anything that can be grasped by the external senses, but the formal object of this sense power is what is known to be harmful or beneficial to the individual or to the species in the objects of sense. It is not something grasped by the external senses. St. Thomas calls this, as we saw, an *intentio insensata* (an unsensed object). On the other hand, when an animal flees from a natural enemy, we need not suppose that the animal has a "blueprint of an enemy" in its imagination; nor need we suppose that in making a nest a bird necessarily has previous experience in making a nest, or has received instruction in a sensory way from other birds. Knowledge of the estimative power is precisely that which is not grasped by the external senses and cannot be explained solely in terms of external sense experience. Rather it belongs to a kind of "prudence" rooted in the nature of the animal.

The Cogitative Power

Because man has a sensory nature with the same basic tendencies of self-preservation and reproduction found in other animals, he has a sense power which corresponds to the estimative sense in irrational animals. But because his sensory powers operate in conjunction with, and in subordination to, reason, this power cannot be identical with that of irrational animals. In man the knowledge of what is harmful or helpful among sensory objects is tempered and directed by reason.

The material objects of the cogitative sense, while differing in no essential way from the material objects of the estimative power, have an excellence in proportion to the goal which they serve. Man's knowledge of self-preservation, the variety of his food and the variety of ways in which he prepares it, his manner of expressing sexual love, and so on, are examples of cogitative actions. These are examples of the types of good that belong to man's sensory nature, but raised to a superior order by the direction of his reason.

In order to acquire the "particular experiences," in the sense in which St. Thomas uses the term, not only reason must be employed, but the cogitative power also, since it is directly concerned in the knowledge of the singular, whether it be an individual of some species, or a particular human action.[16]   In man the cogitative power operates as an instrument of his intellect, both in acquiring knowledge, and in directing his actions.

Prudence is in the interior sense, which is perfected by memory and experience so as to judge particular experiences promptly. This does not mean, however, that prudence is in the interior sense as in its principal subject, for it is chiefly in the reason, yet by a kind of application it extends to this sense.[17]

RELATION OF THE COGITATIVE POWER AND REASON

Just as the estimative power in beasts (which is frequently called "animal prudence") makes it possible for them to judge things useful or harmful to them (judgments which go beyond the image delivered by the external senses), so the cogitative power in man makes it possible for him to judge singular human actions as useful or harmful to him as a human person. Thus, it is employed in his intellectual and moral life, since man's rational powers do not operate independently of his sense powers. Unlike the estimative power in beasts, this cogitative power in man is not predetermined by nature to particular types of impressions. It functions as an instrument of reason, and is thus discursive and quasi-syllogistic, proceeding by the comparison of one impression with another, and coming to a conclusion. Thus, the cogitative power in man shows a greater amount of flexibility than the estimative power in beasts, since reason dominates its activity. In fact, the operations of this power are not distinct and separate from the operations of the intellect, but rather are instruments of the reason in one dynamic activity that terminates in an intellectual grasp of the concrete particular. Hence this power is frequently called the "particular reason" by St. Thomas.

Sense Memory

The last of the internal sense powers is sense memory, by which we are able to recall past experiences of a sensory kind, with a recognition of the past insofar as it has affected us favorably or unfavorably. While the imagination is a "storehouse" of external sensory impressions, it is not sense memory in the strict sense of the word, for it

---

[16] St. Thomas: *Summa Theologiae*, I, 79, 1.
[17] *Ibid*. II–II, 47, 3, *ad*. 3.

does not record the past in its formal aspect of the recognition of the past as it actually affected the knower. Sense memory is the "store-house" of the estimative power rather than of the external senses.

To illustrate the difference between imagination and memory in respect to the same kind of sensory object, let us suppose that a person goes to a movie, enjoys the picture, but after some time forgets the characters, the plot, and even the name of the film. If by chance he goes to see the same film several years later, not realizing that he has seen it before, it may happen that the characters and the plot seem familiar to him, but he cannot recall why they are familiar. He has retained the images of the characters and their actions in his imagination, but they have no direct ties with a recognizable past experience that is the work of his imagination. If, on the contrary, he can identify the movie as one that he has already seen, if he can recall the circumstances of the previous experience and be aware of how he was affected by it, his new experience is an example of memory.

In comparison with memory, the imagination is like a vault in which a film had been stored to be shown again at a later date. Imagination is, then, simply an instrument of memory in that it furnishes the sensory data of the past in which memory operates. Not simply the retention of the past experience, but the recognition of it as having already affected us, makes memory in the formal sense. Memory perfects the imagination by placing the images in their proper setting of time and place, for without memory the images would be unconnected and in a kind of psychical vacuum, without a mooring in personal experience.

RECALL: SENSE MEMORY IN MAN

The power of sense memory in man differs from the sense memory of brute animals in the same way that the cogitative power differs from the estimative power, namely, by being subject to the power of reason. Reason makes it possible for man to employ sense memory deliberately, in a kind of syllogistic way. The sense memory of brute animals, for example, is predetermined by the physical surroundings in which it operates, as when a dog remembers the pain it experienced when the person who once inflicted the pain is seen and smelled again. Unlike irrational animals, man can deliberately provoke his sense memory to act without a new sensory experience, as he does when he wishes to recall the name and features of a person who had injured him. We should not suppose, however, that sense memory in man operates only in the area of sensory objects that have harmed us or benefited us physically. On the contrary, any sensory experience connected with us as human persons, whether in the physical, intellectual, or moral order, is subject to sense memory, since we cannot in fact isolate any of our inferior powers from the power of reason.

In a passage of his *Commentary on Aristotle's On Memory and Recall,* St. Thomas points out the difference between recall, as found in man, and sense memory, as found in irrational animals.

> He (Aristotle) clarifies the term *recall.* He says, first of all, that recall is a return to what was already known. Then he shows that not every return to knowledge already possessed is an example of recall. First of all, it is not the kind of return had in memory in which the knower again knows what he knew or sensed before by means of the external senses or by the central sense. In this regard memory as well as recall refer to knowledge gained at some previous time. But recall is different in this way. When we return to the previous knowledge, recall is not part of what was said, or sensed, or remembered, or imagined, or known. Rather, through recall we remember; it is a kind of movement that makes us remember. Thus memory follows recall as the term of its movement. Or as another reading has it, "recall follows memory," because just as the searching by reason is the way which leads to the knowledge of something else, proceeding as it does from something already known, so it is with recall, which is the way that leads to remembering something, proceeding likewise from something already remembered.[18]

A distinction must be made, however, between the memory of a sensory experience and the memory of an intellectual operation of the past. Intellectual memory differs from sense memory because it deals with a type of object that is strictly intellectual. The ability to recall philosophical proofs, not simply as printed words on a page or sounds of the teacher's voice, but as meaningful statements, comes from intellectual memory. Nevertheless, the intellectual memory can operate only through phantasms by means of which the experience is concretized.

THE UTILITY OF SENSE MEMORY

Sense memory is a very practical instrument of the intellectual life. Too often its training is ignored. It is a rare experience to find a

---

[18] St. Thomas Aquinas: *Commentary on Aristotle's On Memory and Recall,* Lesson 4, Numbers 356, 357.

person so modest that he admits having a poor judgment, but almost as rare to find a person who does not complain of a poor memory. Good memory is just as important to a sound intelligence as acute external sensory powers, good perception, and a creative imagination, because memory makes it possible to employ the experiences of these other powers for our intellectual development. The ability to recall the names, places, dates, definitions, colors, sounds, printed formulae, or any other object of a sensory kind is not an undesirable quality. A person with a poor memory is handicapped; he is like a skilled craftsman without his tools, unable to work because he has nothing to work with.

Memory is important, however, not only because it is an aid to reason in the theoretical and practical details of our lives, but also because it plays a very important part in our total experience of living. Most of us are fortunate in that the memory of pleasant details of the past is sharpened, while the remembrance of the difficult and painful details of the past is dimmed. This is explained only partially by the fact that memory is weakened the further we are removed from the original experience. There is a more important reason. Memory has a broader function than to make us recall isolated experiences of the past; it gives continuity to our lives. Memory makes possible the kind of prudence that comes with experience. By using memory in conjunction with our other powers we can measure a single incident of the present against the background of a life's experience. When the memory of pleasant details is sharpened and that of painful details is erased, it is perhaps because we are able to appreciate more accurately the true value of those experiences in an over-all judgment that memory makes possible. Each one judges his memories of the past in the light of the person that he is at present. In the present he is a person compounded, as it were by means of memory, of all his experiences of the past. St. Thomas wrote:

> It is the role of prudence to direct the prudent man in the immediately practical affairs about which he must make decisions. But it is not merely the present that he (the prudent man) must investigate, but also the past. Thus, in his *Rhetoric,* Tully lists as parts of prudence not only providence by which the future is prepared for, but also intelligence by which the present is investigated, and memory by which the past is apprehended. Other animals, therefore, which have a participated likeness of prudence, must have not only a sensation of the present but also a memory of the past. At the beginning of the *Metaphysics,* therefore,

the Philosopher says that some animals have memory of their sensations and are, consequently, "prudent." [19]

THE TRAINING OF MEMORY

Psychologists have contributed greatly to our knowledge of memory and of memory training. They have given a number of rules, the fruit of their experiments, for training a better memory. In general, these rules stress the importance of strong initial impressions, clear-cut associations, and frequent repetitions. Until more recent studies gave evidence to the contrary, it was held almost universally that memory training could succeed only in the young. A person who had reached maturity was told that he could no longer memorize things easily, but that he should depend more upon reason and experience. He was not expected to remember things that young people could easily remember. But there is no clinical evidence to show that the power of memory deteriorates any more quickly than the other sensory powers. Poor memory in adults is due apparently more to a lack of exercise than to any failure in the sense power itself. Because they depend more on experience and a mature judgment, adults do not use memory as much, perhaps, as they did when they were children, and like any organic power that is not exercised, their power of memory becomes less efficient.

Among other causes of poor memory in adults is the belief that the cultivation of a good memory is impossible in older persons. Having been convinced that they cannot do it, they do not make a serious effort to memorize things. Thus a psychological barrier arises for the adults when they are told, for example, that they cannot learn a foreign language because it is impossible for them to remember the words or the grammar. Another cause of poor memory in adults may be their lack of interest in the kind of experience that sensory memory deals with. These and other extrinsic causes can help explain why adults often complain of a poor memory.

Conclusion

In our discussion of the internal senses we made a distinction between the estimative sense in irrational animals and the cogitative sense in man, and between sense memory in irrational animals and the power of recall in man. The truth of the matter is that all the internal sense powers as well as the external sense powers operate

---

[19] St. Thomas: *Commentary on Aristotle's On Memory and Recall*, I, 298.

under the direction of man's reason and hence do not operate in man in exactly the same way as they do in irrational beings. Our knowledge of these powers in irrational animals comes from an analogy with our own powers. In man all the sense powers are the instruments of reason. It is only when we come to the study of the rational powers of the soul, however, that we shall be able to set up a formal comparison between the powers of sense and the powers of reason, and only then understand the instrumental role of the senses with respect to reason.

Section C: The Sense Appetites

The natural terminus of the estimative power in brute animals and of the cogitative power in man is not the simple act of knowing, but action. The recognition of the sensory good to be pursued or the sensory evil to be avoided is not speculative but practical knowledge, and it causes in the soul what St. Thomas calls a *movement of sensuality*. His use of the term *sensuality,* however, does not have the restrictive or pejorative meaning that belongs to *sensuality* as employed in common usage. In the following passage, St. Thomas gives us the etymology of the word and shows that the movement of sensuality differs from sensory knowledge.

> The name *sensuality* comes from the sensual movement about which Augustine speaks in Book XII, *On the Trinity,* for the name of a power comes from its act, just as the power of sight, for example, receives its name from seeing. The act of a sense-knowing power, unlike the act of the sense *appetite,** is completed when the thing apprehended is in the knower, but the act of the appetitive power is completed when the one who desires actually turns to the desirable object. Therefore the act of the power of knowledge is like rest, but the act of an appetitive power is like movement.[20]

Appetitive Union and Cognitive Union

In no case is the soul perfected absolutely in knowledge alone, because its union of knowledge is an intentional one in which forms exist, not in their natural mode of being, but in that of the knower. It is necessary, therefore, that there be a movement subsequent to the

---

[20] St. Thomas: *Summa Theologiae,* I, 81, 1, Body of the Article.

movement of the cognitive power in which the soul returns to the forms as they exist in their physical mode of existence. The movement of the appetite is, as it were, the completion of a circle which began when the objects acted upon the external sense powers.

Although the cognitive sensory powers and the appetitive powers differ because of movement in opposite directions, there is no conflict between them, for appetitive powers are the natural completion of the cognitive.

> The movement of a cognitive power is terminated in the soul; for the known must be in the knower in the manner of being of the knower. But the movement of an appetitive power terminates in the thing itself. The Philosopher, therefore, in Book III, *On the Soul,* speaks of a kind of circle in the acts of the soul, insofar as the thing which is outside the soul moves the intellect, and the thing understood moves the appetite, and the appetite leads back to the thing itself, from which the movement originally began.[21]

Many different names are used for this sensual movement. *Passion* * is a name which suggests both extreme sensual love as well as being acted upon. *Emotion* * suggests an impulse either towards an object that is helpful or away from one that is harmful. *Affection* * suggests an inclination to love or to enjoy what is pleasant. *Conation* * and *erexsis* * indicate a striving for a goal. No single word can express all that is contained in this movement. We shall continue to use the name *sense appetite,* which suggests a desire for food, but in its etymology and in its traditional usage it has a much broader meaning.

Natural Appetite (Readings: II, C, No. 1)

Every natural being, living or not, has an inclination towards the perfection proper to it. Without entering specifically into the question whether or not they have only one substantial form in the strict sense, we can hold that natural inanimate bodies tend to act according to their nature; that plants tend to reproduce themselves; that the external senses tend to grasp their proper objects, and so on. This general tendency in all things towards what is perfective is called a *natural appetite.* The appetite of cognitive beings is a special kind of natural appetite.

---

[21] St. Thomas: *Disputed Question on Truth,* I, 2, Body of the Article.

Elicited Appetite

Those beings which possess knowledge, however, have a more perfect appetite because form is found in them in a more perfect way. In those beings which lack knowledge the inclination is in only one direction, namely, that in which the being will be perfected by means of a limited, particular form. But in those beings with knowledge there is an appetite also for the things whose forms belong to other things. In its highest form the appetite which follows knowledge is called *elicited appetite*.* The name comes from the Latin *lacere,* which means *to coax*—it is as though the object of knowledge coaxes the knower to seek what is good (or to avoid what is harmful). The appetites that follow knowledge are as varied as the types of object which are known.

> Some things are inclined to a good solely through a natural inclination without knowledge, like plants and inanimate bodies. This inclination to a good is called a *natural appetite*. Other things are inclined to a good by means of knowledge, not insofar as they recognize the thing as having the essence of good, but recognize it as some concrete good. This the sense does when it knows sweetness and whiteness and things of this kind. The inclination which follows this knowledge is called sensitive appetite. Finally, some things are inclined to a good because they recognize the essence of goodness, and this is characteristic of intelligence. Beings of intelligence are most perfectly inclined to the good, not being directed as it were by someone else, like those things that lack knowledge, nor being inclined to the particular good only, like those beings that have only sense knowledge, but being inclined as it were to universal good. This inclination is called will.[22]

The Internal Senses and Appetite

There is certainly some connection between the imagination and the sensory appetites, as both Aristotle and St. Thomas point out.[23] However, the imagination alone cannot move the appetites. There must also be some knowledge of benefit or harm for the individual in the object of sense. This comes from the estimative or cogitative power. Lewd imaginative pictures, for example, do not necessarily excite a person's sexual appetite. It is only when the cogitative

---

[22] St. Thomas: *Summa Theologiae,* I, 59, 1, Body of the Article.

[23] Aristotle: *On the Soul,* III, 10 and 11. St. Thomas: *Commentary on Aristotle's On the Soul,* III, 15 and 16.

power is operative, that is, when the practical notion of good or evil of the sensory order is recognized, that the sense appetites are aroused. Sexual appetite, for instance, would be aroused only when an object capable of rendering sexual pleasure to the individual has an affinity for the particular capacities of the individual.

The intensity of sense appetite depends upon the type of object, the strength of the sensory impression, and the susceptibility of the knower. From the viewpoint of the knower, there is a great diversity of susceptibility to sensible goods, not only among different persons, but even within the same person at different times. On the part of the object, some things tend to move the appetites more than others either because they create a stronger impression on the senses, or because they are the kind of thing that would naturally arouse the appetites, for example, the public execution of criminals or public display of sex acts.

Morality and the Appetitive Union

Because the sensory appetites incline the knower to the object as it is in its natural mode of existence, a person who desires and pursues a sensory good is in a far different relationship to the object than the person who has only knowledge of the object. The difference lies in the two types of union that are effected. Love depends on knowledge; nevertheless, it can go far beyond knowledge in the way that it affects the knower. From the viewpoint of causality, the appetites depend on knowledge; nevertheless the appetites are, in a certain sense, more important than the powers of knowledge. In the two short passages which follow, St. Thomas explains why this is true.

> Love is said to transform the lover into what is loved, because through love the lover is inclined to the actuality of the thing loved; but knowledge gives a likeness only, insofar as the image of the thing known is in the knower.[24]

In another passage, he says:

> When, therefore, the thing in which there is good is nobler than the soul itself, in which the understood likeness is, then, by comparison with such a thing, the will is higher than the intellect. But when the thing which is good is less noble than the soul, then, even in comparison with that thing, the intellect is higher than the will. Hence the love of

---

[24] St. Thomas Aquinas: *Disputed Question on Evil,* Question VI, Article 1, Reply to Objection 13.

God is better than the knowledge of God; but, on the contrary, the knowledge of corporeal things is better than the love of them.[25]

Divisions of the Sense Appetites: Concupiscible and Irascible (Readings: II, C, No. 2)

Within the sensory appetites there is a primary division into what are called the *concupiscible* * and the *irascible* * appetites. Concupiscible comes from the Latin *cupere,* which means *to desire,* while irascible comes from *irasci,* which means *to become angry.* The concupiscible appetites are those by which the animal is inclined to the enjoyment of sensory goods as perfective of the animal nature; the irascible appetites are those which incline the animal to overcome the obstacles that lie in the path of the sensory goods to be enjoyed. Thus the formal object of the one is the *pleasurable sensory object,* and the formal object of the other is the *difficulty connected with the pleasurable object.*

Let us illustrate how the two appetites are related. Suppose a child's appetite for food is aroused by the smell of freshly baked cookies. His mother's threats of a spanking, however, are an obstacle to his enjoyment of the cookies. On the one hand a desire to satisfy his appetite grows; on the other hand, a fear that he will be caught is present. If he takes the cookies and begins to eat them and is caught in the act by his mother, he will be unable to enjoy them and his anger is aroused and the child may show his petulance until the mother gives in.

IRASCIBLE APPETITE AS THE INSTRUMENT OF THE CONCUPISCIBLE

The irascible appetites are related to the concupiscible as means to an end. When nature put into us a tendency to pleasurable goods, she has also provided the means to attain those goods when difficulties arise. By means of irascible appetites we are moved to make the extra effort needed to acquire the pleasurable goods. But if, on the contrary, the pursuit of the pleasurable good is detrimental to our animal nature, the irascible appetites will turn us away from the pursuit of them. Thus, despair or fear would turn a person from a sensory pleasure whose possession might mean pain or death. In this sense, despair and fear are good.

The two sets of appetites, then, are like two balances or springs that tend to keep the tendencies of our animal nature in harmony: the

---

[25] St. Thomas: *Summa Theologiae,* I, 82, 3, Body of the Article.

concupiscible tending toward the pleasurable good, and the irascible pulling with the concupiscible if the task is difficult though worth while; but the irascible pulling against the concupiscible if the pursuit is detrimental to the whole. Just as the tension on one spring is determined by the intensity of the pull by the other, so the intensity of the irascible appetite depends upon the intensity of the concupiscible. The strength of the desire is commensurate with the pleasure which will be given, and this in turn measures the intensity of the courage, anger, or whatever other irascible appetite is aroused. Consequently, because they have an instrumental role, the irascible appetites are employed only during the time and in the measure that they are needed in their relationship to the concupiscible.

The relationship of the two kinds of sense appetites is pointed out in the following passage:

> For sometimes the soul occupies itself with disagreeable things, contrary to its concupiscible inclination, in order to combat obstacles according to its irascible inclination. Hence, movements of the irascible appetite counteract those of the concupiscible for concupiscence, when aroused, diminishes anger, and anger, when aroused, usually diminishes concupiscence. It is clear also that the irascible is like a champion and defender of the concupiscible when it rises against those things which obstruct the attainment of suitable things sought by the concupiscible, or when it opposes the harmful forces, that the concupiscible flees. For this reason, all the movements of the irascible appetite originate and terminate in the movements of the concupiscible appetite. For example, anger originates in sorrow, and when it inflicts vengeance, terminates in joy. For this reason also, the struggles of animals are over concupiscible objects, food and sex, as the Philosopher says in Book VIII, *On the Animals.*[26]

LIST OF THE CONCUPISCIBLE APPETITES

In the interplay of the concupiscible and irascible appetites, we can discern a variety of sub-types within the two general divisions of sense appetite. Thus, in the genus of concupiscible appetite we find that for every concupiscible good to which the appetite is inclined there is a contrary from which the concupiscible appetite turns away. And then within each division of these contraries there are three stages of the movement of the appetite. They are as follows: the first stage of movement toward the pleasurable good is simply the

---

[26] St. Thomas: *Summa Theologiae*, I, 81, 2, Body of the Article.

love of the good; the second stage is the *desire* for the good when it is absent; the third stage is the *enjoyment* in the possession of the good. The contrary division also has three stages. The first is *hatred* of the object causing sensory harm; the second is *aversion,* which is the impulse away from the evil; and the third is *sorrow,* which is *sadness* in the presence of the sensory evil.

LIST OF THE IRASCIBLE APPETITES

The irascible appetite has stages which correspond, with one exception, to the various stages of the concupiscible appetite. The first is found in the pursuit of the pleasurable good is *hope,* which is an inclination to overcome the obstacles to the possession of the good; the second is *courage,* which is the determined stand in overcoming great obstacles to the good. However, there is not a third stage of the irascible appetite corresponding to the enjoyment of the pleasurable good, because there is no need of it, since the goal has been reached—this is the exception mentioned above. On the other side of the picture, where it is a question of sensible harm, there are three stages of the irascible appetite. The first is *despair,* which is an *inclination* to give up in the face of obstacles; the second is *fear* which is the movement to recoil during the struggle because of the threat of harm; and finally anger, which results from the presence of evil which has not been overcome. The following graph shows the stages in the contrary tendencies of the two kinds of sense appetite:

CONCUPISCIBLE

Stage	Positive		Contrary
First	Love	Movement begins	Hatred
Second	Desire	Movement continues	Aversion
Third	Enjoyment	Object is present	
		Movement ends	Sorrow

IRASCIBLE

First	Hope	Movement begins	Despair
Second	Courage	Movement continues	Fear
Third	No irascible	Object is present	
	appetite	Movement ends	Anger

Value of the Sense Appetites

Perhaps no one would dispute the value of the sensory appetites from the standpoint of the needs of irrational animals, but many have questioned their value relative to the spiritual nature of man. Because of a lack of understanding of a natural body-soul relationship, and because of an exaggerated conception of the spiritual nature of man, the sensory appetites have sometimes been regarded as evils rather than as useful powers of the soul. Strong sense appetites may be compared to swift flowing rivers or spirited animals—if they are not controlled, they destroy and ravage. But no one should prefer feeble appetites to strong ones simply because of the difficulty in curbing them, just as no one should prefer a stagnant river or a lethargic horse to swift ones because of the difficulties of controlling them. When the appetites are subordinated to the needs of reason they are most valuable human instruments: the sense appetites—anger, fear and sorrow, love, courage, and all the rest—can help man live more fully the life of reason.

Control of the Appetites

Because of the effect that appetites have on a person far beyond the effect that knowledge has, it is necessary that a person learn how to control his appetites.

In irrational animals the sensory appetites are directed by nature to the higher good of the animal order, which is the perfection of animal existence. In man, they should be directed by reason to the perfection of rational existence. Reason, however, does not exercise a despotic control over the sensory appetites. Consequently, when there is a conflict between the rational and the sensory appetites, the inferior appetite will sometimes overcome the superior. For example, no argument will convince a man to risk his life even for a noble cause, if he is seized by an uncontrollable fear of danger or death. On the other hand, a man can be persuaded to risk his life, perhaps for the sake of justice, if his passions are under the control of reason.

St. Thomas describes the kind of rule that reason has over the sense appetites:

As the Philosopher says (*Politics,* Book I, Chapter 3) we observe in animals both a despotic and a politic [27] rule: for the soul dominates the body by a despotic rule, but the intellect dominates the appetite by a politic and royal rule. *Despotic* describes a power whereby a man rules slaves who do not have the possibility of resisting the power of his rule

[27] It is very difficult, perhaps impossible, to find an adequate rendering of the word *politic.* A politic rule is one exercised over free subjects.

because they have nothing of their own. *Politic* and royal describes a power whereby a man rules free subjects, who, though subject to the direction of the ruler, nevertheless have something of their own, by reason of which they can resist his commands. And so we say the soul dominates the body with a despotic rule, since the members of the body can in no way resist the rule of the soul; at the soul's desire, the hand and the foot and whatever members are subject to voluntary motion, are moved immediately. But the intellect or reason is said to rule the irascible and concupiscible appetites by a politic rule, since the sensitive appetite has something of its own by which it can resist the rule of reason. For the sensitive appetite is moved naturally not only by the estimative power in some animals, and by the cogitative power directed by universal reason in man, but also by the imagination and the sense. Hence, we experience the irascible and concupiscible appetites resisting reason when we sense or imagine something pleasant which reason forbids, or something sad which reason commands. Nevertheless, the fact that the irascible and concupiscible appetites resist reason to some degree does not mean they do not obey reason.[28]

Because the appetites do not always submit to the control of reason, it is necessary for man to employ other means not only to keep them in check but also to employ them most efficaciously. To the control by reason man can add the control by habits. Hence, after studying the powers of reason we take up the subject of habits.

Conclusion

We have come to the third and final stage of our consideration of the sensory powers of the soul. In the course of our consideration we saw how a movement is begun by the action of a sensible object on an external sense power and terminated in sense knowledge. We saw how this movement continued on into the internal senses where knowledge in a more perfect sense takes place—knowledge which included an awareness of the activity of the external world upon the knower, and a recognition of what is harmful or beneficial among the objects of sense. Finally, we saw how the movement is completed by a return, under the impulse of the sense appetites, to the objects of sense which are recognized as harmful or beneficial for the sensory life. This is the first of two such cycles that are found in the life of man. The second is found in the operations of his rational powers, the subject which we shall now take up.

---

[28] St. Thomas: *Summa Theologiae*, I, 81, 1, *ad.* 2.

Bibliography for Part II

Allers, Rudolph: "The Cognitive Aspects of the Emotions."
  The Thomist, Volume IV (1942), 589–648.

Boulogne, Charles-Damian: *My Friends the Senses.*
  Translated by Jane Howes. New York: P. J. Kenedy Sons, 1953.

Flynn, Thomas V.: "The Cogitative Power."
  The Thomist, Volume XVI (1953), 542–563.

Gaffney, Mark A.: *The Psychology of the Interior Senses.*
  St. Louis: B. Herder Co., 1942.

Klubertanz, George P.: *"The Discursive Power."*
  St. Louis: *The Modern Schoolman,* 1952.

Ledvina, Jerome P.: *A Philosophy and Psychology of Sensation According
  to St. Thomas Aquinas.*
  Washington, D.C.: Catholic University, 1941.

Moore, Thomas V.: *Cognitive Psychology.*
  Philadelphia: J. B. Lippincott Co., 1939.
    Part II: "Landmarks in the Theory of Perception."
      Chapters 1, 2, 3, (pages 93–130).
    Part III: "The Psychology of Perception."
      Chapters 1, 2, 3, 4 (pages 209–271).
    Part VI: "The Psychology of Memory."
      Chapter 6, pages 462–472.

Renard, Henri: "The Problem of Knowledge in General."
  The Modern Schoolman, Volume XXIV (1946), 1–11.

Simon, Yves and Peghaire, Julien: "The Philosophical Study of Sensation."
  The Modern Schoolman, Volume XXIII, 111–119.

READINGS FOR PART II

PART II. *THE SENSORY POWERS OF THE SOUL*

SECTION A: EXTERNAL SENSE KNOWLEDGE

No. 1. *The Relationship of the Object to the Power of Sensing*
Aristotle: *On the Soul,* Book II, Chapter 5, Lines 416b32–417a20

St. Thomas: *Commentary on Aristotle's On the Soul,* Book II, Lesson 10, Numbers 350–357

No. 2. *The Definition of a Power of Sensation*
Aristotle: *On the Soul,* Book II, Chapter 12, Lines 424a16–424b19

St. Thomas: *Commentary on Aristotle's On the Soul,* Book II, Lesson 24, Numbers 551–563

No. 3. *A General Division into Proper, Common, and Accidental Objects of Sensation*
Aristotle: *On the Soul,* Book II, Chapter 6, Lines 418a6–418a25

St. Thomas: *Commentary on Aristotle's On the Soul,* Book II, Lesson 13, Numbers 383–398

No. 4. *The Divisions of the External Senses*
St. Thomas: *Summa Theologiae,* Part I, Question 78, Article 3
Is it correct to divide the external senses into five distinct kinds?

SECTION B: INTERNAL SENSE KNOWLEDGE

No. 1. *The Divisions of the Internal Senses*
St. Thomas: *Summa Theologiae,* Part I, Question 78, Article 4
Are the internal senses correctly differentiated?

SECTION C: THE SENSE APPETITES

No. 1. *A General Discussion of Appetite*
St. Thomas: *Summa Theologiae,* Part I, Question 80, Article 1
Is the appetite a special power of the soul?

No. 2. *The Division of the Sense Appetites into Irascible and Concupiscible*
St. Thomas: *Summa Theologiae,* Part I, Question 81, Article 2
Is the sensitive appetite divided into the irascible and concupiscible?

No. 3. *The Relationship of the Sense Appetites to Reason*
St. Thomas: *Summa Theologiae,* Part I, Question 81, Article 3
Do the irascible and concupiscible appetites obey reason?

No. 4. *The Relationship of the Sense Appetites to the Will*
St. Thomas: *Summa Theologiae,* Part I–II, Question 17, Article 7
Is the act of the sensory appetite commanded?

SECTION A: EXTERNAL SENSE KNOWLEDGE
No. 1. The Relationship of the Object to the Power of Sensing
Aristotle: *On the Soul,* Book II, Chapter 5, Lines 416b32–417a20
St. Thomas: *Commentary on Aristotle's On the Soul,* Book II,
Lesson 10, Numbers 350–357

ARISTOTLE:

[¶ 1.] Having settled the previous problems (on the vegetative powers), let us now speak of sensation in general. As has been said, sensation consists of being moved and of being acted upon. Hence, it appears to be some kind of alteration. Some hold that like is acted upon by like. To what extent this is possible or impossible is taken up in the general treatment of activity and passivity.

[¶ 2.] The question arises as to why a sense has no sensation of itself, and why without an external object, the senses do not cause sensation, since they have in themselves fire and earth and the other elements, or the things that happen to these elements, which are the objects of sensation. It is clear that a sense power is not in act (of itself) but only in potency, hence, it does not sense (of itself), just as a combustible object does not burn unless fire is present. Otherwise, it would burn spontaneously and would not need a fire already lit.

[¶ 3.] We speak of sensation in two different ways: first, as a potency, for we say that someone who can hear or see, "sees" or "hears" even if he is asleep; second, as actually operating. So we may speak of a sense in two ways: as in potency and as in act. Similarly, "to sense" is the power to sense or the sense in act.

[¶ 4.] We shall start by saying that being acted upon or moved is the same as acting on or moving. For movement is act, even though it is imperfect, as was stated elsewhere. Everything is acted upon or moved by an agent and a being in act. Hence, we say that to be acted upon is as much by what is like as by what is unlike: What is unlike is acted upon; what has been acted upon is like.

ST. THOMAS:

[¶ 1.] *350.* After treating of the vegetative part of the soul, the Philosopher now begins to treat of the sensitive part. He makes a twofold division: He first deals with what appears in the present section, namely, with the external senses; and second, at the words, "There is no other sense, *etc.*" he deals with what is latent in the notion of sensation. The first part he sub-divides into two: First, he shows the relationship of the sensible object to the sense; second, he defines the sensible object and the sense at the words, "In treating of each sense, *etc.*" In the first of these parts he reiterates some previous statements; and in the second he begins his investigation with the words, "The question arises, *etc.*" After treating of what belongs to the vegetative soul he says that we must make a general investigation of sensa-tion. He will take up later what concerns the individual senses. He re-peats two statements about sensation: The first, that sensation involves being moved and acted upon (for the actual sensation is an alteration—that which is altered is acted upon and is moved); the second, the statement made by some people that like is acted upon by like, thus making sensation an exam-ple of being acted upon.

[¶ 2.] *351.* Some of the early philosophers held that like is known and sensed by like. Empedocles, for example, held that earth is known by earth, fire by fire, and so on. The question of whether like can be affected by like has already been taken up in the general treatment of activity and passivity, in the Book, *On Generation,* where he treats of activity and passivity in general. There it was stated that what is acted upon is at first contrary to the agent, but finally, when it has been acted upon, it is like the agent, for an agent makes what it acts upon like itself.

[¶ 3.] *352.* Then when he says, "The question arises, *etc.*" he gives the solution to the problem: First, he shows that the sense power (of itself) is in potency; second, that sometimes it is in act; third, at the words, "We should distinguish, however, *etc.,*" he shows how the sense power passes from potency to act. Regarding the first point, we should note that Em-pedocles and others who said that like is known by like held that the sense in act is (identified with) the sensible objects. They held that in order to know all sensible objects, the sensory soul must be, in a way, composed of all sensible objects, because they thought that it was made up *of the elements* found in the sensible objects.

[¶ 4.] *353.* Two things follow from this position. First, that the sense and the sensible objects in act are the same, because their elements are the same. And because sensible objects in act can be sensed, it would follow that the senses themselves are objects of sensation. Second, since senses can sense when sensible objects are present, if these sensible objects are actually present in the sense, namely insofar as the senses are composed of them, then it would follow that the sense power can sense without exterior sensible objects. He questions these two untenable consequences of the position of the ancient philosophers and shows that the ancients had no solution for the problem.

This is why he says, "The question arises as to why a sense has no sensation of itself," that is, why the senses themselves are not sensed. This would seem to follow if the senses were like sensible objects.

[¶ 5.] *354.* At the words, "Why, without an external object, *etc.*," he raises the question of why the senses are not active "without an external object, that is, without exterior sensible objects since they exist within the senses themselves." For, "according to the viewpoint of the ancients," fire and earth and the other elements which are sensible objects already exist in the senses, either in themselves, that is, in their substance—they did not differentiate sense knowledge and intellectual knowledge, for the intellect is the proper faculty for knowing substance—or in their proper accidents, namely, heat and cold, and so on, which are, in themselves, sensible objects. Having shown that there is no solution for these problems if the senses are themselves actually the sensible objects, he considers it an evident conclusion that the sensitive soul is not sensible in act but only potentially. Therefore, the senses do not sense without exterior sensible objects, just as something combustible, which is only in potency to burn, does not ignite itself, but must be ignited by an external source. If it were actually the same as fire it would ignite itself, and would not need an external fire in order to burn.

[¶ 6.] *355.* When he says, "We speak of sensation, *etc.*" he points out that the sense power also is sometimes in act. He makes this point by showing that "to sense" has two meanings. Sometimes we say a man sees and hears, when his sight and hearing are potential, for example, when he is asleep. Sometimes we say a man sees and hears, when he is actually using his powers of hearing and sight. And so it is clear that sense and sensation have a twofold meaning, namely, as either actual or potential.

[¶ 7.] *356.* At the words, "We shall start by saying, *etc.*," he explains how we must understand what he has just said, since "to sense is to be in act," seems to be opposed to what he has said, namely, that sensation consists in being acted upon or moved; for to be in act seems to correspond more correctly to acting. To explain this point, he says that "to sense is to be in act" is like saying that being acted upon or moved are a certain acting, that is, being in act, for movement is act, even though it is imperfect, as was said in Book III, *Physics.* It is the act of a being existing in potency, that is, a mobile being. Motion is act, and in the same way being moved or sensing is a certain type of act, or being in act. At the words, "We shall start by saying, *etc.*," he indicates that he will add later other things to show how the senses are activated.

[¶ 8.] *357.* Third, at the words, "Everything is acted upon, *etc.*," he proves from the foregoing the impossibility of the opinion of the ancient philosophers, that like is sensed by like. He says that everything in potency is acted upon or moved by an agent, and a being in act. While it is making them be in act, a being in act makes them like itself. Therefore, something in one way is acted upon by what is like, and in another way, by what is unlike. At first, when the object is being changed and acted upon, it is dissimilar; but finally, when change and action are finished, it is similar. And so after the sense has been actualized by the object of sensation, it resembles it, but not beforehand. The lack of this distinction caused the error of the ancient philosophers.

No. 2. The Definition of a Power of Sensation
    Aristotle: *On the Soul,* Book II, Chapter 12, Lines 424a16–424b19
    St. Thomas: *Commentary on Aristotle's On the Soul,* Book II, Lesson
        24, Numbers 551–563

ARISTOTLE:

[¶ 1.] It must be generally understood of every sense, that it receives forms without matter, as wax receives the imprint of a ring without the iron and gold. Yet it does receive the imprint of gold or bronze, but not as gold or bronze. Likewise, the sense is affected by an object having color, or flavor, or sound, not in respect to what each substance is, but insofar as it is such (a quality) and according to its form.

[¶ 2.] The primary area of sensation is that in which there is a power of this sort. And indeed that part in which the power exists and the power are the same but differ in the manner of existence. What receives the sensation will be an extended magnitude. However, neither being sensitive nor sense is a magnitude but rather a kind of proportion and power of the magnitude.

[¶ 3.] And it is clear from this why an excessive stimulus destroys the sense power. If the movement of the stimulus is too strong for the sense organ, the balance is destroyed—for it was in the balance that the sense consisted— just as harmony and tone are destroyed by a violent striking of the strings. This absence of immaterial receptivity explains why plants do not sense in spite of a kind of participation in the animal soul and of being affected by tangible stimuli (for they become both hot and cold). The explanation is that they have no medium and so no principle capable of receiving sensible forms, but must be acted upon with matter.

[¶ 4.] Some will wonder, if something which cannot smell can be affected by odor, or if a thing which cannot see is affected by color, and likewise for all the senses. But if odor is what can be smelled, whatever causes the sensation of smell causes odor. Wherefore, what cannot have the sensation of smell cannot be affected by odor. The same reasoning holds for the other senses, nor are there potential sensible objects except in view of things that have sensation.

[¶ 5.] This is seen to be true, also, for the following reason. Neither light nor darkness, sound nor odor have any sensible effect on bodies; rather, those things in which these qualities inhere affect bodies, as the air, which accompanies thunder, splits trees.

[¶ 6.] But tangible and moist things do affect bodies. For if they do not, by what are inanimate objects affected and changed? Therefore, do not these other things affect them? Or is not every passive body affected by odor and sound, both those with indeterminate receptors and those which do not remain stable, as air? For air becomes odorous, like something being acted upon.

[¶ 7.] What is the sensation of *smelling* except being acted upon? To smell is to sense. And air, being affected, quickly becomes a sensible object.

ST. THOMAS:

[¶ 1.] *551.* After treating of the individual senses in the preceding section, the Philosopher now treats of sensation in general. And he does three things with respect to this. He shows, first of all, what a sense is. Secondly, he gives the solution of certain problems which arise from the definition of sense, at the words "And it is clear from this, *etc.*" Thirdly, he proposes certain questions with respect to what is affected by the sensible object at the words, "Some will wonder, *etc.*" He does two things with respect to the first point. First, he shows what a sense is. Second, at the words, "The primary area of sensation, *etc.*" he shows what an organ of sense is. First, then, he says that it is necessary to accept, as universally and generally true of all senses, that they receive forms without matter, as wax receives the imprint of a ring without the iron or gold. However, this seems to be the case in all receptivity, for all recipients receive something from the agent insofar as it is an agent. But an agent acts through its form, and not its matter. Therefore, every recipient receives a form without matter. And indeed this is evident to our sense, for air does not receive the matter from the fire affecting it, but its form. Therefore, receiving forms without matter does not seem to be proper to the senses.

[¶ 2.] *552.* Granted that it belongs to all recipients to receive a form from an agent, we must say, nevertheless, that there is a difference in the manner of receiving. For the form which is taken into the recipient from the agent sometimes retains the same mode of existence in the recipient as it has in the agent. This happens when the recipient has the same disposition to the form as the agent, for whatever is received into another is received according to the mode of the receiver. Hence, if the receiver is disposed in the same manner as the agent, the form is received in the same mode in which it existed in the agent; and then form is not received without matter. For, although the same matter in number which belongs to the agent does not become the matter of the receiver, nevertheless, in a certain way, it becomes the same, inasmuch as it takes on a similar material disposition to form as that which is in the agent. In this way air is affected by fire, and whatever else is acted upon by the active or passive qualities of the elements in nature.

[¶ 3.] 553. But sometimes the receiver receives the form under a different mode of existence than the form has in the agent, because the receiver's material disposition to receive is not like the material disposition which is in the agent. And in these cases the receiver becomes like the agent in respect to form but not to matter. And in this way a sense receives a form without matter, because a form has a different mode of existence in the sense than it has in the sensible object, for a form has a natural existence in the sensible thing, but an intentional and spiritual existence in the sense.

[¶ 4.] 554. And appropriately he gives as an example the seal and the wax. For the wax does not have the same disposition to the imprint as the iron and gold had. Therefore, he adds that the wax receives the imprint, that is, the gold or copper image or figure, but not insofar as it is gold or copper. For the wax becomes like the gold seal in respect to the image but not in respect to its disposition to gold. Likewise, a sense is affected by a sensible object having color, sound, or moistness, such as flavor, but not in respect to what each substance is; for example, it is not affected by a colored rock as rock, nor by sweet honey as honey. For a disposition to the form, like that which is in these objects, is not impressed upon the sense, but these objects affect the sense because they are colored, or tasty, or according to the nature, that is, according to form. The sense becomes like the sense object in form but not in its material disposition.

[¶ 5.] 555. Then when he says, "The primary area of sensation, *etc.*" he treats of the organs of sense. Because he has already said that a sense receives forms without matter, which is also true of the intellect, some may think that a sense is not a corporeal power because the intellect is not a corporeal power. To exclude this he says there is an organ of sensation. He says also that the primary area of sensation, that is, the basic organ of sensation, is that which has a power of this kind, namely, one that receives forms without matter. Thus a sense organ with this power, an eye, for example, is the same in subject but exists differently because, by nature, a power differs from a body. The power is like the form of the organ, as was said above. And he adds that "an extended magnitude," the physical organ, for instance, "is what receives the sensation,"—that which receives the sensation is like matter in its relation to form. However, the notion of magnitude and that of sensitive or sense is not the same, for the sense is a kind of perfection, that is, proportion and form and power of a magnitude.

[¶ 6.] 556. Then when he says, "And it is clear from this why, *etc.*" he finds in the previous propositions a solution to two questions which could be asked. He says it is clear, from what has been said, why excessive stimulation destroys the organ of sense. For in a sense organ, there must be a certain "balance," or proportion, as has been said. If, therefore, the motion of the sensible object is stronger than the organ was made to receive, this proportion is destroyed, and the sense is injured, because, as we have said, the sense power consists in a certain proportion of the organ. It is as if someone by striking the strings too violently were to destroy the harmony and tone of the instrument, which consists in a certain proportion.

[¶ 7.] 557. The solution to another question is clear from the foregoing, namely, why plants do not sense, although they have a certain part of the soul, and are affected by certain sensible objects, namely, by what is tangible (for it is obvious that they become hot and cold). The reason why they do not sense is that there is not in them this proportion which is necessary for sensation, for they do not have a medium (for receiving forms) after their connection with tangible objects. This is necessary for an organ of touch, and without it there can be no sensation. Hence, they do not have in themselves a principle of this kind, namely sense, which can receive forms "without matter." But they (plants) can be affected by form with matter, namely, in material alterations.

[¶ 8.] 558. Then at the words, "Some will wonder, if something which cannot smell, *etc.*" he poses a problem about being acted upon by sensible objects. Since he had said that plants are acted upon by certain sensible objects, he poses as a first problem, whether something which does not have sense is able to be affected by any sensible objects. For example, can a being which does not have a sense of smell be affected by an odor, or can what does not have sight be affected by a color, or what does not have hearing be affected by a sound?

[¶ 9.] 559. Secondly, at the words "But if odor is what can be smelled, *etc.*" he gives two reasons showing that what cannot sense cannot be acted upon by sensible objects. The first is this: Since it is the property of what can be smelled to cause smelling, and since odor can be smelled, it follows that, if anything causes smelling, it causes it through odor. Or another reading has it, "odor causes smelling." Thus the proper activity of odor, as odor, is to cause an object to be smelled, or smelling. It follows from this that whatever receives the activity of odor, as odor, possesses the sense of smell. Thus, a being which does not possess a sense of smell cannot be affected by odor. And the same argument holds in all cases, for not anything and everything can be acted upon by sensible objects, but only those things endowed with senses.

[¶ 10.] 560. He gives a second reason at the words, "This is seen to be true, etc." The conclusion of the first argument, he says, is evident from experience: for light, darkness, odor, or sound, have no effect on sensible bodies except accidentally, insofar as bodies, which have these sensible qualities, effect something, as when air splits a tree during a thunder storm. For a tree is not affected by sound, strictly speaking, but by the rushing air.

[¶ 11.] 561. Thirdly, at the words, "But tangible and moist things do affect bodies, etc." he points out that tangible qualities have another type of existence. He says that sensible objects can be affected in a certain way by "tangible and moist things," for example, by savor. But this must be understood of moist things, not insofar as they are moist, but insofar as the tastable is a certain type of tangible object, and taste is a certain type of touch. Now if tangible qualities do not affect insensible bodies, there is no explanation how inanimate bodies are acted upon and changed. The reason for this is that tangible qualities are the active and passive qualities of the elements by means of which all alteration in bodies takes place.

[¶ 12.] 562. Fourthly, at the words, "Or is not every passive body, etc." he shows that other sense objects act on inanimate things, although not on all of them. He asks "is not every passive body," namely, other sensible objects, able to have some effect and to be smelled in inanimate things? He seems to affirm it. Yet not every passive body is affected by odor and sound as they are affected by the hot and cold. Only unstable and indeterminate bodies, such as air and water, which are liquid, and not effectively limited by boundaries of their own, can be affected by these sensible qualities. It is obvious that air can be affected by odor since it itself gives off a foul odor as if being acted upon by the odor. Another reading has "carries" because forms are brought to the sense through the medium of other sensible objects. The reason for this difference is that tangible qualities cause other sensible qualities, and thus possess a more active power and are capable of acting on all bodies. Other sensible qualities, having a less active power, can only act on very passive bodies. There is a similar reason in relation to the light of heavenly bodies, which alters inferior bodies.

[¶ 13.] *563.* Fifthly, at the words, "What is the sensation of smelling, *etc.*" he answers the question posed above. First he asks, if something which does not have a sense of smell is affected by an odor, what does it mean to smell, other than being acted upon by an odor? And he answers that smelling occurs when something is affected by an odor so that it senses that odor. Air is not affected in such a way that it senses, since it lacks the power of sense, but it is acted upon so that it becomes sensible, that is, as the medium of sensation.

No. 3. A General Division into Proper, Common, and Accidental Objects of Sensation

Aristotle: *On the Soul,* Book II, Chapter 6, Lines 418a6–418a25

St. Thomas: *Commentary on Aristotle's On the Soul,* Book II, Lesson 13, Numbers 383–398

ARISTOTLE:

[¶ 1.] We must first of all discuss the sensory objects of each of the senses. The sensory object is of three kinds, two of which are said to be grasped by the senses *per se* and the other *per accidens.* Of these first two, one is proper to each of the senses and the other is common to all of them.

[¶ 2.] By proper sensible I mean the kind that is not sensed by any other power and one about which there is no error, as for example, with color for sight and sound for hearing and savor for taste. Touch has several inner differences. Each of the senses is able to discern these and not be deceived—thus sight does not err regarding color, nor hearing regarding sound. But it may err about what is colored, or about where it is, or about what is giving off sound. These things, then, are called the proper objects of each sense.

[¶ 3.] The common sensible objects are movement, rest, number, figure, and size. These are not proper to any one of the senses but are common to all. The movement of a sensible object is sensed by touch and by sight. These, then, are the *per se* sensible objects.

[¶ 4.] The *per accidens* sensible object is one in which, for example, a white object is seen to be the son of Diares. This is sensed *per accidens* because white happens to belong to what is sensed. The sense is not affected by the sensible insofar as it is of such a kind. Of the *per se* sensory objects those are rightly called *proper sensible objects* to which the substance of each sense is naturally accommodated and from which the sense is defined.

ST. THOMAS:

[¶ 1.] *383.* After the Philosopher shows how the sense is related to sensible objects, he begins to define sensible objects and the senses. He divides his exposition into two parts, and in the first of them he specifies the sensible objects, and in the second he specifies the senses, where he says "It is necessary, *etc.*" He divides the first of these again into two parts. In the first, he differentiates the proper sensibles from other kinds of sensible objects. In the second, he specifies the proper sensible object of each of the senses, where he says "The object of sight is color, *etc.*" In the first division he does two things: He first makes a division of sensible objects; then he explains the members of the division, when he says "By proper sensible I mean, *etc.*" He says, first of all, that before we specify what the senses are, we must define the sensible object for each of the senses, because objects are prior to powers. Sensible objects are of three kinds, one of which is *per accidens* and two of which are *per se.* The two kinds of *per se* objects are: those proper to each of the senses, and those sensed in common by all beings with powers of sensation.

[¶ 2.] *384.* When he says "By proper sensible I mean, *etc.*" he explains the members of the division. First, he explains the proper sensibles. He says that a proper sensible is one that is sensed by one sense only and cannot be sensed by another, and about which the sense cannot err. For example, it is proper for sight to know color, for hearing to know sound, and for taste to know flavor or savor. Touch, however, has many different objects proper to itself, for it knows heat and moisture, cold and dryness, heavy and light, and many things of this kind. Each one of these senses judges of its proper object and is not deceived regarding it. For example, sight is not deceived about the fact that there is such a color nor hearing deceived about sound.

[¶ 3.] *385.* But about accidental or common sensibles the senses can be deceived, as sight would be deceived if a man would judge by means of it *what a colored object is or where it is.* Likewise anyone would be deceived if he would judge by hearing what it is that is giving off sound. These, then, are the proper objects of each of the senses.

[¶ 4.] *386.* Secondly, where he says "The common sensible objects, *etc.*" he explains the second member of the division when he states that the common sensibles are five in number: movement, rest, number, figure, and size. These are the proper objects of no particular sense but are common to all. We should not understand by this that all of them are common to all the senses. Only certain ones, namely, number, movement and rest are common to all the senses. Touch and sight grasp all five. It is clear, then, what the *per se* sensibles are.

[¶ 5.] *387.* Thirdly, he explains the third member of the division. Something is sensible *per accidens* when, for example, we say that Diares or Socrates is accidentally sensible because he happens to be white. The object is sensed *per accidens* because it is something which is accidental to that which is sensed *per se*. It is accidental to the white thing, which is *per se* sensible, that it is Diares, hence, Diares is *per accidens* sensible. The sense power is not acted upon by it insofar as it is this kind of object (Diares). Although the common sensibles and the proper sensibles are *per se* sensibles, nevertheless, only the proper sensibles are properly *per se* sensible, because the nature and definition of each of the senses is derived from the fact that it naturally is capable of being affected by such an object. The essence of each power consists in its relationship to its proper object.

[¶ 6.] *388.* At this point a difficulty arises about the distinction between the common sensibles and the *per accidens* sensible. Just as the *per accidens* sensibles are not grasped except in conjunction with the proper sensibles, so neither are the common sensibles grasped except in conjunction with the proper sensibles. Sight never grasps size or figure except insofar as it apprehends a colored object. It seems therefore that the common sensibles are also *per accidens* sensible.

[¶ 7.] *389.* Some give two reason for saying that the common sensibles are not *per accidens* sensible. The first is that the common sensibles are the proper sensibles of the central sense *(sensus communis),* just as the proper sensibles are proper to the individual sense powers. The second is that proper sensibles cannot exist without common sensibles but they can exist without *per accidens* sensibles.

[¶ 8.] *390.* But both of these reasons are defective. The first because it is false, since common sensibles are not the proper objects of the central sense. The central sense is a power in which the changes of all the senses terminate, as will be clear later on. Therefore, it is impossible for the central sense to have a proper object distinct from the object of the particular senses. It deals with the changes wrought in the particular senses by their objects, which the particular senses themselves cannot grasp. It perceives these changes in the senses and differentiates among the sensible objects of the various senses. By means of the central sense we perceive that we are alive and by it we discern the sensible objects of different senses, for example, whiteness and sweetness.

[¶ 9.] *391.* Moreover, even if the common sensibles were the proper objects of the central sense, this would not keep them from being *per accidens* sensibles in regard to the particular senses. Thus far he is treating of sensible objects according to their relationship to a particular sense power; for he has not yet explained the power of the central sense. Whatever is the proper object of one of the internal sense powers can also be *per accidens* sensible, as will be pointed out later. This is not strange because what is *per se* sensible for one of the external senses is *per accidens* sensible for another, as, for example, a sweet thing is *per accidens* visible.

[¶ 10.] *392.* The second reason also is defective, for it makes no difference to what is *per accidens* sensible whether the subject of sensible quality is *per se* its subject or not. No one would say that fire, which is the proper subject of heat, is *per se* sensible by touch.

[¶ 11.] *393.* Rather, we must say that sensing consists in a kind of receiving and being altered, as was said above. Whatever brings about a difference in the receptivity or alteration of the sense has a direct relationship to the sense and is called *per se* sensible, while that which effects no such change in the sense is called a *per accidens* sensible. Hence, the Philosopher says expressly that the sense is not affected by a *per accidens* sensible as such.

[¶ 12.] *394.* A difference in the alteration of the sense can come about in two ways. In one way, with respect to the form acting upon it, and thus we have a difference caused by the *per se* sensibles, so that this is color, that sound, this is white, that black. The forms of those things which are active in relation to sense are proper sensibles in act and the sense power has a natural affinity for them. Thus, because of a difference in these sensible objects, the senses themselves are diversified. Certain other things cause a difference in the receptivity of the senses, not with respect to the form of the agent, but from the difference in the mode of action of the sensible object. For sensory qualities affect the senses corporeally and by position. Thus, they affect them differently depending on whether they are in a large or small body, or in different positions, that is, near or far, or whether they are in the same body or in a different one. In this way, the common sensibles make a difference in the change of the senses. It is clear that size or position is diversified according to all these five. Because they do not have the same relationship to the sense as the form of that which activates the sense (that is, the proper sensible object), it follows that they do not diversify the sensory powers but are common to many senses.

[¶ 13.] *395.* After seeing why both the proper and the common *per se* sensibles are so named, it remains to be seen why something is called *per accidens* sensible. We must keep in mind that in order to be *per accidens* sensible, something must first of all be accidental to what is *per se* sensible, as, for example, it is accidental to whiteness to be man or to be sweet. Secondly, it is necessary that it be grasped by a sentient being, for if something were accidental to a sensible object, but remained unknown to the one sensing, it could not be said to be sensed. It is necessary, therefore, that it be *per se* an object of knowledge for some knowing power of a sentient being, other than the sense in question. It may be another sense power, or the intellect, or the cogitative, or the estimative sense. I say that it is another sense power when, for example, what is sweet is *per accidens* visible because what is sweet happens to be white, which is apprehended by sight. Sweet is known *per se* by another sense power, that is, by taste.

[¶ 14.] *396.* Strictly speaking, this is not entirely *per accidens sensible,* but only *per accidens visible* and *per se sensible.* What is not known by a particular sense power, if it is something universal, is grasped by the intellect. But even here not everything which the intellect can apprehend in a sensory object can be called *per accidens* sensible, but only what is apprehended immediately by the intellect on coming in contact with a sensed thing. For example, as soon as I see someone talking or moving about, I grasp by my intellect that he is alive, so that I can say that *I see* he is alive. But if I grasp a particular object, as when I see a colored object, and I perceive that it is this man or this animal, an apprehension of this kind belongs to the cogitative power, which in man is called "particular reason," since it combines individual intentions, just as universal reason combines universal ideas.

[¶ 15.] *397.* This power, however, belongs to the sensitive part, for in its highest activity the sensory power participates in the intellectual power, inasmuch as the senses are joined to intellect in man. But in a brute animal the apprehension of individual intentions is made through the natural estimative power, by which a sheep, for example, knows her young when she hears or sees them. And so with other things of this kind.

[¶ 16.] *398.* There is a difference between the cogitative power and the estimative on this point. The cogitative power apprehends an individual as existing under a common nature, for it is united to the intellectual power in the same subject. Therefore, it knows *this* man as this *man,* and *this* wood as this *wood.* But the estimative power does not grasp the individual as having a common nature, but only as being the term or origin of some activity or passivity. Thus, a sheep knows this particular lamb not as this *lamb* but insofar as it is milkable by it, and knows this plant insofar as it is its food. Therefore, it cannot grasp with the natural estimative sense other individual objects which do not come under its own activity or passivity. The natural estimative sense is given animals to direct them to seek or to avoid whatever affects them according to the needs of their nature, or to act in a way required by those needs.

No. 4. The Divisions of the External Senses
     St. Thomas: *Summa Theologiae,* Part I, Question 78, Article 3
     Is it correct to distinguish five external senses?

[¶ 1.] *Objection 1.* The senses are cognizant of accidents, and there are many kinds of accidents. Since the powers are differentiated by their objects, it seems that there must be as many senses as there are kinds of accidents.

[¶ 2.] *Objection 2.* It is said in Book II, *On the Soul,* that magnitude and figure and the other "common sensibles" are not *per accidens* sensible objects but are distinct from them. Now, since powers are diversified according to the *per se* diversity of their objects, and since magnitude and figure differ more from color than sound, it seems more necessary to have another sensitive power to apprehend magnitude or figure than to grasp color and sound.

[¶ 3.] *Objection 3.* Each sense apprehends one set of contraries, as sight, for example, apprehends white and black. Touch, however, apprehends several sets of contraries, such as hot and cold, moist and dry, and the like. Therefore, touch is not a single sense, but several, and hence, there are more than five senses.

[¶ 4.] *Objection 4.* A species is not divided against its genus. Since taste is a kind of touch, it should not be considered as a sense distinct from touch.

[¶ 5.] *On the contrary,* the Philosopher says that "there are only five senses." (Book III, *On the Soul.*)

[¶ 6.] As their criterion for distinguishing and enumerating the external senses, some have wished to take the organs in which some element—water, air, or the like—predominates. Others have made a distinction from the viewpoint of medium, whether internal or external, such as air, water, or the like. Still others have differentiated the senses according to the diverse nature of sensible qualities, depending on whether the quality belongs to a simple body, or results from complexity.

[¶ 7.] But none of these views is accurate. Powers do not exist for the sake of organs, but organs for the sake of powers. Thus, there are not diverse powers, because there are diverse organs, but nature has established a diversity in organs to correspond to the diversity in powers. Likewise, there are different media for different senses, insofar as the media are suitable for the act of those powers. The intellect, not the sense, knows the natures of sensible qualities.

[¶ 8.] We must employ as criterion for enumerating and differentiating the external senses what belongs properly and primarily to the senses. A sense is a type of passive power, which is capable of being altered by external sensible objects. The external object which causes the change in the sense is that which *per se* is grasped by the sense. The powers are differentiated in relation to the diversity of these external sensible objects.

[¶ 9.] There are two kinds of alteration in the sense; one is natural, the other spiritual. The natural alteration results from the reception of the form by the subject. The form in this case is received according to its natural mode of existence, as, for example, when heat is received into the thing heated. A spiritual alteration results when the form which causes the change in the subject is received according to a spiritual mode of being, as, for example, when the form of color is received by the pupil, without physically being colored. A spiritual impression is needed for the operation of the senses in which an intentional form of the sensible object is present in the sense organ. Besides, if a natural impression sufficed for sensation, every natural body would sense, whenever it underwent alteration.

[¶ 10.] In certain senses only a spiritual change is found, as in sight. In other senses, a natural change occurs along with the spiritual, either of the object alone, or even of the organ. A natural change in the object occurs, according to place, in sound, which is the object of hearing, since sound is caused by percussion and the movement of air. Natural changes of alteration occur in odor, which is the object of smell, since a body must be altered in some way by heat before it produces an odor. A natural change on the part of the organ occurs in touch and taste, since the hand is heated by touching something hot and the tongue is moistened by the moisture of flavors. The olfactory and auditory organs are not affected in the act of sensing by any natural change except accidentally.

[¶ 11.] Since sight has no natural change in the organ or in the object, it is the most spiritual, the most perfect, and the most universal of all the senses. Next are hearing and smelling, which have a natural change in their object. The local motion is more perfect and naturally prior to the motion of alteration as is proved in Book VIII, *Physics*. Touch and taste are the most material senses and will be differentiated in replies 3 and 4. Thus, the first three senses (sight, hearing and smell) do not operate through a medium connected with them. This is to prevent some natural change from extending to the organ, as happens in these two senses, taste and touch.

[¶ 12.] *Reply to Objection 1.* Not all accidents have of themselves a power of causing change but only the qualities of the third species, according to which alteration is possible. Thus, only qualities of this kind are objects of the senses; as is said in Book VII, *Physics:* "A sense is altered by the same things which alter inanimate bodies."

[¶ 13.] *Reply to Objection 2.* Magnitude and figure and the other "common sensibles" are midway between "accidental sensibles" and "proper sensibles," which are the objects of the senses. The proper sensibles immediately and *per se* effect a change in the senses, since they are qualities causing alteration. All the common sensibles are reducible to quantity; magnitude and number are clearly species of quantity; figure is a quality about quantity, since the essence of figure is the termination of magnitude. Motion and rest are sensed insofar as the subject is in one mode or in many modes according to its size or distance away, in the case of growth or local motion; or also, according to sensible qualities as in the movement of alteration.

[¶ 14.] Therefore, the sensing of motion and rest is in a way the sensing of one and many. Quantity is the proximate subject of qualities causing alteration as, for example, a surface is the proximate subject of color. Thus, the common sensibles do not immediately and *per se* affect the senses but through the intermediacy of sensible qualities, as a surface (is sensed) through its color. Nevertheless these are not accidental sensibles, because sensibles of this kind cause a certain diversity in the alteration of the senses. A large surface, for example, alters the senses in a different way than a small one, for even the whiteness is itself said to be large or small; hence, it is divided according to its proper subject.

[¶ 15.] *Reply to Objection 3.* As the Philosopher seems to say in Book II, *On the Soul,* the sense of touch is a single genus, but is divided into many senses according to species; hence, touch apprehends various contrarieties. Nevertheless, the species of touch are not separated from one another by reason of an organ, but are conjoined through the whole body, and thus their distinction (as individual senses) is not apparent.

[¶ 16.] Taste, which senses the sweet and the bitter, accompanies touch in the tongue but not in the whole of the body and so is easily distinguished from touch. Nevertheless, it could be said that all these single contrarieties agree in one proximate genus, and all in one common genus, which is the object of touch according to its common form. This common genus does not have a name, just as the proximate genus of hot and cold is without a name.

[¶ 17.] *Reply to Objection 4.* The sense of taste, according to the Philosopher, is a certain species of touch located only in the tongue. Taste is not generically different from touch but differs from touch with respect to the other species which are diffused throughout the entire body. If touch is really only one sense on account of the one common form of the object, it should be stated that taste is differentiated from touch inasmuch as it has a different way of being changed. Touch is changed not only by a spiritual alteration but also by a natural alteration with respect to its organ, according to the quality which is properly its object. The organ of taste is not necessarily changed by a natural alteration according to the quality which is its proper object; for example, the tongue may become sweet or bitter. But this is according to a prior quality, which is the basis of flavor, namely, moisture, which is the object of touch.

SECTION B: INTERNAL SENSE KNOWLEDGE

No. 1. The Divisions of the Internal Senses

St. Thomas: *Summa Theologiae*, Part I, Question 78, Article 4

Are the internal senses correctly differentiated?

[¶ 1.] *Objection 1.* Since what is common is not divided against what is proper, the central sense should not be numbered among the inner sensory powers in addition to the proper external senses.

[¶ 2.] *Objection 2.* There is no need of an inner power of apprehension if a proper external sense suffices. The proper external senses are able to judge about sensible objects, since each sense judges its proper object. Likewise, they seem able to perceive their own acts. Since the activity of sense is, in a way, between the power and the object, sight would seemingly be more able to perceive its own vision than to perceive color itself, because sight is nearer to the power of vision. The same is true of the other senses. Thus, there is no need for the inner power which is called the central sense.

[¶ 3.] *Objection 3.* According to the Philosopher, in the book, *On Memory and Recall*, imagination and memory are effects of the movement of the first sensitive powers. Since such an effect is not divided against its subject, memory and imagination should not be considered as powers separate from the central sense.

[¶ 4.] *Objection 4.* The intellect depends less on the senses than any power of the sensory part; but the intellect knows only by receiving from the senses; hence, "whoever lacks one sense, lacks one kind of knowledge," as is said in Book I, *Posterior Analytics.* Therefore, we have even less reason to assign a power of the sensitive soul (which is called the estimative power) to perceive forms *(intentiones)* which the senses do not perceive.

[¶ 5.] *Objection 5.* The act of the cogitative power (which is to collect, compose, and divide) and reminiscence (which is to use a certain kind of syllogism for the sake of inquiry) are not less distinct from acts of the estimative power and memory than the act of the estimative power is distinct from the act of the imagination. Hence, either the cogitative power and the power of recall should be considered as powers distinct from the estimative power and memory; or the estimative power and memory should not be considered as distinct from the imagination.

[¶ 6.] *Objection 6.* Augustine (Book XII, *Commentary on the Text of Genesis*) defines three types of vision: corporeal, which takes place through sense; spiritual, which occurs through the imagination; and intellectual, which comes about through the intellect. Thus, the only other sense which comes between the senses and the intellect is the imagination.

[¶ 7.] *On the contrary, Avicenna,** in his book, *On the Soul,* posits five internal sense powers: the central sense, phantasy, imagination, memory, and the estimative power.

[¶ 8.] Since nature cannot be defective in necessary things, there must be as many actions of the sensitive soul as a perfect animal needs to live. If these actions are irreducible to one principle, they require different powers, since a power of the soul is the proximate principle of the soul's operation. We should note that the life of a perfect animal requires the apprehension of a thing not only when the sensible object is present, but even when it is absent. Otherwise, since the motion and action of an animal follow apprehension, an animal would not be moved to seek something absent. The contrary is readily seen in perfect animals, which are moved by a progressive motion, since they are moved by something absent yet apprehended. Hence, an animal must receive through its sensitive soul not only the species of sensible things (when the soul is changed by them in their presence) but also must retain and preserve them. In corporeal bodies, *receiving* and *retaining* belong to different principles, for humid things receive well, but retain poorly, while the opposite is true of dry things. Thus, it is necessary, since the sensitive power is the act of a corporeal organ, that there be a power to retain the species distinct from the power which receives it.

[¶ 9.] We must also consider that if an animal were moved solely by things which are pleasant or disagreeable to sense, the animal would need only to apprehend the sense perceived forms which it liked or disliked. But an animal must necessarily seek some things and avoid others not simply because these things are suitable or unsuitable to the senses, but because of other benefits and advantages or disadvantages. For example, a sheep flees when it sees a wolf approaching, not because of its unsightly color or shape but because it is a natural enemy; likewise, birds gather straw, not because it pleases their senses, but because it is useful for building a nest. Therefore, the animal must perceive forms of this kind which the external senses do not perceive. Now there must be some other principle for this type of perception, for although the receiving of sensible forms is from an impression by a sensible object, the same is not true of these other forms.

[¶ 10.] So there is a "proper sense" and a "central sense" ordained for the reception of sensible forms. (They will be distinguished in the first and second replies.) The *"phantasy"* * or "imagination," which are the same, is ordained to retain or preserve (sensible) forms; the "phantasy" or "imagination" is a kind of storehouse for forms received through the senses. The "estimative" power is ordained for the apprehension of forms which are not received through the senses, while the "memory" is the storehouse to preserve these forms. A sign of this is that the beginning of remembering comes about in animals from some form of this kind; for example, that something is harmful or desirable. The very character of something as past to which memory is directed includes the intentions of this kind.

[¶ 11.] We must also note that there is no difference between man and the other animals as regards sensible forms, for both men and animals are changed by external sensible objects in similar ways. But there is this difference about the previously mentioned forms: Other animals perceive such forms only by a kind of natural instinct, while man perceives them by a kind of comparison. Hence, what is called the natural *estimative power* in other animals, is called *cogitative power* in man. This latter power arrives at these forms by a kind of comparison. Therefore, it is called the *particular reason;* and doctors assign to it a particular organ in the middle part of the head. It compares individual intentions just as the intellectual reason compares universal intentions.

[¶ 12.] As to remembering, man not only has a memory, like other animals, which suddenly recalls past events, but also a power of recall which is the remembrance of past events by a kind of syllogistic inquiry in respect to individual intentions.

[¶ 13.] Avicenna posits a fifth power, midway between the estimative power and imagination. This power composes and divides imagined forms, as when from the imagined form of gold and the imagined form of mountain we compose the single form of a gold mountain, which has never been seen by man. This operation is not evident in any other animal except man, whose imaginative power is sufficient to perform this operation. *Averroes* * likewise attributes this operation to the imagination in his book, *On the Sense and Sensible Objects.*[29] Thus, it is necessary to posit only four inner sense powers: the central sense and the imagination, and the estimative sense and memory.

---

[29] *De sensu et sensibilibus.*

[¶ 14.] *Reply to Objection 1.* The inner sense is not called "common" *(communis)* by predication as if it were a genus, but as the common root and principle of the external senses.

[¶ 15.] *Reply to Objection 2.* The particular sense power judges about its proper sensible by differentiating one object from several others which the same sense receives, for example, by distinguishing white from black or green. Neither sight nor taste can distinguish white from sweet, since whatever distinguishes between them must know both. Hence the power of discerning must belong to the central sense; and to it, as to a common term, all apprehensions of the senses are referred; and by it the actions of the senses are perceived, for example, when someone sees that he sees. This cannot take place through the proper senses, which know only the forms of the sensible thing by which it is altered, and in which alteration vision is effected; but from this alteration another alteration follows in the central sense, which perceives the act of seeing.

[¶ 16.] *Reply to Objection 3.* Just as one power arises from the soul by means of another, as was stated above (*S.T.*, I, 77, 7), likewise the soul is the subject of one power by means of another. In this sense, imagination and memory are said to be effects of the movement of the first sensitive powers.

[¶ 17.] *Reply to Objection 4.* Although the operation of the intellect has its origin in sense, the intellect, nevertheless, knows much about the object apprehended by the sense which the sense itself cannot grasp; likewise, the estimative power, though in an inferior way.

[¶ 18.] *Reply to Objection 5.* The cogitative power and the power of recall in man have a certain eminence, not in virtue of what is proper to the sensory part but because of a certain affinity and proximity to the power of universal reason, which overflows into them in a certain way. Hence, these are not different powers but the same as those found in other animals, although they are more perfect.

[¶ 19.] *Reply to Objection 6.* Augustine defines a spiritual vision as one taking place through the likenesses of bodies, when those bodies are absent, which is clearly common to all internal apprehension.

SECTION C: THE SENSE APPETITE
  No. 1. A General Discussion of Appetite
      St. Thomas: *Summa Theologiae,* Part I, Question 80, Article 1
      Is the appetite a special power of the soul?

[¶ 1.] *Objection 1.* Whatever is common to both animate and inanimate things should not be considered as a power of the soul. Appetency is common to both animate and inanimate; because, as is said in Book I, *Ethics* "The good is that which everything desires."

[¶ 2.] *Objection 2.* Powers are differentiated by their objects. Since what we know and desire is the same thing, it is not necessary that there be an appetitive power over and above the apprehensive power.

[¶ 3.] *Objection 3.* The common is not differentiated from the proper. Now every power of the soul desires some particular thing, namely, an object suitable to it. In relation to this object, which is a common object of desire, a distinct appetitive power is not necessary.

[¶ 4.] *On the contrary,* the Philosopher makes a distinction between the appetitive and the other powers in Book II, *On the Soul;* Damascene in Book II, *On the True Faith,*[30] also differentiates the appetitive powers from the cognitive.

[¶ 5.] There must necessarily be some appetitive power of soul. This is evident if we consider that some inclination follows upon any form; fire, for example, on account of its form, tends to rise and to reproduce itself. Now form is found in a higher mode in those things which have knowledge than in those which lack knowledge. In those things which lack knowledge, form is found only as determining that thing to the one proper state of being natural to it. This natural inclination, which follows from the natural form, is called "natural appetite." In those things which have knowledge the individual is determined to its proper natural state of existence by a natural form, which, however, is receptive of the species of other things. For example, the senses receive the species of all sensible things, and the intellect the species of all intelligible things, so that the soul of man becomes, in a certain way, all things by his senses and intellect. In having such knowledge they approach in a certain way the image of God, "in Whom," as Dionysius says, "all things pre-exist."

[¶ 6.] Therefore, since forms exist in a higher mode in those beings having

---

[30] *De Fide Orthodoxa.*

knowledge, beyond the mode of natural forms, it is necessary that there be in them some inclination superior to the natural inclination, which is called "natural appetite." This superior inclination belongs to the appetitive power by which an animal can desire not only those things to which it is inclined by its natural form, but also things that it apprehends. Therefore, it is necessary to posit some appetitive power of the soul.

[¶ 7.] *Reply to Objection 1.* It must be noted again that appetite is found in those things having knowledge beyond the common mode in which it is found in all things; thus, it is necessary that a particular power of soul be assigned to it.

[¶ 8.] *Reply to Objection 2.* What we know and what we desire is in the same subject, but different in definition; for we know an object insofar as it is sensible or intelligible being, but we desire an object as suitable or good. A diversity in the definition of the objects is needed for diversity of powers, not a material diversity.

[¶ 9.] *Reply to Objection 3.* Every power of the soul is a kind of form or nature with a natural tendency towards something. Thus, every power desires the object suited to its natural appetite. Superior to the natural appetite is the animal appetite which follows apprehension. It does not desire something because it is fitting for the act of a particular power, for example, sight for the sake of seeing or the power of hearing for hearing, but because it is fitting absolutely for the animal.

No. 2. The Division of the Sense Appetites into Irascible and Concupiscible
   St. Thomas: *Summa Theologiae,* Part I, Question 81, Article 2
   Is the sensitive appetite divided into the irascible and concupiscible?

[¶ 1.] *Objection 1.* It seems that the sensitive appetite is not divided into the irascible and concupiscible as separate appetites, for the same power of the soul deals with one contrariety, as sight grasps both black and white, according to the Philosopher, in Book II, *On the Soul.* But *beneficial* and *injurious* are contraries. Since, therefore, the concupiscible appetite deals with what is beneficial and the irascible with what is injurious, it seems that they are the same power of the soul.

[¶ 2.] *Objection 2.* The sensitive appetite deals only with what is beneficial according to sense. But this is the object of the concupiscible appetite. Therefore, there is no sensitive appetite differing from the concupiscible.

[¶ 3.] *Objection 3.* Hatred is in the irascible appetite. Jerome, in his *Commentary on St. Matthew's Gospel,* XIII, 33 says, "Let us have a hatred of vices in our irascible appetite." But hatred, since it is contrary to love, is in the concupiscible appetite. Therefore, the concupiscible and the irascible appetites are the same power.

[¶ 4.] *On the contrary,* Gregory of Nyssa (Nemesius, *On the Nature of Man,*[31] Chapter 16) and Damascene (*On the True Faith,* Chapter 22) assign two powers, the irascible and concupiscible, as parts of the sensitive appetite.

[¶ 5.] The sensitive appetite is generically one power, which is called sensuality. It is divided into two potencies which are species of the sensitive appetite, namely, the irascible and the concupiscible. As evidence of this, we see that natural, corruptible things must have an inclination not only to attain what is beneficial and to avoid what is injurious, but also to resist the corruptive and contrary forces, which hinder attainment of what is beneficial and cause what is harmful. For example, fire has a natural inclination not only to rise from a lower place which is not beneficial to it, to a higher, more suitable place, but also to resist anything that destroys or impedes it. There must be, then, two appetitive powers in the sensitive part, since the sensitive appetite is an inclination following upon sensitive apprehension (as natural appetite follows upon natural form). The one, by which the animal is simply inclined to pursue things beneficial according to sense and to flee things harmful, is called the concupiscible. The other, by which an animal resists those forces which oppose the beneficial and inflict harm, is called the irascible. Hence, we say its object is that which is difficult, since it tends to conquer and rise above obstacles.

[¶ 6.] Now these two inclinations cannot be reduced to one principle, for sometimes the soul occupies itself with disagreeable things, contrary to its concupiscible inclination, in order to combat by means of the irascible appetite what is of the nature of an obstacle. Hence, the movements of the irascible appetite seem to be opposed to those of the concupiscible, for concupiscence when aroused diminishes anger, and anger when aroused diminishes concupiscence, in most cases. It is clear also that the irascible is a kind of champion and defender of the concupiscible, when it rises against those things which obstruct the attainment of the suitable things sought by the concupiscible, or when it opposes the harmful forces which the concupiscible flees. For this reason, all the movements of the irascible appetite originate and terminate in the movements of the concupiscible appetite. For example, anger originates in sorrow, and when it inflicts vengeance, terminates in joy. For this reason also, the struggles of the animals are over concupiscible objects, food and sex.

---

[31] Nemesius, *De Natura Hominis.*

[¶ 7.] *Reply to Objection 1.* The concupiscible appetite deals with both the beneficial and the harmful, but the irascible appetite resists the harmful, which it attacks.

[¶ 8.] *Reply to Objection 2.* As in the apprehensive powers of the sensitive part there is an estimative power which perceives things that are not received through the senses, as we have said (*S.T.,* I, 78, 2), so also there is in the sensitive appetite a certain appetitive power that desires something not because it is pleasing to the senses, but because it is useful to the animal in self-defense. This is the irascible appetite.

[¶ 9.] *Reply to Objection 3.* Hatred belongs directly to the concupiscible appetite, but because of the strife it causes, it can pertain to the irascible appetite.

No. 3. *The Relationship of the Sense Appetites to Reason*
  St. Thomas: *Summa Theologiae,* Part I, Question 81, Article 3
  Do the irascible and concupiscible appetites obey reason?

[¶ 1.] *Objection 1.* The irascible and concupiscible appetites are parts of sensuality. But sensuality does not obey reason, and hence, it is signified by the serpent, as Augustine says (XII, *On the Trinity,* Chapter 13). Therefore, the irascible and concupiscible appetites do not obey reason.

[¶ 2.] *Objection 2.* What obeys a thing does not resist it. But the irascible and the concupiscible appetites resist reason, as the Apostle says: "I see another law in my members, warring against the law of my mind," (Roman VII, 23). Therefore, the irascible and concupiscible appetites do not obey reason.

[¶ 3.] *Objection 3.* As the appetitive power is inferior to the rational part of the soul, so also is the sensitive power. But the sensitive part does not obey reason, for we do not hear and see only when we wish to. Therefore, neither do the powers of the sensitive appetite, the irascible and the concupiscible, obey reason.

[¶ 4.] *On the contrary,* Damascene says (XII, *On the True Faith,* Chapter 12) that the part of the soul obedient and amenable to reason is divided into concupiscence and anger.

[¶ 5.] The irascible and concupiscible appetites obey the superior part, in which is the intellect or reason, and the will, in two ways: in one way as related to reason; and in another way, to the will. The sensitive appetites are subject to reason with respect to their own acts. The sensitive appetite in other animals is made by nature to be moved by the estimative power, for example, a sheep, seeing the wolf as an enemy, is afraid. In place of the estimative power there is in man a cogitative power, as we have said, (*S.T.,* I, 78, 4), which is called by some the *particular reason,* because it combines individual intentions. Hence, in man the sensitive appetite is made by nature to be moved by the cogitative power. But this same particular reason is made to be moved and directed in man by universal reason; hence, in syllogistic reasoning, particular conclusions are drawn from universal propositions. Therefore, it is clear that universal reason rules the sensitive appetite (which is divided into irascible and concupiscible) and this appetite obeys. To draw particular conclusions from universal principles is not simply the work of understanding, but of reason; hence, we say the irascible and concupiscible appetites obey reason rather than the intellect. Anyone can experience this in himself, for by applying certain universal considerations, anger or fear, or similar movements, may be tempered or even stimulated.

[¶ 6.] The sensitive appetite is also subject to the will in the execution of an act through the motive power. In other animals, movement follows immediately upon the irascible and concupiscible appetites; for example, a sheep, fearing a wolf, flees at once because it has no counteracting superior appetite. In contrast, man is not moved immediately by the irascible and concupiscible appetites. He awaits the command of the will, which is a superior appetite, for in all co-ordinated motive powers, the second moves only by virtue of the first; hence, the lower appetite is not sufficient to move someone unless the higher appetite consents. The Philosopher says this in Book III, *On the Soul,* "the higher appetite moves the lower, as the higher sphere moves the lower." In this way, therefore, the irascible and the concupiscible appetites are subject to reason.

[¶ 7.] *Reply to Objection 1.* Sensuality is signified by the serpent with respect to the sensory part of the soul. But *irascible* and *concupiscible* designate the sensitive appetite on the part of the act to which reason leads them, as we have said. (*S.T.,* I, 81, 1 and 2.)

[¶ 8.] *Reply to Objection 2.* As the Philosopher says in Book I, *Politics,* Chapter 3, we observe in animals a despotic and a politic rule: For the soul dominates the body by a despotic rule, but the intellect dominates the appetite by a politic and royal rule. *Despotic* describes a power whereby a man rules slaves who do not have the possibility of resisting the power of his rule because they have nothing of their own. *Politic* and *royal* describe a power whereby a man rules free subjects who, though subject to the direction of the ruler, nevertheless have something of their own by reason of which they can resist his commands. And so we say the soul dominates the body with a despotic rule, since the members of the body can in no way resist the rule of the soul; at the soul's desire, the hand, the foot and whatever members are subject to voluntary motion, are moved immediately. But the intellect or reason is said to rule the irascible and concupiscible appetites by a politic rule, since the sensitive appetite has something of its own by which it can resist the rule of reason. For the sensitive appetite is moved naturally not only by the estimative power in some animals, and by the cogitative power directed by universal reason in man, but also by the imagination and the sense. Hence, we experience the irascible and concupiscible appetites resisting reason, when we sense or imagine something pleasant which reason forbids, or something sad which reason commands. Nevertheless, the fact that the irascible and concupiscible appetites resist reason to some degree, does not mean that they do not obey reason.

[¶ 9.] *Reply to Objection 3.* The external senses require for their acts external objects to stimulate them, and the presence of these objects is not under the rule of reason. But the interior powers, both appetitive and perceptive, do not need exterior things. Hence, they are subject to reason which can stimulate or modify the desires of the appetitive power, and also form phantasms in the imagination.

No. 4. *The Relationship of the Sense Appetites to the Will*
St. Thomas: *Summa Theologiae,* Part I–II, Question 17, Article 7
Is the act of the sensory appetite commanded?

[¶ 1.] *Objection 1.* It seems that the act of the sensitive appetite is not commanded, for the Apostle says: "For that good which I will I do not," (*Romans,* Chapter VII, Verse 15) and the *Gloss* explains that "man does not want to lust, yet lust he does." But to have concupiscence is an act of the sensitive appetite. Therefore, the act of the sensitive appetite is not subject to our command.

[¶ 2.] *Objection 2.* Corporeal matter obeys God alone with respect to change in form, as we said earlier. (*S.T.,* I, 105, 1; and I, 110, 2.) But the act of the sensory appetite effects a kind of change of form in a body, namely, heat or cold. Therefore, the act of the sensitive appetite is not subject to human command.

[¶ 3.] *Objection 3.* The proper moving principle of our sensory appetite is something apprehended according to sense or imagination. But it is not always within our power to apprehend something by means of our senses or imagination. Therefore, the act of the sensory appetite is not subject to our command.

[¶ 4.] *On the contrary,* Gregory of Nyssa says that whatever obeys reason is of two kinds: the desirable (concupiscible) and the irascible, and these refer to the sensory appetite. Therefore, the act of the sensory appetite is subject to the command of reason.

[¶ 5.] Any act comes under our command if it lies within our power, as we said before (*S.T.,* I–II, 17, 6). Accordingly, in order to understand how the act of the sensitive appetite comes under the command of reason, we must consider how it is within our power. We should note that the sensitive appetite differs from the intellectual appetite (which we call the will) in that the sensory appetite is a power of a corporeal organ, while the will is not. Now, every act of a power that uses a corporeal organ, depends both on the power of the soul and the disposition of the organ, as sight depends on the power to see and the condition of the eye by which vision is aided or impeded. Hence, the act of the sensitive appetite depends not only on the appetitive power but also on the disposition of the body. But that which is on the part of the power of the soul depends on apprehension. The imagination's apprehension (which is of a particular thing) is ruled by the apprehension of reason (which is universal) as a particular, active power is ruled by a universal active power. In this respect, then, the act of the sensitive appetite is subject to the command of reason. However, the quality and disposition of the body is not subject to the command of reason, and in this respect, the movements of the sensitive appetite are kept from being completely subject to reason.

[¶ 6.] It sometimes happens, as a result of the apprehension of our imagination or senses, that our sensitive appetite is set in motion suddenly and then that motion is beyond the control of our reason, although it could have been prevented by our reason if it had foreseen it.

[¶ 7.] Hence, the Philosopher says, in Book I, *Politics,* "that reason rules over the irascible and concupiscible, not with a despotic rule, which is that of a master over a slave, but with a politic or a royal rule, which is exercised over free men who are not completely subject to the ruler.

[¶ 8.] *Reply to Objection 1.* Whenever a man lusts after something which he does not want to lust after, this is a result of the body's disposition, through which the sensitive appetite is prevented from being completely subject to the command of reason. Therefore, the Apostle also says: "I see another law in my members, fighting against the law of my mind." This can also be the result of a sudden movement of concupiscence, as we have said.

[¶ 9.] *Reply to Objection 2.* The quality of the body is related in two ways to the act of the sensitive appetite: first, as prior to it, insofar as his body disposes a man in some way towards this or that passion; and second, as following it, for instance, when someone becomes flushed with anger. Therefore, the quality of the body which is prior to the movement is not subject to the command of reason, either because it belongs to the nature of the body or because it follows a previous movement which it cannot immediately quiet. But the quality which is consequent to the sensitive appetite is under the command of reason, because it follows the local motion of the heart which is moved in various ways by the different acts of the sense appetite.

[¶ 10.] *Reply to Objection 3.* Because there must be an external object for an apprehension by the external senses, it is not within our power to apprehend anything through our senses unless that object is sensibly present, and this presence is not always within our power. At such a time (when it is present) man can employ his senses whenever he wants, unless there is some impediment on the part of the organ. But the apprehension of the imagination is subject to the rule of reason, according to the mode of the power or the weakness of the imaginative power. The explanation why a man cannot imagine what his reason is considering is either that the objects are unimaginable, as when they are incorporeal, or that there is a weakness of the imaginative power, because of some indisposition of the organ.

Part III

THE RATIONAL POWERS OF THE SOUL

Section A: The Human Intellect

Nominalism and Realism in the Middle Ages

In the universities of Europe during the two centuries prior to the time of St. Thomas, bitter controversies waged over the meaning of *universal* * ideas. Some held that universal ideas are only concepts, without a real foundation in the world of experience where only the individuals exist. Those who held this view were called *nominalists,* * a name coming from their ascribing universality not to natures or things, but only to names *(nomina)*. There were others who held that there are universal ideas which do really correspond to universal names, because in their view every concept of the mind to which a universal name is applied must have an identical form in reality; otherwise intellectual knowledge would be false. Those who held this view were called *realists* * or, more properly, extreme realists. This dilemma of the philosophers seemed insoluble, for it appeared that either one or the other of these positions had to be true. Yet both of them contained difficulties that common sense could not disregard. St. Thomas, in offering a solution, took the view that there was a middle ground between what seemed to be contradictory positions. His view, called *moderate realism,* * will be taken up later in this section.

Contemporary Nominalism

In our times the problem of nominalism has appeared in a somewhat different frame of reference from the one of the Middle Ages. At that time it has seen as a problem of logic and of dogmatic theology; now it is seen more particularly as a problem of morals or ethics. We shall begin this chapter by raising this problem of contemporary nominalism, for it is by studying the power of intellect with reference to such a problem that we shall understand better the meaning and the importance of this power of the soul. In the passage that follows we see the problem as it is raised by a contemporary author who writes psychology for the layman.

> Today, much of our vocabulary that deals with personal relationships is based upon philosophical daydreams. This applies especially to such concepts as "goodness," "virtue," "truth" and the like. The philosopher takes a word, such as "evil" or "justice" or some other abstraction that never has existed in nature, and investigates it as he would a thing or an animal. Havelock Ellis spends a chapter of his *Studies in the Psychology of Sex* explaining "chastity." These verbalisms, inventions of philosophers, magic-makers, witch-doctors and devil hunters are weighted with emotional meanings to befuddle and confuse. They upset troubled people in their attempts to adjust themselves to the world of reality.[1]

In this passage the author holds that such concepts as "goodness," "virtue" and "truth" and the like are based upon philosophical daydreams. The implication is that they do not have objective validity because they are not based immediately upon a concrete experience such as we have in sense knowledge. The conclusion that one might draw from this view is that intellectual knowledge does not have a formal object really distinct from sense knowledge, and that it is only a more refined kind of knowledge than that found in brute animals. We shall try to prove the falsity of this view. It will be our task to employ again the arguments of St. Thomas used against the earlier nominalists. Through those arguments we hope to establish that human intelligence is a power of knowledge essentially superior to sense knowledge. Our immediate purpose, then, is not ethical but psychological, for the ethical problem can have a sound answer only if there is a sound answer to the psychological problem.

---

[1] David Fink: *Release from Nervous Tension.* Simon and Shuster, New York: 1943, 140–141.

Intellectual Knowledge Compared to Sense Knowledge
(Readings: III, A, No. 1)

Our method will consist in examining the objects and acts of intelligence or reason, and, by comparing them to the objects and acts of sensory knowledge, prove that we are engaged here with two essentially different types of knowledge. The investigation of the two types of knowledge must proceed along the general lines of the definition of knowledge as *an immaterial union between the knower and the known*.

Now if the intellect is essentially different from the senses, the union of the form of knowledge with the knower will constitute a different mode of immateriality in intelligence than it does in sensation. Aristotle defined the sense as a power that can receive forms without matter as wax receives the form of the signet ring without the bronze or the gold. Though it is immaterial by the fact that it exists in the sense power without the physical subject that it has in nature, the sense form is not completely immaterial because, by definition, it is grasped by a power existing in a corporeal organ. Both the power which senses and the sensible form are dependent upon time and space as conditions of their being. To prove that the intellect is essentially superior we shall have to show that it can transcend even these material conditions of time and space and arrive at a universal idea, not in a merely artificial maneuver which does not get at reality (as the nominalists say), but in an act of knowledge that is at once both abstractive and objective.

A Dialectical Argument for the Essential Superiority of
Intelligence Over Sensation

Instead of beginning immediately with a strictly philosophic argument based upon the mind's ability to grasp universal ideas, we will begin with a *dialectical argument* * with which we are more familiar. When reduced to its philosophical principles, the dialectical argument is found to be, like the *demonstrative argument,** based on the ability to form universal ideas.

We shall examine two typical examples of man's use of reason, the first of which is man's ability to construct machines, and the second, his ability to construct artificial language. If there is nothing comparable to these examples among animals, we may infer that animals do not have the kind of knowledge that can produce those effects. We shall not argue that these activities prove that man is

uniquely a thinking spirit (as Descartes defined him), for we know
he has a body, powers of sensation, and sense appetites similar to
those of higher brute animals. Nor shall we try to prove that the
so-called "intelligence" of animals is owing fundamentally to the laws
of matter (as mechanistic psychologists suppose), for there is "intelligence" in animal behavior even though it does not belong formally
to an animal nature. While it is difficult to determine clearly in a
concrete example where sense knowledge leaves off and reason begins, we shall try to point out in the examples we cite why a person
might conclude to the existence of a higher power of knowledge than
that of the senses.

THE POWER OF INVENTION

Intelligence, as the French philosopher Bergson [2] points out, is the
only power that can make artificial objects like machines. It is the
property possessed in some degree by all men, but not at all by even
the highest of the brute animals. Animals can construct, but their
constructions merely copy what is already found in nature; and though
they can be taught *to use* machines, they cannot be taught *to invent*
them.

Invention requires reason in order to take an object that exists only
in the mind and make it real; it implies an ability to see *means and end*
relationships in a universal way, as for instance, when a man invents
a machine to make shoes. An animal skin becomes the material of
shoes; cotton becomes the stitching; iron ore becomes the parts of
the machine; oil serves as fuel—these objects of nature have nothing
that would ostensibly suggest to the senses the final image of shoe-
production. If the idea does not come from the senses, it must obviously come from a power of knowledge that goes beyond them.
Guided by its estimative sense, an animal may take certain objects
and put them together to form a crude instrument, as when an animal
makes a kind of ladder out of boxes. However, in this activity the
animal is merely accomplishing something predetermined by its own
nature and experience and by the nature of the objects it knows.
The relationship of means to end verified in activity of this kind is

---

[2] Henri Bergson: *Creative Evolution,* translated by Arthur Mitchell. New York:
Henry Holt and Company, 1911, 139 *ff*. We give this reference to Bergson's *Creative
Evolution* not because we fully accept his philosophy, but because Bergson who is not
in the tradition of scholastic philosophy offers material for our dialectical argument on
human intelligence.

already a familiar factor in the pattern of the animal's instinctive behavior and is already implicated in the materials used. Therefore, only the animal's sensory powers are required for the realization of animal "inventiveness."

This kind of knowing does entail a rudimentary kind of judgment, but it is not the abstractive judgment which belongs to intelligence. The estimative sense suffices to explain the "judgment" of what is beneficial for the animal sense memory, and the central sense operating in conjunction with the external senses makes it possible to "judge" distances, continuity, shapes, and so on, in the list of previous experience. Unlike the example of the invention of a machine for making shoes, the construction of a ladder from boxes does not contain anything that is not already found within the experience of the animal or within the capacity of the estimative sense. In animals there is no evidence of knowledge that can go beyond the capacity of the external and internal sense powers. The animal can "see" only what is proper to the sense powers and that forms the basis of the judgments that the animal makes. But man can "see" characteristics that are not obvious in sensible phenomena, and by reason of this insight, can invent something that nature does not produce. Nature produces the materials, but man produces a new form.

THE CONSTRUCTION OF ARTIFICIAL LANGUAGE

Let us take a second example. Languages, like machines, are the products of invention. A language is made up of signs that have no natural relationship to what they are to express. It is true that human language employs some natural signs, like those used by animals; a cry of pain, for example, is common to men and to brute animals. In these signs there is a predetermined connection between the expression and what it signified, and the signs are invariable and need not be learned. But artificial language owes its existence to reason and the choice of man, who can select his signs at random and use them in any way that he chooses. Just as men can freely choose to live in different geographical areas of the earth and under different forms of government, so they can freely choose the language by which they will communicate with each other. This kind of construction transcends the powers of the sense order.

The gist of the preceding dialectical argument is that man can do by means of intelligence what higher brute animals with a full assortment of external and internal sensory powers cannot do even in an imperfect way. The explanation of man's ability and of the animal's inability must lie in the type of knowledge present in each. In all examples given, we find that man's knowledge goes deeper than the phenomena of sense experience and penetrates to what is universal in things. Because he can see the universal nature of different substances he can apply them to ends that are not found in sense experience, and because he understands the universal significance of signs, he can assign a variety of meanings to sounds and gestures, and convey to his fellow men a meaning that is hidden from the senses.

The differences between the animal's "intelligence" and man's intelligence can be summed up in man's ability to abstract universal concepts. In a passage of his *Commentary on Aristotle's On the Soul,* St. Thomas points out that powers of the soul differ because different types of objects act upon the powers and act upon them in different ways.[3] We now make an application of this principle to intellectual knowledge in order to show by a strict philosophical argument that it differs from sense knowledge. For the sake of the clarity that opposing views may provide, we put the argument in its historical setting.

Views on the Nature of Intellectual Knowledge
(Readings: III, A, No. 2)

(a) Materialistic

The early Greek philosophers of nature thought that nothing existed in the world except bodies, and that knowledge itself consisted in a union of tiny physical images with the sense organs. Democritus, for one, held that there is no other cause of knowledge than the sensible images that come from bodies and enter into our minds. Mind itself, in his opinion, is composed of physical particles. Because bodies are naturally in a state of constant flux, these philosophers of nature thought that no knowledge about the physical world could be certain, since permanence is a necessary condition for certitude. Hence, they ascribe only *opinion* to all natural knowledge.

(b) Platonic

Plato's doctrine of knowledge, while granting the uncertainty of sense knowledge, upheld the scientific character of intellectual knowledge. He taught that the sensory forms were only participations of the necessary and eternal universal forms of intellectual knowledge. Sensory forms could stimulate the intellectual memory so that it could

---

[3] St. Thomas: *Commentary on Aristotle's On the Soul,* II, 13, No. 394.

recall the innate forms of universal ideas which lay hidden in the soul of every man; and every form of thought in the soul of man had a corresponding universal form in the higher world of reality where forms existed in a pure state, unmixed with the imperfections of matter. But intellectual knowledge was not derived from sense knowledge.

(c) Aristotelian

Aristotle agreed with Democritus that intellectual knowledge begins with the impressions that bodies make upon our senses and agreed with Plato that intellectual knowledge must deal with universal ideas in order to have the certitude required by science. Contrary to the atomist view, Aristotle taught that nothing corporeal can act upon the intellect because it is immaterial. Against Plato, he held that forms are individuated when they are received into matter as into a subject, and that these forms become universal when they are abstracted by the mind from the individuating principle of matter. Aristotle taught that intellectual knowledge has its origin in sense knowledge because the senses deal with the singular realities in which the potentially intelligible universal forms of the intellect exist. Thus, he held that the universal idea was consequent to sensory knowledge and not antecedent to it, as Plato had held.

(d) Thomistic

The Aristotelian doctrine of knowledge, elaborated by St. Thomas, is called the doctrine of *moderate realism: realism* because the universal nature or form abstracted by the mind is thought to correspond to a form that exists in reality; *moderate,* because the universal mode of existence of the form is only in the mind and not in reality, for it is not necessary to suppose that a form as it exists in the mind must have all and exactly the same characteristics that it has in reality.

The Universal in the Intellect and in Nature

In the following passages, St. Thomas indicates that the solution to the problem of intellectual knowledge lies in the distinction between the universal as it exists in nature and as it exists in our intellect.

The term *universal* can be taken in two ways: first, universal can mean the common nature according as it underlies the intention of universality; second, universal can be taken as it is considered in itself. *White,* for example, can be taken in two ways: either as the subject in which white happens to be; and second, whiteness by itself as a form.

Now the nature to which is added the intention of universality, human nature, for example, has a twofold existence. The one is a material existence, according as nature is in natural existence. The other is immaterial, according as it is in the intellect. Hence, according as a nature has existence in natural matter, the intention of universality cannot be added to it, because it is individuated by matter. The intention of universality comes only when it is abstracted from individual matter. But what is abstracted from individual matter cannot be abstracted really, as the Platonists thought. For a natural man, that is, a real one, exists only in this flesh and these bones, as the Philosopher proves in VII, *Metaphysics.*[4]

And a little farther on in the same work he says:

Thus, the intention of universality can be predicated of a common nature only when it has existence in the intellect. It can be considered common to many things only when it is thought of without those principles by which one is divided into many. We can conclude, therefore, that universals as such exist only in the soul, but that the natures themselves, to which the intention of universality is added, exist in things. Therefore, common names which signify the natures themselves can be predicated of individuals, but not names that signify the intentions of universality. Socrates, for example, is a man but he is not the species, even though man is a species.[5]

The Process of Abstraction (Readings: III, A, No. 3)

When the intellect grasps a universal idea, it grasps the nature of something without the individuating differences that are found in the thing as it exists outside the mind, since the meaning of *man,* for example, is clear without the characteristics belonging to a man's individuality. The individual differences do not come from the nature itself, but from the mode of existence which the nature has as an individual. Hence, in abstraction everything that belongs to form as form must be included in the universal concept and nothing must be added that does not belong to it. But it is not necessary to include the mode of existence that belongs to the nature as it is found existing outside the mind, because the mode of existence adds nothing to the intelligibility of the form.

---

[4] St. Thomas: *Commentary on Aristotle's On the Soul,* II, 12, 378.
[5] *Ibid.,* 380.

ABSTRACTION INCLUDES FORM BUT PRESCINDS FROM THE MODE OF INDIVIDUAL EXISTENCE

St. Thomas thus explains why we include the essential form but why it is not necessary to include the mode:

Abstraction may take place in two ways. First, by way of composition and division, as when we know that something does not exist in another thing, or exists separate from it. Second, by way of simple and absolute consideration, as when we know one thing without considering another. Therefore, to abstract by the intellect things which in reality are not abstract does involve falsity according to the first mode of abstraction. But in the second mode, this does not involve falsity, as is manifest in the case of the senses. For if we understood or said that color is not in a colored body, or is separated from it, there would be falsity in our judgment or speech. But if we consider color or its properties without reference to the apple which is colored, or if we express by voice what we understand, we would not be in error, because the apple is not essential to color. Therefore, nothing prevents the color from being understood, though we know nothing of the apple. Likewise, the things which belong to the species of a material thing, such as a stone or a man or a horse, can be thought of apart from the individual principles, which do not belong to the notion of the species. And to do this is to abstract the universal from the particular, or the intelligible species from the phantasms, that is, to consider the nature of the species without considering its individual principles represented by the phantasms. Therefore, if the intellect is called false when it understands something other than as it is, this is true, only if the word *otherwise* refers to the thing understood, for the intellect is false when it understands a thing to be otherwise than it is. Hence, the intellect would be false if it abstracted the species of a stone from matter in such a way as to understand the species as not existing in matter, as Plato held. But this is not so, if the word *otherwise* is taken as referring to the knower, for it involves no falsity if the mode of understanding in one who understands differs from the mode of the thing in entitative existence. For the thing understood is in the knower immaterially, according to the mode of the intellect, and not materially, according to the mode of the material thing.[6]

---

[6] St. Thomas: *Summa Theologiae,* I, 85, 1, ad. 1.

The Natural Object of Man's Intellect: The Essence of Natural Substances

Man's intellectual knowledge is conditioned by sense experience. It is from the phenomena of sense that the intellect draws the material which becomes the object of understanding. The natural object of the human intellect, then, is the kind of nature that exists individuated in matter and which comes to us by means of the senses. The proof of this is that the intellect continually employs the senses to gather data about the material beings from which an essence is abstracted, and that it goes back to the senses to confirm the data and to refine and complete its first act of knowledge.

Limitation of the Human Mode of Knowing Essences

To say that the intellect abstracts the essences of corporeal things, without qualifying the statement, is to invite an exaggerated optimism about human intelligence. We should not suppose that our intellect has such great powers of penetration that as soon as it begins to abstract from sensory experience, it achieves the knowledge of universal essences once and for all. Rather, it begins a long process which sometimes ends with universal and necessary knowledge of essences, but more often than not, ends with fragmentary and dialectical definitions. Often it is necessary for the intellect to see a substance from many different angles, through many different sense experiences. In looking at essences in different ways, the intellect multiples its concepts. However, it is not because the object demands a plurality of concepts, but because the human approach to universal knowledge of the truly scientific kind is often along a wearisome route where one travels slowly from potency to act.

Because we have to multiply concepts before arriving at universal scientific knowledge, we should not fear that our preliminary concepts are false or arbitrary or simply provisionary. They are objectively true and in an obscure way they are essential concepts, without the whole essence having been refined and made clear. Each concept is like a facet of a crystal which permits a ray of light to enter and shine on the essence. The stronger our powers of penetration are, the fewer angles we have to look from. But it would be a mistake to think that human knowledge could ever be privileged to grasp the essence of anything except by seeing it through multiple formalities of sense experience.

The Platonists thought that every formality grasped by the mind exists objectively outside the mind as a distinct form. They held that man, for example, is composed of a plurality of forms because there are many essential predicates that can be attributed to him. He is, for example, substantial, corporeal, spiritual, living, rational, and so on. St. Thomas, however, in the passage quoted earlier,[7] pointed out that the act of understanding is true as long as there is a basis in reality for the concept which the mind forms, and it is not necessary that forms be multiplied in reality because they are multiplied by the mind.

We may attribute, then, to the intellect the knowledge of natural essences, if we mean that this knowledge begins in a most imperfect way, in the simple act of understanding in which we see, as it were, the essence out of the corner of our intellectual eye; and that this knowledge, if pursued, naturally tends to an actual knowledge of the essence in scientific form. Or the statement about knowing essences may mean that whatever we know intellectually about an object is in the form of a universal and essential concept. Any intellectual object whatsoever becomes a kind of universal knowledge of the essence, since the intellect must always grasp an object first of all by removing it from the contingency of sense experience.

Intellectual Knowledge of Singulars

The intellect can know individual things in a kind of knowledge that takes them outside their natural conditions of mobility. It is not the individuality of an object, but its materiality, that makes it unintelligible for the intellect. But because individuality is coincident with materiality, it is necessary for the intellect to form universal concepts in the process of abstracting from matter. This does not mean, however, that we cannot know the individual intellectually.

Disregarding for the moment the difficulty of explaining how an intellect which necessarily has universal knowledge can know individual objects, let us see if we are sure that we have such knowledge. Each one of us is fairly certain, we may suppose, that he has firm convictions about himself as an individual. Each one probably feels also that he can make an intellectual judgment about the people he lives with. Every day we are obliged to make intellectual judgments about individual objects, because every moral judgment is concerned with particular people, events, and things. It seems fairly certain, then, that we can know individual people and things intellectually.

---

[7] St. Thomas: *Summa Theologiae*, I, 85, 2, Body of the Article.

In commenting on the ability of the mind to know singulars, St. Thomas uses a number of different expressions to explain how the intellect comes into contact with the individual. In one place he says: "Our intellect has some knowledge of the singular according to a certain continuity with the imagination." [8]   In another place he says: "For it (the intellect) knows the universal nature or the essence (what a thing is) by directly extending itself, but it knows the singular by a *reflection,* inasmuch as it returns to the phantasms from which the intelligible species are abstracted." [9]   In another place he says: "Singulars which are individuated by matter are not known except by a certain *bending back* of the intellect to the imagination and sense, that is, the intellect applies the universal species which it has abstracted from singulars to the singular form retained in the imagination." [10] Hence, in St. Thomas' explanation, it is by means of the continuity which the intellect has with the sensory powers of the soul in the act of consciousness that we are able to know singulars. This cannot be a continuity in the organic sense, for the intellect operates without an organ; nor is it a continuity in the same mode of knowing, for the intellect knows universal and necessary intelligible objects; but it is a continuity through consciousness, by which it can bend back completely upon the origin of its own act in the sensory powers of the soul.

Human Knowledge: A Progression from the Imperfect to the More Perfect

The very first concept of the mind, according to the commentator Cajetan, is the concept of being as seen individualized in the essence of a sensible object *(ens concretum quidditate sensibili).* From the first awakening of thought until the mind reaches the heights of metaphysical knowledge, being is the object of the mind. But in the very first contact with it, the mind does not penetrate it as an intelligible object, but knows it only as something that exists. At this stage, the concept of being contains for the mind only the notion of an "existing something" known by the senses, but already this is the seed from which the metaphysical knowledge of being can grow.

---

[8] St. Thomas: *Disputed Question on Truth,* II, 6. *Cf.* article by Klubertanz, "St. Thomas and the Knowledge of the Singular," *The New Scholasticism,* Vol. XXV, 135–166.

[9] St. Thomas: *Commentary on Aristotle's On the Soul,* III, 8, No. 713.

[10] St. Thomas: *Commentary on the Sentences,* Book II, Distinction 2, Question 3, Article 3, Reply to Objection 1.

Knowledge shifts back and forth between the senses and the intellect, each area of knowledge increasing its scope from its initial state of potentiality until the object is more or less definitely grasped by each power. Neither the sense nor the intellect ever leave the individual. Not the knowledge of abstract essences, but the knowledge of the individual is the goal of learning. However, the intellect never reaches the point where it can make a truly scientific judgment about the individual as an individual, because it can never adequately know with necessary and universal knowledge the causes that make the individual precisely what it is. It is only when it makes an application of general principles that the mind can make a statement about an individual that will have scientific validity. That is why, for example, the mind can judge that a particular body is corruptible, that another living body belongs to the class of animals, that another is the type that reproduces its kind, and so on. It does not have strictly scientific knowledge about the particular principles and causes of individual persons and things but about its common principles and causes.

The more we know about the contingent circumstances of the individual the more we approach the ideal of scientific knowledge. Though we can never see fully beyond the shadow or reflection of the intrinsic causes, the knowledge of the individual becomes more and more definite with each new experience. It is in this sense that two people who have lived together for many years may have knowledge of each other that approaches universal scientific knowledge. The imperfect knowledge of the individual is not *ipso facto* confused or uncertain knowledge. By grasping the individual even imperfectly, we form a quasi-universal by which we can identify it, though we do not penetrate the mystery of its individuality.

THE POWER OF TRANSCENDING THE PHYSICAL ORDER

From its connatural object, which is the essence of sensory objects, the intellect can rise by means of abstraction to the knowledge of forms that have no matter of any kind necessary to them either for their existence or for their definition. Because it is a spiritual power that does not depend upon a corporeal organ, the intellect is subjectively unlimited in the extent of its knowledge. Sensory powers, on the other hand, are limited in the type of objects they grasp by the organic structure of the sense organ. Thus, the eye can see only what properly affects the sense organ, and so on for the other senses. Because of its spirituality, however, the intellect can grasp the universal concept of being as it pertains to all reality. Being as such is fundamental to beings of all the categories, and in an analogical way, to the Transcendent Being who is beyond the categories. The limitation of the human intellect is only in the manner in which it can know all being and truth: it must know through the process of abstraction from sensory experience, and even when it transcends this experience by means of analogy, it must employ an imaginative form to symbolize in concrete fashion what is of its nature purely spiritual.

The Infinite Capacity of the Human Intellect

In commenting on St. Thomas' reason for saying that the human intellect has the capacity to know all things, John of St. Thomas points out that this power is rooted in our spiritual nature.

In regard to the capacity of the intellect, there is one reason taken from St. Thomas (*Summa Theologiae*, I, 79, 7) which is valid for all intellects: "An intellect grasps its object under the common notion of being, in that the possible intellect is that in which all comes to be. Hence, the possible intellect is not specified by any particular kind of being." In this place Cajetan rightly points out that the intellectual capacity cannot be filled by any particular object which moves the intellect to know, but only by one which terminates its activity. The capacity of the intellect exceeds any specification given by an object, and therefore, as St. Thomas says, it takes as its object all being.[11]

Then he goes on:

The *a priori* reason for this statement is that the intellectual power is based upon immateriality, which excludes all matter and corporeality and leaves it a purely spiritual potency. By the fact that it has immateriality and is separated from matter, it has a capacity for any intelligible object, because its manner of being specified and moved on the part of the object is a spiritual and immaterial mode.[12]

He finally adds:

There is a difference between the intellect and the sense on this score, because the capacity of the intellect goes beyond the connatural way of being specified by its object. The specification is effected by the object as an agent cause. In sensation, the capacity is completely limited to the connatural operation of the sense, insofar as it is moved by a sensible

---

[11] John of St. Thomas: *Cursus Philosophicus,* Part IV, Question 10, Article 3, 315b18.
[12] *Ibid.,* 316a40.

object. The reason for this difference is that the capacity of a knowing power comes from one basic source, namely, from immateriality.[13]

No object is absolutely unintelligible for the human mind, for every object is being in some way or other. Positively or negatively, literally or symbolically, scientifically or dialectically, we can know something about any object, because when we know universal being we know something about everything.

THE GENESIS OF MAN'S INTELLECTUAL KNOWLEDGE
(READINGS: III, A, NO. 4)

Aristotle spoke of the possible intellect as a pure potency, to be compared with prime matter in the natural order, because it is capable of becoming in an intentional way the forms of all things. The intellect is at first, he said, like a slate upon which nothing has been written. But we should not suppose that the intellect is passive in the same way that prime matter or any other subject that undergoes alteration is passive. St. Thomas points out the different meanings of passivity:

> To be passive may be understood in three ways: first, and most strictly, when something suitable either according to the nature or its proper inclination is taken away from a being, for example, when water loses its coolness by being heated, or when a man becomes ill or sad. Second, and less strictly, someone is said to be passive when something either suitable or unsuitable is taken away from a being. In this sense not only is he who becomes ill said to be passive but also he who is cured; not only he who is saddened but also he who is made joyful—hence, it means being changed or moved in any way whatever. Thirdly, in a broad sense, a thing is said to be called passive simply because it receives something it was in potency to receive, without being deprived of anything. In this sense anything which passes from potency to act can be called *passive,* even when it is perfected. In this way "to know" is to be passive.[14]

The act of understanding has been compared to be act of generation because just as a woman is made fertile by a man so that she can conceive and give birth to a child, so the intellect must be made fertile by the activity of another principle in order to conceive knowledge and give it birth in the form of truth. The analogy of repro-

---

[13] *Ibid.,* 317a5.
[14] St. Thomas: *Summa Theologiae,* I, 79, 2, Body of the Article.

duction is apt in many respects, because like the child that is conceived, knowledge must grow from an imperfect and potential status, developing quantitatively and qualitatively through the food that is supplied to it, until it reaches the condition of being a fully formed and viable truth.   But the analogy falls short in one very important aspect, because unlike the process of natural reproduction in which the mother and her child are distinct persons and become, in a sense, ever more distinct, the intellect tends to become more and more identified with the truth that it conceives.

Transition from the Sensory to the Intelligible Form

At this point some questions arise about the passivity of the intellect. How can the senses, which supposedly supply the material to the intellect, activate a power of the soul which is on a superior plane of existence?   How can a sensory form which is both contingent and material act upon the intellect whose object is an intelligible form? Can we say that a sensory form is made intelligible by being received into an intellectual potency, according to the axiom: "Whatever is received, is received according to the manner of existence of the recipient"?   We must answer that the sensory form cannot become intelligible by being received into the intellect, because it must first be shown that it can be received.   The axiom just quoted does not mean every potency can receive any form whatsoever, but means that *if a form is received,* it must be received according to the mode of being of the recipient.

The Agent Intellect (Readings: III, A, No. 5)

The possible intellect cannot make sensory forms intelligible, for this would suppose that the possible intellect is active prior to its act of knowing.   There is only one formal object and one formal act of the possible intellect, consisting only in the intelligible object and the act of becoming identified with it.   Consequently, there must be another power of the soul distinct both from the sensory powers whose objects are only potentially intelligible, and from the possible intellect which must be specified by an intelligible object before it can produce its own immanent acts of understanding.   This other power cannot be passive with respect to the sensory forms which are to be made intelligible; otherwise, it would need a further power to make the forms intelligible, *ad infinitum.*   Therefore, it must be at the same time an active power and an intellectual power.   We call it the *agent intellect.*

Though the agent intellect is a distinct power of the soul, its act does not constitute a distinct act of understanding. The possible intellect and the agent intellect together make up one act of understanding that is peculiar to the intellect of man. In his *Disputed Question On the Soul,* St. Thomas says:

> There are two actions proper to the two intellects, the agent and the possible. For the act of the possible intellect is to receive intelligible objects; the act of the agent intellect is to abstract the intelligible objects. From this it does not follow that there is a twofold understanding in man, because both of these acts combine to form one act of understanding.[15]

ROLE OF THE AGENT INTELLECT

The work of the agent intellect is described as an "illumination." This illumination is not, strictly speaking, a leaving behind as some would suppose, of sensory data, but rather an act which makes intelligible what is contained in things known by the senses. For the more perfectly we know an object intellectually, the more we understand it in its individual sensible reality, since the perfection of intellectual knowledge consists in knowing things that actually exist. The better we understand things, the more precisely we grasp them in their individual differences.

Nor should we imagine that the agent intellect simply lights up what is hidden or only potentially intelligible in the phenomena of sense knowledge—the way that a candle throws light on the walls of a darkened room. The objects of a sensory experience are not intelligible in the same way that colors are sensible before a light shines on them. An object becomes intelligible for our possible intellect only in the species formed by the agent intellect. There is not actually an intelligibility in the species of the senses; they are radically unintelligible. Sensory species are instruments through which the agent intellect produces a new species. Because sense objects and intellectual objects are on two essentially different planes of being, the agent intellect cannot simply "dress up" the species of sense knowledge.

SENSORY SPECIES AS INSTRUMENTAL CAUSES

The sensory species contain the material out of which the agent intellect produces the intelligible species. It is by means of a sensory

---

[15] St. Thomas: *Disputed Question On the Soul,* Article 4, Reply to Objection 8.

species that our intellect ultimately comes to know intellectual realities. Therefore, even though we deny that there is intelligibility hidden in the *species* of sensory knowledge, we must admit that there is radically an intelligibility in the *things* known by the senses: By means of our senses we know physical reality and not merely sensory species, and physical realities contain natures that are radically intelligible. Natures are "reason implanted in things" (*rationes inditae rebus*). Our manner of knowing, which is the grasping of these natures from the impressions that physical things make upon our senses, makes an agent intellect necessary. Material things and the possible intellect are on two different levels of existence, and the material things can become intelligible for us only when their natures are removed from their subjectivity in matter. This is what the agent intellect does when it produces an intelligible species, and in this consists its acts of "illumination."

UNDERSTANDING IS AN IMMANENT ACTIVITY

After the possible intellect receives the intelligible species, its own immanent act of understanding begins. The act of understanding is not like the act by which a figure is imprinted on a photographic plate. The film is completely passive; not so the possible intellect. For the passivity of the possible intellect is in the order of specification and not in the order of operation. Understanding is the most perfect of all immanent activity and the most vital of human activity.

Both the agent intellect and the possible intellect operate in the act of understanding. Nevertheless, most properly it is in the possible intellect that the act of understanding takes place. For in the act of understanding the knower becomes identified intentionally with what he knows, and this is the immanent activity proper to the possible intellect.

The Production of an Expressed Species or Concept

In the immanent act of understanding the possible intellect produces within itself a *concept*.* The concept is also called the *mental word,** the *idea** or the expressed species. Whenever powers of knowledge grasp their objects, not in their physical presence, but indirectly (because the objects are absent), it is necessary that they produce an *expressed species* in which the object is represented. Since the act of understanding takes place after an abstraction from the sensory data in which the object was first grasped, it requires an intelligible representation or concept. The concept is the immaterial likeness by which the intellect represents to itself the object that it knows. It has the name *concept* because it is the fruit of the reproductive power of the intellect; it has the name *expressed species* because it expresses what the intellect grasps in the act of knowing; it has the name *mental word*,[16] because it is that which the intellect speaks in the act of knowing.

Though it produces a concept which is an effect distinct from the act of understanding, the intellect's act remains immanent. The production of the concept is necessitated not by the essence of the act of knowing but by the mode of knowing. In abstraction, the intellect no longer has immediate contact with the object and it must, therefore, reproduce the object to be able to look at it.

EVIDENCE FOR THE EXISTENCE OF EXPRESSED SPECIES OR CONCEPTS

Is there any evidence apart from that of inference for positing the existence of concepts or expressed species? We know from experience that we are able to think of objects, intellectual in nature, which cannot be grasped through sense experience. The intellect knows, for example, what blindness is and what falsehood is; it knows truths that are deducible by reason and completely beyond the scope of sense knowledge. In these instances, it forms a concept of what is understood. The concept is not the same as the image in the imagination which accompanies the concept. It is, indeed, impossible to form a concept without an accompanying imaginative representation, but we do not identify the sensory representation of an act of justice, for example, with our conception of justice in general. The imaginative representation is variable and incidental to the meaning of what is grasped by the mind, since the same image could represent many other kinds of concepts. But the intellectual representation can in no way deviate from what is known, so that the conception of *justice,* for example, cannot apply to anything else.

If there were no concept produced in the act of understanding, the whole process of learning would have to be renewed every time we thought about an object. There would be no such thing as intellectual memory. But we know that we have an intellectual memory of things that we have understood, and this is distinct from the representations of sense memory. We do not have to abstract again from

---

[16] The mental word is not the same as the written or spoken word which is a part of language. A word in this latter sense is an artificial symbol which signifies the mental word.

sense experience; we can go directly to concepts already possessed. This is shown by the fact that we can compare immediately new concepts with the old. The intellect must produce, therefore, a concept in which the thing that is known is represented in an intellectual way.

THE CONCEPT AS A FORMAL SIGN

The representation by the species in intellectual knowledge does not prevent our knowledge from having an identity with the object. Concepts, as representations, are signs, but they are not mere symbols. A symbol, like a metaphor, is not the very essence of what it represents but an instrumental sign of it. In general, a sign is something that is used to represent something else. A flag, for instance, is a sign that represents a country; a handshake is a sign of friendship; smoke is a sign of fire. Since a sign is an instrument of knowledge, it must convey meaning; when it represents, it must make something known. An instrumental sign is one that conveys meaning in the way that a tool conveys the activity of an agent. It is something that is extrinsic to the agent; it is something that has, first of all, an existence of its own which is not one of representation. A flag is an example of an instrumental sign. A formal sign, on the contrary, is one whose whole essence is to be a sign. A concept is a formal sign. It exists only for the sake of conveying meaning; its entitative existence as a quality inhering in a power of knowledge is incidental to its role of being an objective representation.

Now the species produced by the intellect in the act of knowing is a formal sign and not an instrumental sign. If it were an instrumental sign, our intellectual knowledge would terminate with the knowledge of a symbol and not with the knowledge of reality. The concept is more than a symbol of reality, as a flag is a symbol of a country. It is reality itself, the same reality that exists outside the mind, except that in the one case it is a form existing intentionally and immaterially, while in the other it is a form embodied in a material subject and existing materially.

Knowledge of Reality Through the Species
(Readings: III, A, No. 6)

Thus, the mind understands the reality of things when it employs the intellectual species. We shall quote a lengthy passage in which St. Thomas shows that the contrary view would destroy intellectual knowledge:

Some held that the cognitive powers in us know nothing except their own impressions, for example, that the sense power senses only the activity upon the organ. According to this view, the intellect understands only what actually affects it, that is, the intelligible species received in itself. Thus, the species is the thing that is understood.

This opinion is evidently false for two reasons. First, because the things we understand are the same things about which we have scientific knowledge. If the thing we understand were only the species that are in the soul, it would follow that no science would treat of things that exist outside the soul, but only of intelligible species that are in the souls. Following this view, the Platonists held that all science treats of ideas, which, they said, are the things that are actually understood. Secondly, (the opinion is false) because the error of those early philosophers would follow those who said that *everything which appears to be true is true*. Hence, they held that contradictories could be true at the same time. It is true that if the power knows only its own impressions, it can judge only of them. Now a thing appears to be according as the power of knowing is affected. Every judgment of the cognitive power will be concerned with its own impression as such, and so every judgment will be true. If taste, for example, senses only its own impression, it will follow that when someone with a healthy sense of taste judges honey to be sweet, he will judge it truly, and if a person with a defective sense of taste judges honey to be bitter, this likewise will be a true judgment. For each of them judges according to the way that his sense of taste is affected. It follows, therefore, that every opinion will be equally true, and universally every impression.

We must hold, therefore, that the intelligible species is related to the intellect as that by which it understands. This is clear from the following argument. There are two kinds of activity, as was stated in Book IX of the *Metaphysics,* one which remains in the agent, for example, seeing and understanding, and another which passes into an external thing, for example, heating or cutting. Each of these kinds of action is effected according to a form. Just as the form by which an action tending to an external thing proceeds is the likeness of the object of the action (as heat in the thing causing heat is the likeness of the thing heated), in the same way, the form by which immanent activity is caused is the likeness of the object. Hence, the likeness of the visible object is the form by which sight sees, and the likeness of the thing understood, namely, the intelligible species, is the form by which the intellect understands.[17]

---

[17] St. Thomas: *Summa Theologiae,* I, 85, 2, Body of the Article.

The ultimate evidence for our certainty that our knowledge corresponds to objective reality is provided by the reflective power of consciousness: The mind can reflect not only upon the object of knowledge, but also upon its own activity—the very act of knowing in which the concept is produced—as well as upon the acts of our sensory apparatus. From its position of universal observer, the intellect can see the various steps that enter into the process of understanding. To ask for a proof of objectivity other than this act of consciousness is to ask for a proof of that which is obvious by what is hidden. It is also to ask for a proof of the objectivity of the intellect by a proof which must again be evaluated by the intellect. Hence, any attempt to prove the objectivity of our knowledge must come back to the mind's ability to reflect upon itself and upon the operations of the other powers of the soul.

The Movement Proper to the Human Intellect

The growth of human knowledge is a kind of movement. The human intellect is a potency comparable to prime matter in that it has a capacity for all intelligible forms as prime matter has a capacity for all natural forms. The intellect is a potency; that is why it is called the *possible intellect*. Its first concepts are imperfect and have to be developed through a continuous process of sense experience and intellectual abstraction. Because of this potentiality, the human intellect does not have only one type of operation but several.

The first operation of the intellect, which is called *simple apprehension,* is only the beginning of the knowing process. Simple apprehension does not completely actualize the capacity of the intellect or satisfy its appetite, even in regard to a simple object of knowledge. Simple apprehension consists in grasping the essence of an object without affirming or denying anything about it; it is mere conceptual knowledge, and does not as yet include a reference to a judgment about real existence.

Two other operations of the mind follow simple apprehension: one of them consists in a composition or division which the intellect makes to form propositions; and the other consists in deriving from such propositions new conclusions that were not immediately evident to the mind in the original propositions. The second operation is called *judgment* and the third is called *reasoning*. The goal of all our intellectual activity, however, is a judgment about the real existence of some kind of being. Therefore, both simple apprehension and reasoning are directed towards making a judgment in the strictest sense of the term, that is, one in which truth in the formal sense is found most perfectly for man.

St. Thomas gives the reason for the threefold operation of the intellect in the following passage:

> The human intellect necessarily understands by composing and dividing. Since the intellect moves from potency to act, it is in a way like things able to be generated, which do not acquire their perfection all at once, but attain it successively. In the same way, the human intellect does not acquire a perfect knowledge of a thing in the first apprehension, but first apprehends something about a thing, namely, its essential "whatness," which is the immediate and proper object of the intellect. Then it understands properties, accidents, and various dispositions affecting the essence of the thing. Accordingly, it is necessary to relate one thing with another by composition or division, and finally to proceed from one composition or division to another, which is reasoning.
>
> But the angelic and the divine intellects, like all incorruptible things, have their total perfection immediately from the beginning; therefore, the angelic and the divine intellects have immediate and perfectly total knowledge of the thing. Hence, in knowing the essence of a thing, they know immediately whatever we know about it by composing, dividing, or reasoning. And so the human intellect knows by composing and dividing, as well as by reasoning. The divine and angelic intellects, however, know the composition or division, and reasoning, not by composing or dividing, and reasoning, but by a simple understanding of the essence.[18]

SIMPLE APPREHENSION

We defined the first operation of the mind, simple apprehension, as the grasping of the essences of objects without further comparison or relationship. It is only the first stage of intellectual knowledge. What we have said until now about the activity of the intellect—its relationship to sense knowledge, its process of abstraction, its passivity, its knowledge of essences, the production of the expressed species—applies initially to simple apprehension. But this is only the beginning of the movement that St. Thomas has described. It is the first stage

---

[18] St. Thomas: *Summa Theologiae*, I, 85, 5, Body of the Article.

in the change from potency to act in the intellect. What follows is the very heart of human knowledge.

JUDGMENT

The first concept holds for the mind no complexity of meaning, but on re-examination, the intellect can discover by means of comparison and distinction a fuller meaning than that which was first grasped. Not content with seeing the richness and the diversity, the intellect now affirms its own discovery in the form of a judgment. This judgment, in which the union of formalities is made by means of the copula *is,* or in which the union of formalities is denied by means of the negative *is not,* may refer to different kinds of unions. There is, first of all, the kind of union which is proper to objects that can exist only as objects of thought like genera and species or subject and predicate. The intellect may judge, for example, that the species "rational" is an immediate division of the genus "animal" and not of the genus "substance." Secondly, there is the kind of union that belongs to natures which have an existence outside the mind as well as in the mind. In this case, the intellect may judge that human nature contains rationality as well as animality. But nothing is affirmed about the actual existence of human nature. These first two examples of judgment can be called a judgment of composition and division. Finally, the union may be one of a nature or essence with real existence outside the mind. In this case, the intellect will judge that a nature has real existence outside the mind. It is in this latter kind of judgment that the perfection of knowledge consists, for truth is the conformity of what is in the mind with what exists in reality. Judgment, therefore, is completed only when it includes existence. The goal of intellectual knowledge cannot be the kind of judgment that prescinds from real existence and is content to affirm or deny concepts of the conceptual order.

The existential judgment comes as the result of the intellect's ability to reflect upon its own acts and upon the acts of the other powers of the soul. It judges of its own power of abstraction and understanding in which universal concepts are formed, and of the activity of the external senses through which the note of existence is learned, and sees that it must affirm the union of the essential with the existential.

REASONING

The third operation of the mind, reasoning, is related to the second as movement to rest. The imperfection of the human intellect makes

reasoning necessary, and only in a relative sense is reasoning a perfection. Truth is the goal and reasoning is the means. The intellect
can rest in the affirmation of truth, but there is no natural goal for
the intellect in the process of reason as such.

Reason and intellect do not constitute two distinct powers, since
they are both related to the same act of understanding. There is no
essential difference between the imperfect state of a form and its
complete realization; neither is there an essential difference between
movement and rest in the intellect. St. Thomas describes the relationship of the two operations in the following passage:

> Reason and intellect in man cannot be two distinct powers. This is
> evident if we consider the act of each. Understanding (the act of
> the intellect) is the apprehending of an intelligible truth absolutely.
> Reasoning, however, is going from one thing that is understood to
> something else in order to know an intelligible truth. Hence, the
> angels, who possess perfectly the knowledge of intelligible truth,
> according to the capacity of their nature, do not have to go from one
> truth to another, but by a simple grasp, without discourse, they appre-
> hend the truth of things, as Dionysius says in Chapter 7 of *On the
> Divine Names*. Men, however, come to the knowledge of intelligible
> truth, by going from one thing to another, as it is stated in that passage,
> and, therefore, they are called rational. It is evident that reasoning is
> to be compared to understanding as movement is compared to rest,
> or as seeking to having, for the one belongs to the perfect or completed
> state and the other to the imperfect. Since movement always proceeds
> from something immobile and terminates in something at rest, so human
> reasoning, in its movement of inquiry and discovery, proceeds from some
> things that are understood absolutely, namely, the first principles, and
> returns, by way of judgment, to those first principles in whose light it
> examines what it has discovered.[19]

Truth and Error (Readings: III, A, No. 7)

Truth, we said, belongs formally only in the judgment where affirmation or denial is made of the relation of the subject of a proposition
to its predicate. Error, then, in the formal sense, can also be only
in the judgment, since it is the contrary of truth. As long as the
intellect is dealing with its proper object, false judgment is impossible,
for no power can fail in the apprehension of its proper object. Just
as the external senses are infallible with respect to their proper objects,

---

[19] St. Thomas: *Summa Theologiae*, I, 79, 8, Body of the Article.

so the intellect is infallible with respect to its proper object, which is the essence of sensory things. It can make no mistake about what is *per se* intelligible for it.

Every power, as such, is essentially directed to its proper object. Things of this kind are always uniform. So long as the power exists, its judgments concerning its own proper object do not fail. Now the proper object of the intellect is the *quiddity* of a thing. Hence, properly speaking, the intellect is not deceived concerning this quiddity in the thing.[20]

THE CAUSE OF ERROR

The intellect can err not only in making a false judgment, but also in forming concepts and in reasoning, for it is immune from error only when it deals with simple concepts or when it forms judgments based upon the immediately intelligible objects. It may be in error about things that accompany the essence, and this can happen in any of the three operations of the mind. It can err in simple apprehension, as when the essence is thought to be composed of contradictory forms, for example, if an irrational animal were thought to have a spiritual soul; or when it falsely attributes the definition of one thing to something else—if it were to attribute the definition of polygon to a circle. It can err in judgment by falsely attributing existence to what is only a possibility. Finally, it can err when it assigns a false conclusion to correct premises—as when it employs four terms in a syllogism.

Regarding things which accompany the essence or quiddity, the intellect can err, when it refers one thing to another, either in composing or dividing, or even in reasoning. Therefore, it cannot be wrong about those propositions which are immediately known once the meaning of their terms is known, as in first principles from which we arrive at the infallibility of truth in the certitude of science as regards its conclusions. Accidentally, the intellect may be deceived about the essence of composite things, not because of the organ, since the intellect is not a power which uses an organ, but because of the composition entering into the definition—either when the definition of one thing is false when applied to something, as for example, if the definition of circle is applied to a triangle, or when some definition is false in itself, since it involves an impossible composition, as if we were to define something as "a ra-

---

[20] St. Thomas: *Summa Theologiae*, I, 85, 6, Body of the Article.

tional animal with wings." Hence, in simple things, in whose definition there is no intervening composition, we cannot be deceived; but if we err, we grasp nothing, as is said in IX, *Metaphysics*.[21]

Descartes was unwilling to admit that the basis of error could be in the intellect because he regarded the intellect as a power whose essence consisted in the intuition of fundamentally simple essences. Thus, he ascribed universally to the intellect the same infallibility that St. Thomas had ascribed to its apprehension of simple essences. But, in Descartes' opinion, complex essences were constituted of simple essences and should, therefore, offer no occasion for error, unless the will interfered with the act of understanding. Hence, he considered an unregulated will the immediate cause of error, inasmuch as it could cause the intellect to make precipitate and faulty judgments and to draw erroneous conclusions. The psychology of St. Thomas does not lend itself to such optimism about the power of the human mind —man has the weakest of all intellects. But neither does it extend to the extreme voluntarism of Cartesian psychology, according to which all things, even truth itself, must be explained through an act of free will.

Conclusion

In this section we have investigated the nature of human intellectual knowledge and have seen that it rises to an essentially higher plane than that on which the sense powers operate. Nevertheless, rational knowledge maintains a bond with sense knowledge as the *sine qua non* condition for its operation. This dependency on the animal side of man's nature makes it evident that in the rational process of knowing, with its three distinct operations, man exists and operates as a mobile being. Hence, the possibility of human error does not remain completely inexplicable.

We can now move on to the question of the human *will* * and human *free choice,* * which in Aristotelian and Thomistic philosophy, presupposes the existence of rational knowledge and which marks the second stage of the intellectual movement that is analogous to the circular movement of knowledge and sense appetite that we saw in the previous part.

---

[21] St. Thomas: *Summa Theologiae,* I, 85, 6, Body of the Article.

Section B: The Human Will

The Relationship of Knowledge and Appetite
(Readings: III, B, No. 1)

Just as the powers of sensation are incomplete without sensory appetite, so the power of intelligence is incomplete without a rational appetite, for the mutual relationship of the intellect and the intellectual appetite is of the same type as that between the senses and the sense appetite. Sense appetite and intellectual appetite differ, however, by reason of their formal objects, since the knowledge which specifies each of them is formally different. St. Thomas puts the reason for this difference and for the superiority of the rational appetite in the immateriality and universality of its object.

> We must realize that the appetitive power in all beings is proportionate to the power of apprehension by which it is moved, just as the mobile being is related to the mover. For the sensitive appetite tends to a particular good, and the will to universal good, as was said above, just as the sense powers apprehend singulars, and the intellect apprehends universals.[22]

How can an intellectual appetite tend to its objects as universal if it tends to goods as they exist in reality outside the mind? St. Thomas answers by saying that the will does indeed tend to objects in their individuality, but under a universal aspect of goodness.

> The intellectual appetite, even though it tends towards things which are singulars outside the soul, nevertheless tends towards them according to a certain universal aspect—for example, when it desires something *because it is good*. Hence, the Philosopher says in II, *Rhetoric* that hatred can be of something universal, for example, "when we have hatred for every kind of thief." Likewise, by our intellectual appetite we can desire immaterial goods, which the sense does not apprehend, such as knowledge, virtues, and similar things.[23]

THE RELATIONSHIP OF INTELLECTUAL KNOWLEDGE AND THE INTELLECTUAL APPETITE

The relationship of intellect to the will—the intellectual appetite—is so essential that unless we understand it, we shall understand nothing

---

[22] St. Thomas: *Summa Theologiae*, I, 64, 2, Body of the Article.
[23] *Ibid.*, I, 80, 2, *ad.* 2.

of the nature of the will, nor of its property of freedom, nor of its act, which is free choice. For the will follows the intellect not only in the choice of objects towards which it tends, but also in the manner in which it tends towards these objects. In this respect the intellect is superior to the will; the intellect moves the will because it specifies the act of the will, thus moving it as an end (a final cause) moves an efficient cause. The will, on the other hand, moves the intellect, as it moves all other powers of the soul, as an agent oversees, commands, and directs the particular and proper activity of any one thing toward a common goal. Will and intellect are seen, consequently, to be mutual causes, each moving the other according to different modes of causality and different goals.

The Identity of the Good and the True

It is sometimes said that the object of the intellect is truth and the object of the will is the good. Though truth is, properly speaking, the object of the intellect, and good the object of the will, when we take man in the concrete, the good and the true are not so sharply separated. Both the good and the true are objects of the intellect, and both are objects of the will. On the one hand, the intellect recognizes the aspect of good in different objects, and on the other hand, the will pursues truth as a desirable object.

THE UNIVERSALITY OF THE OBJECT OF THE WILL

The will, therefore, does not seek only its own good as an isolated power of the soul. It seeks the good of the whole person and of all his powers, since its object is universal good. If the term *universal good* means *good without limit,* it surely means, above all, that the will seeks the goods that pertain to all the powers of a person's soul. A "faculty theory" that would isolate the will from its organic unity with all the other powers of the soul could never explain the universality of the will and could not, therefore, explain how man has *freedom.** For if we were to suppose that in the natural order there were one kind of good to which the will tended and that it could be completely happy in its possession, then the will could not be free. It would be necessitated by that particular good. It is precisely because it is not constrained by any particular good or the good of a particular power of the soul that it can desire all things and consequently be free.

The reason for the eminent role of the will lies in the fact that its object is universal good. Therefore, the good of the intellect and of all the other powers is within the scope of the will. Acting like the supreme authority in government, it has the office of moving the particular powers to their particular goods, and in so doing it moves all the powers towards the common good, which is the ultimate goal. All the powers of man are under the will for the sake of man's common welfare, his ultimate happiness.

The following passage from St. Thomas contains the basis for these statements:

> A thing moves in two ways: first, by way of an end, as when we say that the end moves the agent. The intellect moves the will in this way, for the good as known is the object of the will and so moves it as an end. Second, a thing moves another as an agent, as that which alters moves what is altered, and that which pushes moves what is pushed. In this way, the will moves the intellect and all the powers of the soul as Anselm says in Book II, *On Spiritual Topics*.[24] The reason is that wherever there is order among several active powers, that power related to the universal end moves the powers which are related to particular ends. We can see this in nature as well as in government. For the heavens, which strive for the preservation of all generable and corruptible things, move all the inferior bodies. Each of these inferior bodies strives for the preservation of its proper species or of the individual. A king, too, in whose keeping is the common good of his whole realm, moves by his command the individual governors who rule over their own cities. Now the object of the will is the good, and the end in general. But each power is directed toward some proper good suitable to it, as sight to the sensing of color and the intellect towards the knowledge of truth. Therefore, the will as an agent moves all the powers of the soul to their proper acts except the natural vegetative powers which are not subject to free choice.[25]

Comparison of the Intellect and Will (Readings: III, B, No. 2)

The question whether the intellect or the will is the more excellent power has no simple answer. St. Thomas asks himself the question, and answers it by making several distinctions.

> We can consider the superiority of one thing over another in two ways: absolutely and relatively. We consider a thing absolutely when we consider it in itself, but relatively when we consider it in relation to something else. If, therefore, we consider the intellect and the will

---

[24] St. Anselm: *De Similitudinibus.*
[25] St. Thomas: *Summa Theologiae*, I, 82, 4, Body of the Article.

absolutely, the intellect is the superior power. We can see this if we compare their respective objects, for the object of the intellect is more simple and more absolute than the object of the will, since the object of the intellect is the very essence of the desirable good, but the object of the will is the concrete desired good, the essence of which is in the intellect. Now the more simple and the more abstract a thing is, the more excellent and superior it is in itself, and, therefore, the object of the intellect is higher than that of the will. Since, therefore, the proper nature of a power is in its relationship to its object, it follows that in itself and absolutely the intellect is higher and more excellent than the will. But relative to something else, the will is sometimes higher than the intellect, since the object of the will may reside in something higher than the object of the intellect. For instance, I might say that what I hear is relatively more excellent than what I see, because something in which there is sound is more excellent than the thing in which I see color, although color is more excellent and simpler than sound. For, as we stated above, the action of the intellect consists in the essence of the thing understood being present in the knower, but the act of the will is completed when the will is inclined to the thing as it exists in itself. So the Philosopher says (VI, *Metaphysics*) that good and evil which are objects of the will *are in things:* but true and false, which are objects of the intellect, are *in the mind.* When, therefore, a thing in which there is goodness is more excellent than the soul itself in which the essence of the thing understood is present, in respect to such a thing, the will is more excellent than the intellect. But when the thing in which the good exists is inferior to the soul, then in respect to such a thing the intellect is higher than the will. From this we see that the love of God is better than knowledge of Him, but that the knowledge of corporeal things is better than love of them. Absolutely, however, the intellect is more excellent than the will.[26]

Freedom

The primary property that follows immediately from the nature of the human will is freedom, and the primary act which follows is free choice. We shall examine each of these in its relationship to intellectual knowledge in which each has its explanation. But before we take up the first point, we shall examine briefly several widely accepted views on the meaning of freedom. Freedom is a topic that is widely discussed in psychology, and one about which opinions differ sharply.

---

[26] St. Thomas: *Summa Theologiae,* I, 82, 3, Body of the Article.

It should be worth while, therefore, to compare some of these views with the notion of freedom found in the philosophy of St. Thomas.

VARIOUS VIEWS OF FREEDOM

Freedom cannot be easily categorized or explained. It is, in fact, the most elusive of all human experiences, much more mysterious than the workings of our intellect, even though the cause of freedom is in intellectual knowledge. In an analysis of the act of the intellect we can trace, to some extent, the causes of the act, and we can lay down certain rules of logic which the intellect must follow to pursue knowledge successfully. But there are no rules for human choice which parallel those of logic. We experience the movements of decision, but we cannot calculate them. We cannot set down the rules that will tell what choice follows from certain premises. We do not comprehend the motives of our choice. Our reasons are often hidden in the veils of the subconscious. We cannot explain even to ourselves why we have made a particular choice. At the conclusion of such an experience, the only answer that may satisfy us, if we inquire into the causes of our action, is this: "Because I wanted to." There have been many opinions on the nature of the human will and many attempts to define its rules of action, but none that are undisputed.

According to some, the essential note of freedom is the subjective inclination that makes us do the thing we want to do. It is as if they said: "Freedom makes man choose what he likes; that is, makes him free." That is precisely the point to be questioned. Can freedom and the human will be given some explanation, can the motives be discovered, which will infallibly tell us why a person has made a particular choice? Or is freedom to be explained rather in terms of ignorance of the prevailing or motivating cause.

FREEDOM AS KNOWLEDGE OF NECESSITY

Freedom has been defined as *the knowledge of necessity*. *Friedrich Engels,** the collaborator of Karl Marx, thus defined freedom. A person, in this point of view, is thought to be free as long as he understands the laws of matter that inevitably carry him to a destination that is predetermined not by powers of intelligence, but by chance. Freedom, consequently, is a real contradiction, inasmuch as it is identified with necessity. If a person understands the necessity that carries him like a tide that cannot be resisted, he is to that extent free;

but if he is ignorant of what causes makes him act, he is said to be coerced.

FREEDOM AND KNOWLEDGE OF THE GOOD

One of the earliest and greatest of all philosophers, Plato, identified freedom with knowledge. But in his view, it is not the knowledge of irresistible, necessitating forces acting as efficient causes, but rather the knowledge of the good which attracts the will as a magnet attracts iron. Knowledge of the good becomes identified with good will itself, because it is supposed that a person inevitably chooses the good, if he really understands what is good. Only an ignorant person will choose evil. Though Plato's opinion is chronologically an ancient one, it is by no means out of date; in every court of law it has been repeated countless times, but never in a way more forceful than in its first expression.

> Nearly all reproaches about unbridled and shameful lusts, made with the notion that evil is voluntary, are unjustified. The reasons why a man becomes evil are a bad disposition of the body and a neglected education. But each one experiences this as something disagreeable and against his will . . . And if everywhere in the city, both in private and in public, evil conversations take place, and if, in addition, the educational material absorbed from youth is in no way suited to curb these evils, then for these two reasons all bad individuals become bad, and that contrary to their wills. The blame, therefore, must be placed more on the parents than on the children, more on the educators than on those being educated. We should take advantage of every opportunity to exert all our effort to make use of the means of education, of our profession, and of science, to escape vice and to attain its opposite, virtue.[27]

In this opinion, virtue becomes identified with knowledge. A man acts because of the knowledge that he has gained from his environment and education. Sin is but another name for ignorance, for if a man sees what is best for him it is impossible for him not to choose it. A good state, then, is one which sees to it that its citizens are educated, so that they may become virtuous citizens. The state should not punish a citizen for having made a bad choice. It should punish

---

[27] Plato: *Timaeus,* 86d *ff.*

him only to enlighten him and to cure him, for an "evil person" is a "sick person."

FREEDOM AS VEILED DETERMINISM

The opinion that the will is physically predetermined by the condition of the body is also among those philosophical opinions that are constantly reappearing. Each new era in the history of science and philosophy bursts with optimism over the "discovery" of the physiological explanation of human freedom. But between the atomism of Democritus and the biological determinism of William James, or between the evolutionary determinism of Freud and the physical determinism of *Eddington* * there is little difference except in terminology, because in each of these and in similar opinions it is held that the radical principle governing choice is the material structure of the human body. William James held that the question of free will was insoluble on strictly psychological grounds. Illogically, his reasoning was based upon the impossibility of proving freedom of will by the strictly scientific method as he understood it, a view that is understandable in James because of his preconception that psychology can deal only with the material elements of man. He says of freedom:

> My own belief is that the question of free will is insoluble on strictly psychologic grounds. After a certain amount of effort of attention has been given to an idea, it is manifestly impossible to tell whether either more or less of it *might* have been given or not. To tell that, we should have to ascend to the antecedents of the effort, and defining them with mathematical exactitude, prove, by laws of which we have not at present even an inkling, that the only amount of sequent effort which could possibly comport with them was the precise amount which actually came. Measurements, whether of psychic or of neural quantities, and deductive reasonings such as this method of proof implies, will surely be forever beyond human reach. No serious psychologist or physiologist will venture even to suggest a notion of how they might be practically made. We are thrown back therefore upon the crude evidences of introspection on the one hand, with all its liabilities to deception, and, on the other hand, upon *a priori* postulates and probabilities.[28]

FREEDOM AND CONTINGENCY

Contrary to the doubts expressed by James, Sigmund Freud thought that he could give his psychoanalytic method the status of a strictly

---

[28] William James: *Psychology*, Vol. II. New York: Henry Holt & Co., 1902, 572.

natural science and by means of it explain the mysteries of human choice. But what remains of human freedom after he has applied his analytical method bears little affinity with a spiritual power of self-determination rooted in intelligence. His notion of the human will is, for all practical purposes, identical with instinctive animal emotions of fear and pleasure, more complex, indeed, because of its evolutionary gestation in the womb of human history, but no more conscious than the earth from which it originated.

In contrast to Freud, Arthur Eddington holds that man has free will because all things material are indeterminate and unpredictable in their behavior. The opposition between the teaching of Freud and that of Eddington is not as radical as it may appear at first. Eddington, too, is fundamentally a *determinist* * because unpredictability does not relate to a proximate freely determining cause of action wherein freedom actually lies, but in an observer who is extrinsic to the concept of freedom. When Eddington says that man is free because his actions, like the movement of electronic particles, cannot be charted or accurately predicted, he does not make freedom consist in an objective indeterminism, but rather in ignorance of established and determined laws of matter.

FREEDOM AS SELF-DETERMINATION (READINGS: III, B, NO. 3)

All of these views are in one way or another a form of determinism: a rudimentary materialistic determinism in the view of Engels; an intellectual determinism in the view of Plato; a biological determinism in the view of James; an evolutionary determinism in the view of Freud. But what we should note is that in each case it is a determinism that is imposed on the will from the outside. In none of these views is the will a self-determining power. Therefore, in none of these views can there be freedom in the proper sense of the term.

Freedom in the true sense is the property of a being by which it is self-determinant. Or to say it in a negative way: Freedom is the absence of compulsion in the determination of the activity by which a being tends towards or loves what is its good. By *compulsion* we understand the exercise of violence upon an agent so that it is forced to do what is contrary to its natural striving or self-determination; and by *good* we understand that which is perfective of a nature or is the perfection of a nature. For example, seeking knowledge is seeking what is perfective of man's rational nature; and the possession of knowledge is the perfection of his nature.

It is thought by some that freedom is incompatible with every kind of necessity. But this is not true, because freedom is incompatible only with the kind of necessity that destroys the self-determination we have just spoken of. Necessity is predicated according to the kinds of causes that are found to belong to a being and its activity. First, there is a necessity that comes from the formal cause. For example, it is necessary that man be rational. It is nonsense to suppose that this kind of necessity is incompatible with freedom, because the very basis of man's freedom is in his rational nature. Saying that man must be free even from the necessity of the formal cause would be the same as saying that man must be free not to be a man, if he so chooses; or man must be free not to be free, if he chooses.

Second, there is a necessity which comes from the material cause. Thus, certain properties naturally and necessarily characterize any object that is composed of matter: for example, corruptibility, extension, divisibility, movement, and the like. Insofar as matter belongs to the nature of man, certain effects must follow. But material causality does not destroy man's freedom, because his freedom is rooted not in the material principle of his nature but in the spiritual principle, namely, in the intellectual part. Nevertheless, the imperfection of man's freedom comes precisely because he is a being in whose nature matter has an essential role, and because his intellectual operations are conditioned by the necessary properties of matter, such as movement, extension, situation in space, and so on.

Third, there is a necessity that comes by reason of an efficient cause, for example, the necessity that the child has to move when it is carried in the arms of its mother. This kind of necessity may or may not be incompatible with freedom, depending on whether the activity of the efficient cause is such that it cannot be resisted and on whether the activity of the efficient cause is really violence or compulsion. That is, not every necessity by reason of efficient causality, even when it is absolute, destroys freedom, because it is possible that the activity of the efficient cause be in the very direction of the good to which the intellectual being himself is going by the impulse of his own love. This distinction between coercion or compulsion and the cooperative necessity of the efficient cause is a very important one for certain theological discussions where it is question of the unfailing necessity of an absolute First Mover both in the order of nature and in the order of grace.

Finally, there is a necessity that comes by reason of the final cause. The final cause, as we know, is the good to which a being is attracted or the good which a being enjoys. The necessity that comes from the final cause does not destroy freedom, because the *good* which attracts man is that to which he would naturally determine himself. Therefore, there would be no compulsion or violence, because it is in that that man's freedom consists. Where there is no coercion, no violence, there is no destruction of freedom. Even when it is question of a good that is absolutely necessitating, such as happiness, there is no destruction of freedom, since there is no conflict between the end and the natural strivings of man. Whatever is perfective of man's nature cannot be an obstacle to his freedom.

From this it follows that, strictly speaking, there is no true freedom with respect to evil, and that the possibility of evil choice is not of the very definition of free choice. The possibility of evil, which means the possibility of defect in regard to a good that is proper to one's nature, can come about only because of the imperfect orientation of the intellectual appetite towards the good proper to a nature; and evil choice can come about only because of the radical imperfection of the judgment which deals with objects of choice. However, we shall take up this point more extensively when we undertake a formal discussion of free choice.

The Basis of Freedom: The Infinite Capacity of the Will (Readings: III, B, No. 4)

The cause of freedom lies in man's intellectual nature. We have seen that the intellectual appetite is related to the intellectual knowledge as sense appetite to sense knowledge. Since the extent of intellectual knowledge is being and truth in all its universality, so the extent of intellectual appetite is goodness in all its universality. Just as the human intellect is a capacity for becoming all things in an intentional way, so the human will is a capacity for pursuing all things for the goodness that is in them. Since the intellect is indeterminate with respect to all kinds of being and truth, it follows that the will is indeterminate (free) with respect to all kinds of good. Because of its universality, the will cannot be determinately acted upon by any particular source. It is true that the will is acted upon by the intellect, because in knowing all being the intellect specifies the intellectual appetite—the universal formal causality of the intellect becomes the universal final causality of the will. Thus, the all-inclusive object of the intellect becomes the all-inclusive object of the will. Nevertheless, the intellect does not coerce the will, since it operates not in the order of efficient cause but in the order of formal cause. The efficient causality lies within the will itself.

All other goods, including the good of the intellect, lie within the scope of the universal good of the will. It is for this reason that the will is supreme and is not under the domination of any power, not even of the intellect. The will is moved with necessity only by the good in its universality. But that is not in the order of efficient causality and in a direction contrary to the natural impulse of the will's self-determination. Therefore, the will is not coerced by any extrinsic cause; it moves always from an immanent principle.

This is the very heart of freedom. The power of self-determination is so immanent that it cannot be violated by any extrinsic force. Thus, every act of the will itself is beyond compulsion. It is only when the will exercises its power of command over the other powers of man that it is possible for violence to enter in and destroy the act which was freely commanded by the will. Thus, violence cannot directly affect the act of the will itself, but it can prevent the command of the will from being carried out. The will, in its inner sanctuary, always remains free as long as intellectual knowledge, which is the cause of freedom, is present. Nothing can destroy freedom except that which destroys intellectual knowledge also.

Even when the will is acted upon by divine causality which unfailingly attains the ends designated in Providence, the will must always remain free because freedom is inseparable from any being possessing an intellectual nature. Indeed, the freedom of man under the impulse of divine causality is increased by that very fact, because the good to which the divine impulse directs the will can only be in the direction of the good that is perfective of man's nature; instead of being violent movement, it is movement most in accord with the immanent activity of the will itself.

The will is free because its object is good in its entirety. The intellect, which ranges from the material to the spiritual, can find in each new experience a good capable of attracting the will. But no particular object can completely satisfy man's present desire for good, just as no particular object in human experience can completely satisfy his intellectual striving for knowledge. If there is any way to express man's unlimited desire for good, we might say that it is his total striving for happiness. But for man, happiness is not to be identified with a thing; it is a *state* in which all the tendencies of human nature find complete satisfaction.

That no object in this life can confer complete happiness is the conclusion not only of philosophers and theologians but of anyone who has reflected on life at all. There are defects in everything,

unpleasant memories in every experience. Because our intellect sees
the limitation of goodness in the finite objects of our experience, our
will is free to choose them or to reject them. Nevertheless, we must
seek happiness in whatever we do, and whatever we choose is part
of our search for happiness. But complete happiness in this life is
a goal that stays outside our reach, for anything that we achieve has
some limitation to it.

Thus, intellectual appetite is unlike the sensory appetites in that
it cannot be completely satisfied by any particular experience or series
of experiences. The sensory appetites, limited as they are by their
organic structure, are capable of reaching a saturation point where
appetite ceases. But the rational will, like the intellect, transcends
the limitations of matter and lies beyond the possibility of a saturation
point. The capacity of both powers is infinite.

The infinity of the intellect and the will is qualitative rather than
quantitative. This means that a mere numerical increase of goods
does not of itself satisfy more fully. It is not the number of things
we love that makes life more satisfying but the quality of those things,
perhaps few in number, that are more valuable and satisfying in the
ontological sense. Indeed, numerical increase would inevitably result in dissatisfaction, because, confronted with a variety of imperfect
goods, the will could cling to nothing permanently. In this respect
the perfection of the will is like the perfection of the intellect. Wisdom, the perfection of knowledge, consists in a unity wherein all
things are seen in the light of one principle. Like the universality and
simplicity of wisdom, the universality and simplicity of love is superior
to multiplied loves. The object, therefore, which would confer complete happiness could not consist in the addition of all individual goods
which partially satisfy, but would have to be a supreme good which
can perfectly satisfy all desires simultaneously.

Freedom and the Universal Good

If there is an object which is recognized as universally good, the
will cannot refuse it, for it would satisfy the infinite desire of the
will. But before we accept the conclusion, it must be proved that such
an object, possessing all perfection and capable of bestowing complete
happiness, actually exists and can be known by the intellect. It is
not enough that an object be very good, possibly the most satisfying
that we have ever experienced; it must be a supreme and universal
good and known as such. Finally, the knowledge of such an object
cannot be through hearsay or even based on faith of a supernatural

kind. It must be knowledge through intrinsic evidence of the object itself, because the will is moved necessarily only by what *is seen* to confer perfect happiness. Any object that is or appears to be imperfect, is from one point of view undesirable. Being deficient, it will fail to satisfy some desire. Since it does not completely satisfy the infinite capacity of the will it need not be willed, even though it may hold great advantages. Only good in an unlimited sense must be willed.

THE WILL MUST CHOOSE THE GOOD (READINGS: III, B, NO. 5)

Because the formal definition of the will includes its universal relationship to good, it is possible to reverse the order of the proposition and say that by definition the will must seek good whenever it acts. The seeking of good is inseparable from its act. This does not mean that whatever a man chooses must actually be a good for him. It must, however, appear good. Even the most blasphemous and immoral acts must hold out for the will of the agent something that appears good. For whatever a man does deliberately, he does with an eye to satisfying an appetite for what is good. Man cannot will what is evil as evil, but only as an apparent good. Every good is willed ultimately because it is thought to contribute something towards making man happy.

The Essence of Free Choice (Readings: III, B, No. 6)

After studying the meaning and cause of freedom we now take up the *act of choice* which follows the property of freedom. It is necessary at the outset to make a distinction between the will as the rational appetite and the will as the power of choice. Sometimes the two expressions are used interchangeably; but the same kind of distinction must be made between them that is made between understanding and reason. St. Thomas explains the distinction in the passage which follows:

> Just as on the part of the intellectual apprehension there is a relationship of understanding and reason, so on the part of the intellectual appetite there is a relationship between the will and the power of choosing *(liberum arbitrium)*. This is clear from the relationship of objects and acts (of the powers). For *understanding* implies a simple acceptation of something, as when we speak of *understanding* first principles which are known in themselves without any comparisons with something else. But *to reason,* properly speaking, means to go from

the knowledge of one thing to the knowledge of another. Properly speaking, then, we reason about conclusions which are made known through their principles. In like manner, on the part of appetite, *willing* implies the simple appetite for something, hence, the will is said to be of the end which is desired for itself. But choosing means to desire something for the sake of something else, and so properly speaking, it is concerned with the means to an end. Just as in the cognitive order there is a relation of principles to conclusion, to which assent is given because of the principles, so in the appetitive order an end is related to the means to the end, which are chosen because of the end. It is clear, then, that the same relationship holds between understanding and reason as between will and the power of choosing, that is, freedom of choice. But it was shown above that it belongs to the same power to understand and to reason, just as it belongs to the same power to rest and to be moved. Hence, it also belongs to the same power to will and to choose. The will and freedom of choice are not two powers, then, but one.[29]

CHOICE DEALS WITH MEANS TO AN END (READINGS: III, B, NO. 7)

The simple act of the will is directed towards the good as its object or end, but choice is directed towards the means leading to that good. Some goods are desirable as ends because they are desirable in and for themselves, while other goods are desirable only as means, and only participate, therefore, in the notion of goodness. Knowledge, for example, can be good as an end in itself, but a knife is good only because it is a means or an instrument for attaining a good that is an end in itself.

The act of choice (election) is analogous to a syllogistic process. The good, which is the end of the process, is like a principle in a syllogism from which a conclusion is derived, for the end is the principle from which the goodness of the means is derived. Since choice is concerned with means to an end, it follows that there cannot be choice about an end that is an absolute and not a means. Now something can be both an end and a means: an end because it is the term of a particular process, and a means because it is for the sake of something else. Speculative knowledge, for example, is an end in itself, since truth is something to be valued for its own sake; but it is, at the same time, a means with respect to the will, for speculative knowledge is a means of attaining happiness. Similarly, health is

---

[29] St. Thomas: *Summa Theologiae,* I, 83, 4, Body of the Article.

the goal of the art of medicine, but health is also a means of attaining happiness.

It follows that the only thing which is outside the scope of choice is happiness itself because it is an absolute end. No choice is possible about happiness because it cannot be looked upon as a means. It is the absolute end to which all particular goods are directed. But a choice is possible with respect to anything else insofar as it is regarded as a means to happiness. Thus, one type of vocation is selected over another, one political system over another, a game of cards over a game of football, a poem over short story—these are some of the things with which choice deals. They are examples of means that are chosen ultimately because a person wants to be happy; the choice of means is free because none of them is the absolute end, the only object that necessitates the human will.

Thus, St. Thomas explains the reason for the possibility of choice through the relationship of the object to happiness:

> In every particular good the man can consider the goodness as well as the lack of goodness, which implies the idea of evil. In this way the mind can apprehend any one of these goods as one to be chosen or rejected. The only good which the mind cannot apprehend as evil or as defective in any way is the perfect good, which is happiness. For this reason, man of necessity wills happiness and he cannot will not to be happy, that is, to be unhappy. Now since choice is not concerned with the end but with the means to the end, as we said above, it is not concerned with the perfect good which is happiness, but with other particular goods. Therefore, man does not choose of necessity but freely.[30]

The possibility of choice, therefore, lies, from one point of view, in the limitation of goodness in the object. For whatever is limited lacks some element of perfection and cannot completely satisfy the infinite capacity of the will. And this note of imperfection has the aspect of evil, as St. Thomas says. Evil cannot attract the will, but on the contrary repels it. Therefore, the will can reject any imperfect thing or whatever appears to be imperfect.

Neither the more perfect good nor the most perfect good in any particular order must be chosen, when it is a question of means, because neither the one or the other is seen to lead infallibly and necessarily to happiness. Hence, neither equality of means nor the superiority of one means over another makes freedom of choice im-

---

[30] St. Thomas: *Summa Theologiae*, I–II, 13, 6, Body of the Article.

possible, since in the last analysis it is a will with a capacity and a desire for perfect happiness and not the object that makes for freedom of choice. If our choice were determined infallibly by virtue of the means, we should not be free at all. On the contrary, free will implies the power to choose a good means or a poor means, if one decides to act; or it means the power to reject any and all means, if in a particular situation, one decides not to act.

The self-determination in the act of choice is sometimes divided into what is called the *freedom of specification* and the *freedom of exercise*. We would exercise our freedom of choice in the first way, for example, if when we were asked to choose between watching a baseball game or going for a ride, we decided on seeing the baseball game. We should exercise our freedom of exercise, however, if we decided that we would do neither the one nor the other. Thus, freedom of specification is concerned with selecting one of several objects proposed as desirable in a given situation. Freedom of exercise is concerned with the decision to act or not to act in a given situation. Even though there is a formal distinction between these two kinds of choice, nevertheless, in the concrete the freedom of exercise actually comes down to the freedom of specification. For it is necessary that a man makes some kind of specific choice, since he must exist in some concrete situation where he will be affected one way or another. A man cannot simply decide not to act at all. Thus, in a concrete situation the freedom of exercise will be reducible to the freedom of specification.

CHOICE, AN ACT OF BOTH INTELLECT AND WILL (READINGS: III, B, NO. 8)

Is the act of free choice primarily an act of the will or an act of the intellect? Actually, the choice must come from both powers, each giving a formality of its own to the act. St. Thomas says:

> The name choice implies something belonging to reason or the intellect, and something belonging also to the will, for the Philosopher says in VI, *Ethics* that choice is either an appetitive intellect or an intellectual appetite. Now, whenever two things come together to form one, one of these is as form in respect to the other. Hence, Gregory of Nyssa says that choice is neither appetite alone nor deliberation alone, but a composite of both. For just as we say that an animal is composed of both body and soul, and not of body alone, nor of soul alone, but of both, so it is with choice.

But when considering the acts of the soul, we must keep in mind that the act or habit which belongs to one power, essentially, receives its form and species from a higher power or habit, according as the inferior power is directed by the superior power. For example, if a man performs an act of courage for the love of God, materially this is an act of fortitude, but formally an act of charity. Now we can see that reason, in a sense, acts before the will and specifies its act, insofar as the will tends toward its object according to the direction of reason, because a power of knowing represents the object to the appetite. Therefore, that act by which the will tends to a thing presented to it as a good, through being ordered to an end by reason, is materially an act of the will but formally an act of the reason. Now, in acts of this kind the substance of the act is as matter in relation to the order which the higher power imposes. Therefore, choice is substantially an act of the will and not of reason, for choice is completed through a kind of movement of the soul toward the good which is chosen. Hence, it is evidently the act of an appetite.[31]

The Ultimate Practical Judgment

The control which the will exercises over reason gives us some explanation of the ultimate practical judgments involved in moral action. All moral acts, good and bad alike, involve such practical judgments. Now the intellect is the only power that can make judgments in the proper sense of the term, whether they are speculative and practical, universal or particular. The intellect, for example, makes a universal practical judgment when it judges that "all knowledge is good." Or the intellect may make a more immediately practical judgment when, in knowing particulars, it judges a particular means suitable to a particular end. Thus, the intellect might judge, for example, that the knowledge of mathematics is good for me because I need the knowledge of this subject to pass a course in engineering.

But the intellect can also make a still more practical judgment, when it immediately refers a particular good to a particular subject at the very moment in which the intellect is making the judgment, and judges that this good is to be sought. Here the will enters in. The will commands that this last judgment, the ultimate practical one, be made; and the intellect can only obey, because it is under the domination of the will, for the will has the role of supreme governor of the powers of the soul. When it is a question of the very nature

---

[31] St. Thomas: *Summa Theologiae,* I–II, 13, 1, Body of the Article.

of the intellect, however, as in a judgment involving first principles of the speculative intellect, the will cannot command the intellect actually to judge falsely. However, even here it can turn the intellect away from the evidence, so that no speculative judgment can take place. Thus, the will can restrict, shut off, divert, and control the activity of the intellect in such a way that it can force the intellect to make the ultimate practical judgment which it desires. Hence, it is that moral good or evil is in the last analysis attributed to the will.

THE POSSIBILITY OF MORAL EVIL

If the ontological cause of freedom is knowledge, it follows that the perfection of freedom is proportionate to the perfection of knowledge. The intellect of man, however, even at its best, is an imperfect power. In proportion to the degree of abstraction required, it apprehends the truth of what confronts it only with great labor and by a slow process of extricating itself from the data of sense experience and from the influence of the passions. The property of mobility is applicable to man's intellectual activity: his intellect suffers from its condition of potency, making it necessary to move haltingly from ignorance to truth; his knowledge is corruptible, at least indirectly; it is subject to error because of prejudice, or the influence of passion, or simply because of the natural weakness of the intellectual power itself. Because of all this, human freedom is itself imperfect. In its own order the will is subject to error, but in this case it will be a practical error and not a speculative error as in the case of the intellect. Moral evil is an example of a practical error.

Thinking more of an idealistic condition of human nature than of its actual state, Plato went further than saying that freedom depends on knowledge—he said that virtue is a property of knowledge. He thought that no one could deliberately choose what is evil, for one would certainly avoid choosing evil if he knew what the consequences of his act would be. In his opinion, moral evil was due to ignorance, prejudice or a faulty education, and the like.

In an absolute sense, it is correct to say that moral evil is due to ignorance, because no one would make a practical error—and that is what evil choice is—if he understood *perfectly* all the consequences of his act. But we must judge of knowledge and freedom as they are found in man's natural condition, and not in some kind of idealistic condition. Though our intellectual vision in this life is, as Aristotle said, like that of owls in the daylight, it is sufficient to give us certitude about what is right and wrong. Our knowledge is not comprehensive, but, it need not be. It is possible to have enough certitude to make a correct judgment without our knowledge being clear, distinct, and comprehensive. It is not necessary, nor is it possible, that in a moral choice a man have a clear and distinct knowledge of all the details, or all the contingencies involved in his choice.

To assert a basic human freedom does not mean that we are always able to exercise our freedom. Extrinsic agents and interior motives may so affect us that we cannot make a free choice. Not all the acts of a man are free. Many of our acts are what the moralists call the *acts of a man (actus hominis)* rather than *human acts* * *(actus humani)*. The *acts of a man* are those produced by a rational being, even though they do not issue immediately from reason and will as from their principles. In this category are many acts of our vegetative and sensory powers, as well as many of those acts which have the appearance of rationality, but which belong in fact to the area of the unconscious of subconscious over which reason has no immediate control. Human acts are those which are properly called "free acts" because they have the will as their immediate principle.

Conclusion

Because the will is attracted by anything having the semblance of good, its dominant and decisive role in the matter of free choice is a dangerous one. It is necessary, therefore, to put safeguards around the will so as to direct the will effectively toward the kinds of goods that are perfective of man's rational nature. The instruments for the effective direction of the will are the *moral habits*.* But the same general reason that makes habits necessary in the will also makes habits necessary in the intellect. The intellect has a capacity for all knowledge, but every man has particular intellectual needs according to his vocation in life. The effective direction of the energies of mind are just as necessary in its order as is the direction of the will. In the following section, we shall study the nature of habits in general and then make application to the will and intellect.

Section C: The Psychology of Habits

The Meaning of Habit (Readings: III, C, No. 1)

One difficulty with the term *habit* is that, like many other terms used in philosophy, it has both a technical and a popular meaning.

There is a further difficulty in that even as a technical philosophical term, *habit* has several meanings, only one of which is fully applicable when we speak of habits in the rational powers of the soul.

In the Aristotelian divisions of the category of quality, the first of the four divisions contains habit and disposition. Habit is there defined as a *permanent* quality whereby a thing is poorly or well disposed either in itself or in relation to something else. A disposition, on the other hand, is a *transitory* quality whereby a thing is poorly or well disposed either in itself or in relation to something else. Thus, the science of mathematics is a habit whereby a teacher, for example, has the intellectual grasp of mathematical principles by means of which he can readily solve problems in mathematics. But a nervousness, for example, before teaching his first group of students, would be called a disposition.

Again, some authors speak of two kinds of habits and dispositions, the entitative and operative, the one to dispose the substance of the being and the other to dispose its powers. Thus, any kind of permanent disposition in a person's body, like muscular development, would be called an entitative habit, while a permanent disposition of the intellect or will would be called an operative habit. This terminology is not favored by St. Thomas himself, for he did not use the term *habit* for dispositions like health and beauty, but rather he called them "habitual dispositions." It is to the operative habits that he applied the term *habit* in its strictest philosophical meaning.

An operative habit is a kind of second nature that is added to the native power of the soul and disposes its operation with respect to the object. Habit lies midway between the pure potency of the power and the actual realization of the object, and thus participates in both potency and act. St. Thomas says:

> A habit is act, insofar as it is a quality, and in this respect it can be
> a principle of operation; but it is a potency with respect to operation.
> Therefore, a habit is called first act, and operation, second act.[32]

As we shall see later on, habits in the strict sense belong to the intellectual powers of the soul. To a certain extent there are habits in those powers of the soul that are subject to reason, as, for example, in the sensory powers of cognition and in the appetites, but these are considered by St. Thomas to be extensions of the meaning of habit as found in the rational powers of the soul. Not all psycholo-

---

[32] St. Thomas: *Summa Theologiae*, I–II, 49, 3, *ad.* 1.

gists are agreed, however, that habits are necessarily or even primarily found in the intellectual powers. Indeed, some psychologists regard habits as being fundamentally dispositions of the body.

WILLIAM JAMES' NOTION OF HABIT

According to William James, all habits are structural modifications of the body and they are found not only in man but in animals as well as in inorganic bodies. In summing up his teaching on the origin of habits he goes to the science of physics for the analogies by which he illustrates his notion of habits.

> So nothing is easier than to imagine how, when a current has once traversed a path, it should traverse it more readily still a second time. But what made it ever traverse it the first time? In answering this we can only fall back on our general conception of a nervous system as a mass of matter whose parts, constantly kept in states of different tension, are as constantly tending to equalize their states. The equalization between any two points occurs through whatever part may at the moment be most previous. But, as a given point of the system may belong, actually or potentially, to many different paths, and, as the play of nutrition is subject to accidental changes, *blocks* may from time to time occur, and make currents shoot toward unwonted lines. Such an unwonted line would be a new-created path, which if traversed repeatedly would become the beginning of a new reflex arc.[33]

In this perspective, not only men, but animals, plants, and lifeless compounds can acquire habits. We hold, however, a more restricted notion of habit, one which is applicable only to rational powers. Although we hold that habits are basically spiritual, we do not say they are purely spiritual, either in their origin or their effects. For if an act of the intellect entails a concomitant movement in the sensory faculties, it is logical to suppose that a spiritual habit also has its physical counterpart. Thus, a moral habit, like temperance, for example, while belonging to the rational part of man insofar as it is a virtue, has its effects upon the body, and can by analogy be called a *bodily habit*. In the same way, other moral, scientific, and artistic habits leave their impress upon the human body in the form of muscular and neural patterns, or conditioned reflexes.

The physical qualities which accompany rational habits are not

---

[33] William James: *Psychology,* Volume I. New York: 1902, Henry Holt & Co., 109.

only signs of the existence of such habits, but they actually contribute to the operation of the habits. The artist, the scientist, the philosopher, the man of moral virtue, all employ conditioned physical powers in the exercise of rational habits. The matter-form doctrine of human nature is not limited to the original union of the body and soul as co-principles of human substance, but applies equally well to all the activities that belong to the composite.

Habits Exist Essentially in the Rational Powers of the Soul (Readings: III, C, No. 2)

Taking the term habit in the strict sense as employed by St. Thomas, habits have the function of perfecting and specifying the powers of the intellectual soul, which of themselves are universal and not predetermined to any particular kind of object. The infinite capacity of the intellect, with universal truth as its object, and the infinite capacity of the will, with universal good as its object, makes it necessary that man possess habits which incline him towards particular kinds of objects of the intellect and will. Habits, then, are added to the powers of intellect and will in the manner of second natures, which dispose the powers more definitely to their objects. This is the argument St. Thomas employs in the following passage from the *Disputed Question On the Virtues in General*:

Because of the perfection of his soul, which as an active principle extends in a certain way to an infinity of things, man has a plurality and a diversity of operations. Therefore, a natural appetite for what is good and a natural judgment about what is to be done according to right order do not suffice for man. There must be a further perfection and determination.

By means of his natural appetite a man is inclined to seek his proper good. But since there is a manifold variety of goods and the good of man consists in many different things, there cannot be in him a natural appetite for a determined kind of good that contains all that is necessary to constitute good in man. For what is good is varied in many ways in accordance with the diverse conditions of peoples, of times, of places, and so on.

This same reason would hold for a uniform natural judgment and it would not suffice for the pursuit of this kind of good. Hence, it is necessary that man employ reason, whose function it is to compare diverse things, so that he may discover and judge of his proper good

determined here and now in all its conditions. Without the comple-
ment of habits, reason in this case would be as it is in speculative matters
when it is without a habit of science to effect the conclusions of the
science—it can do so only imperfectly and with great difficulty.

Thus, just as speculative reason needs habits of science to judge
correctly about the intelligible objects belonging to that science, so the
practical reason needs to be perfected by habits in order to judge correctly about the human good that is to be pursued among particular
things.[34]

In a different context, though in a slightly different form, St.
Thomas gives the same reason for the necessity of habits in the intellectual powers of the soul. He points out that as a rational being,
man is the master of his acts and should have, therefore, control over
them so that he can employ them whenever he desires. It is precisely
by means of habits that he gains control over the exercise of his intellect and will. In comparison with the rational powers of the soul,
the sense powers are more passive and act more according to an
impulse of nature than according to a principle of freedom and therefore do not need habits.

What is added to a sensory power is not in the order of habit but
rather in the order of passivity. But in the intellectual powers of the
soul it is an addition by way of habit. Rather than being active, the
sensitive part is acted upon by an impulse of nature, but the intellectual
part is the master of its act, and therefore should have a promptitude
in its acts, so that it can act whenever it chooses to do so.[35]

HABITS IN THE OTHER POWERS OF THE SOUL (READINGS: III, C, NO. 3)

From this we can see that habits in the strict sense are not found
in other powers of the soul except as extensions of the habits in the
intellect and will. The other powers are already predisposed by
nature for the particular type of object which they are made: the
eye, for example, to color; the ear to sound, and so on. There can
be no question here of specification of these powers. A habit could
not more fully predetermine these powers to their natural objects.
So-called "habits" of the sense powers of knowledge and sense appetites are extrinsic to the powers themselves, and are not, therefore,
habits in the strict sense. Rather, they are dispositions in the composite in which these powers exist.

---

[34] St. Thomas Aquinas: *Disputed Question On the Virtues in General*, Single Question, Article 6, Body of the Article.

[35] St. Thomas: *Disputed Question on Truth*, 20, 2, Body of the Article.

Habits and Habitudes

The indiscriminate use of the word *habit* for both physical and rational habits not only confuses the issue, but leads to serious divergence in the practical application of the psychology of habits. In an Aristotelian context, habit is applicable immediately only to the qualities which perfect the rational powers of intellect and will, and only by analogy to the sensory, vegetative and motor powers.

Our language does not have a specific word for each of these different meanings. Some philosophers would prefer to use the Latin term *habitus* for rational habits rather than risk the possibility of having them identified with habits as defined in modern psychology. A term like *habitude* * comes close to expressing the type of permanent way of acting that is proper to a conditioned reflex, which is what William James takes for *habit*. We shall continue to use the word *habit* as a generic term and modify it with the adjectives demanded by the context, such as *moral, intellectual, artistic, supernatural,* and the like.

THE EFFECTS OF HABITS

A short text from St. Thomas tells of the effects that habits have upon the subject in whom the habits exist:

From these considerations it is clear that we need habits for three reasons: first, in order that there be uniformity in operation. Things that depend on operation alone are easily changed, unless they have been stabilized by some kind of habitual inclination;

Second, in order that a perfect operation (of the power) be readily had. Unless a rational power is inclined by a habit towards one object, there will always be necessarily a hesitancy prior to the operation (*oportebit semper praecedere inquisitione de operatione*). It is in this way that a person will act who wants to think out some problem but does not have a habit of science, or the way another will act who wants to be virtuous but lacks a habit of virtue. Therefore, the Philosopher says in V, *Ethics* (Chapter 3) that things are done quickly by means of habits;

Third, in order that the operation be performed with pleasure. This does take place if it is done through habit. Since a habit is like a nature, it makes its own act a kind of natural act, and consequently makes it pleasant, for what is naturally adapted gives pleasure. Therefore, the Philosopher in II, *Ethics* gives as a sign of habit the pleasure that is present in doing the work.[36]

---

[36] St. Thomas: *Disputed Question On the Virtues in General*, 1, Body of the Article.

THE MOMENTUM OF HABITS

Habit is called "second nature" because it acts like the intrinsic principle of movement and of rest which belongs innately to substances. It is like a second carburetor on a gasoline motor, giving to nature the extra boost that makes for efficient, easy, secure and pleasurable operation. Habit is like the momentum of a moving body, the effortless turning of a wheel, the controlled descent of an expert skier, the power of a train in motion. Though difficult to put in motion, the nature becomes, under the influence of habit, equally difficult to turn from its course of action.

THE INDELIBERATION OF HABITS

Habits diminish the need for deliberation. This might seem to be a disadvantage, since awareness of what our actions entail is a condition for a free moral act. Because they are accompanied, moreover, by conditioned reflexes which are themselves outside the field of morality, it seems that habits would diminish freedom, which is the basis of morality. Thus, the acquiring of habits poses a question: Are they really perfective of the will or do they hinder its free exercise?

It may happen that attention to an individual act is diminished or completely absent in the operation of a habit. This is the result not of the habit itself but of the physical conditioning that accompanies habits. With respect to responsibility for conditioned reflexes, it would seem that since moral habits are formed through deliberate choice, the effects of habits, if they are foreseen, are also said to be deliberate. If the habits are never freely revoked, the consequent effects are morally attributed to the moral agent even though at the moment of execution there is no deliberation. Such effects are called "voluntary in cause," and they partake of the morality of the decision which led to the formation of habits. If, on the contrary, a person wills to break a bad moral habit, and employs suitable means to do so, he is not held morally responsible for the effects which follow from the physical aspects of the habit. We may conclude that moral habits, in the philosophical sense, do not diminish free choice, though the physical conditioning which accompanies these habits may do so.

THE PLEASURE OF HABITS

The pleasure which accompanies habits contributes greatly to their efficiency. The pleasure found in the exercise of habits has a number of possible explanations. One of them is that by habits we escape the doubt and indecision which accompany new tasks. Initial actions, without the benefit of habits are often painful. Habit likewise diminishes conscious effort, so that more attention can be given to doing the work well, and a work done well gives pleasure. The pleasure of habitual actions may also be explained by the well-being of powers conditioned through exercise. Or the pleasure may arise simply from the fact of repetition, or from a sense of accomplishment. Young and old may find pleasure in habit: the child simply because he likes to imitate and repeat; the older person, because he feels a measure of security in habits. Whatever motive may be predominant, the fact of pleasure cannot be denied, and it has, therefore, important ethical significance, because both good and evil habits give pleasure.

THE ROLE OF HABITS IN THE MORAL ORDER

Habits play a primary role in ethical conduct. Good moral habits, which are called virtues, facilitate moral choice, assure its constancy, and give pleasure in exercise. Bad moral habits, which are called vices, have the same effects in the contrary direction. Thus, the immediate effect of either good or bad moral habits is to fix the will in the direction of a particular type of moral object. In its etymology the word *character* designates a seal of ownership or permanent title of possession. A man of well-established moral virtues, who had some kind of permanent title to their possession and use, was known as a man of character. Just as a seal or title is a means by which ownership of property can be judged, so the character or seal of moral habits is the means by which others can judge the person in whom these qualities exist.

THE DANGERS OF HABITUDES

The advantages of habits are sometimes counteracted by the routine and lack of spontaneity which habits seem to endanger. But even good habits may have some undesirable side effects. One danger against which we should be alerted is the degeneration of a habit into mere habitude. A mere habitude can create monotony and paralyze initiative by inviting a person to act always in the same way, because the familiar way is easier. A rational habit, however, is by nature self-perfective, for it is, like the power to which it is attached, a vital principle. Rational habits tend to produce new efforts rather than to repeat the old. Good rational habits, therefore, free the mind, promote originality and enhance freedom, whereas habitudes create routine and kill spontaneity and growth.

To illustrate, let us see how a good habit of art and a habitude would operate in the artist. Because the artist is a man living in a particular segment of history, he is conditioned by his environment, by the examples of art that surround him, and by interests that lie predominantly in some particular school of art. But if he is a good artist, his experience in a particular area will not stifle him, for his good habit of art will make him creative within his own school and medium of expression. He will not simply duplicate his own work or repeat the work of other men; he will be interested in and sympathetic with new forms that grow naturally out of his school. In short, he will be an artist who will not let mere habitude dominate his habit of good art.

GOOD HABITS INCREASE FREEDOM

Far from hindering the natural spontaneity of man's natural powers, good habits tend to increase it by removing the difficulties that prevent the power from achieving its natural perfection. It is the erroneous opinion of some philosophers that indetermination in the intellect and will is a desirable condition and that control by habits destroys the natural spontaneity of these powers. They would assign to chance events the greatest freedom and perfection, because a chance cause is not directed to a definite end. But the truth of the matter is that chance really excludes freedom since it excludes the deliberate choice by which an agent acts for a particular end. When the human mind and will act without the direction of habits they are actually further from spontaneity and closer to blind determinism. It is a specious kind of freedom that is associated with chance. Good habits make a person more free because they perfect the powers of intellect and will, which are the causes of freedom. Good habits incline man to those goods that perfect his nature; good habits overcome his inertia and enhance the spontaneous activity of his intellect and will. Thus, his good habits tend to make him more fully a person.

THE DEVELOPMENT OF HABITS (READINGS: III, C, NO. 4 AND NO. 5)

The growth and decline of rational habits is not measurable quantitatively, since habits are qualities that belong directly to the spiritual powers. Hence, an increase and decrease in habits is qualitative rather than quantitative. Just as increased strength in the physiological order is acquired through systematic exercise, so, analogously, the strength of habits is increased through systematic and continued exercise of our habits. It is essential, however, that new activity be qualitatively equal or superior to the actual status of the habit, because not any and all exercise of a habit makes for qualitative improvement. On the contrary, feeble acts diminish the intensity of the habits. For example, an artist who contents himself with mediocre imitations, or a mathematician or scientist who merely repeats solutions to problems, does not perfect his intellectual habit of art or science. It is by meeting new challenges, by seeing problems still on the horizon and attempting to solve them, that there is a growth in the habits of the artist, scientist or virtuous person. If habits were only skills, mere repetition would suffice. But they are more than skills; they are our intellectual powers operating with a new impetus. No one need fear that a habit will grow ineffective through too frequent exercise, because the potentialities for growth in all intellectual and moral habits are infinite.

The slow growth of a habit follows naturally from the potentiality of the intellect and will. In the natural order, at least, habits can be acquired only through slow growth and continuous exercise. Slow growth has its advantages. For if habits could be formed quickly through one or several acts, a person could too easily become entangled in habits from which he might want to escape but could not easily do so. Since habits grow slowly, just as life itself develops slowly, we are able to make needed corrections, and to direct our habits to the formation of a balanced personality.

THE BREAKING OF HABITS (READINGS: III, C, NO. 6)

The breaking of habits is not simply the reverse of the process of their formation. Habits begin in powers orientated to the good and true in general, but without positive dispositions towards particular types of goodness and truth. The native state of the rational being is neither one of virtue nor of vice. An infant is not virtuous simply because he has no vices, nor is he vicious simply because of the absence of virtue in him. With contraries, it is not necessary that *one or the other* be present, because it can happen that both are absent. Since virtues and vices are contraries and not contradictories, it is not necessary to conclude that a person is either virtuous or vicious.

Thus, in the breaking of habits, we do not return to an original state of potentiality in our intellectual powers in which neither good nor bad habits exist. On the contrary, we must try to overcome bad habits by promoting the immediately contrary good habits. This method is most efficacious, first of all, because of the strength of positive motivation. When habits are deeply rooted, it requires a strong will and deliberate effort to change them. A negative attitude, that is, the desire to be rid of the habit, is not enough; the contrary habit, with an equally strong appeal, must be cultivated. Second, the development of a contrary habit is efficacious in overcoming previously acquired habits because it attacks the habit in its essence, namely, in the object. Since contraries belong to the same genus of object, the growth of one contrary destroys the other. Tapering off is not to be recommended *per se,* because it does not directly attack the habit. Diminishing the frequency of an act may affect the extrinsic properties of habits, but it does not directly touch the essence. Thus, a vice is not eradicated by indulging it less frequently. It follows from the nature of spiritual beings—the category to which habits belong—that habits are not *per se* corrupted merely by the passage of time.

Conclusion

Let us sum up what we have said about habits. While the term *habit* has a variety of meanings, habit in its strictest philosophical meaning is a permanent quality added to an intellectual power of the soul to facilitate its operation. Habit lies midway between the pure potency of the power and its actual operation. Though habits in the strict philosophical sense reside only in the rational powers, habits engender certain bodily effects that help man in the exercise of habits. Habits are necessary in the rational powers because by nature they are unspecified capacities for infinite truth and infinite good. Habit is a "second nature" that gives momentum, ease, and pleasure in the operation of our rational powers with respect to particular kinds of intellectual and moral objects.

In this third part on the rational powers of the soul, we have made many comparisons with the sense powers from the viewpoint of operations in order to show how the one order rises essentially above the other. This was necessary in order to understand the part that follows, where we treat of the nature and origin of the human soul. It is from the operation of the human soul we can infer its essential properties, as well as the kind of origin it must have.

Bibliography for Part III

Allers, Rudolph: "Intellection Cognition," in *Essays in Thomism*, Edited by Robert E. Brennan.
  New York: Sheed and Ward, 1942, 41–62.
  "On Intellectual Operations."
  The New Scholasticism, Volume 26, 1–36.

Bourke, Vernon: "The Role of Habitus in the Thomistic Metaphysics of Potency and Act," in *Essays in Thomism*, 103–109.

Brennan, Robert E.: "The Habits of Man," *Thomistic Psychology*.
  New York: The Macmillan Company, 1941, 260–279.

Cunningham, Francis: "Judgment in St. Thomas."
  The Modern Schoolman, Volume 31, 185–212.

Dunne, Peter: "The Production of the Intelligible Species."
  The New Scholasticism, Volume 27, 176–197.

Franz, Edward: *"The Thomistic Doctrine of the Possible Intellect."*
  Washington, D.C.: The Catholic University of America Press, 1950.

Gilson, Etienne: "The Intellect and its Object," and "Love and its Object," in *The Spirit of Medieval Philosophy*.
  New York: Charles Scribner's Sons, 1936, 248–268; 269–288.

Lauer, Rosemary: "Intellectual Causality in Election."
  The New Scholasticism, Volume 28, 299–319.

O'Connor, William: "Natural Appetite."
  The Thomist, Volume 16, 361–409.

Quesnell, Quentin: "Participated Understanding; the Three Acts of the Mind."
  The Modern Schoolman, Volume 31, 281–288.

Renard, Henri: "The Functions of Intellect and Will in the Act of Free Choice."
  The Modern Schoolman, Volume 24, 85–92.

Sullivan, Robert: "Natural Necessitation of the Human Will."
  The Thomist, Volume 14, 351–399; 490–528.

Tyrell, Francis: "Concerning the Nature and Function of the Act of Judgment."
  The New Scholasticism, Volume 26, 393–423.

READINGS FOR PART III

PART III. THE RATIONAL POWERS OF THE SOUL

SECTION A: THE POWER OF INTELLIGENCE

No. 1. Man Can Know Natural Bodies in an Intellectual Way
St. Thomas: *Summa Theologiae,* Part I, Question 84, Article 1
Does the soul know bodies by means of the intellect?

No. 2. The Relationship Between the Intellect and the Senses
St. Thomas: *Summa Theologiae,* Part I, Question 84, Article 6
Is intellectual knowledge derived from sensible things?

No. 3. The Intellect Abstracts Intelligible Forms from Sense Experience
St. Thomas: *Summa Theologiae,* Part I, Question 85, Article 1
Does our intellect know corporeal and material things by abstraction?

No. 4. The Human Intellect Is a Passive Power
St. Thomas: *Summa Theologiae,* Part I, Question 79, Article 2
Is the intellect a passive power?

No. 5. The Existence and Function of an Agent Intellect
St. Thomas: *Summa Theologiae,* Part I, Question 79, Article 3
Is there an agent intellect?

No. 6. The Objectivity of Our Intellectual Knowledge
St. Thomas: *Summa Theologiae,* Part I, Question 85, Article 2
Is the intelligible species that is abstracted from the phantasm the object that is understood?

No. 7. The Possibility of Error in the Human Intellect
St. Thomas: *Summa Theologiae,* Part I, Question 85, Article 6
Can the intellect be false?

SECTION B: THE POWER OF FREE WILL

No. 1. How the Intellect and Will Are Mutual Causes
St. Thomas: *Summa Theologiae,* Part I, Question 82, Article 4
Does the will move the intellect?

No. 2. Comparison of the Intellect and the Will
St. Thomas: *Summa Theologiae,* Part I, Question 82, Article 3
Is the will a higher power than the intellect?

No. 3. The Different Kinds of Necessity
St. Thomas: *Summa Theologiae,* Part I, Question 82, Article 1
Does the will necessarily desire anything?

No. 4. Man Has Freedom of Will
St. Thomas: *Disputed Question on Evil,* Question 6, Article 1

No. 5. The Will Can Desire Only What Appears Good
St. Thomas: *Summa Theologiae,* Part I–II, Question 8, Article 1
Does the will desire only the good?

No. 6. The Will Is Not Moved with Necessity by Particular Objects
St. Thomas: *Summa Theologiae,* Part I–II, Question 10, Article 2
Is the will moved with necessity by its objects?

No. 7. Man Has the Power of Free Choice
St. Thomas: *Summa Theologiae,* Part I–II, Question 13, Article 6
Does man choose freely or by necessity?

No. 8. Choice Is an Act of Both Will and Reason
St. Thomas: *Summa Theologiae,* Part I–II, Question 13, Article 1
Is choice an act of the will or of reason?

SECTION C: THE PSYCHOLOGY OF HABITS

No. 1. The Necessity of Habits
St. Thomas: *Summa Theologiae,* Part I–II, Question 49, Article 4
Are habits necessary?

No. 2. The Subject of Habits
St. Thomas: *Summa Theologiae,* Part I–II, Question 50, Article 2
Is the soul the subject of habits by reason of its essence or by reason of its powers?

No. 3. How Habits Can Be in the Sensory Powers of the Soul
St. Thomas: *Summa Theologiae,* Part I–II, Question 50, Article 3
Can there be habits in the powers of the sensory part of the soul?

No. 4. The Formation of Habits
St. Thomas: *Summa Theologiae,* Part I–II, Question 51, Article 3
Can a habit be caused by one act?

No. 5. The Increase of Habits
St. Thomas: *Summa Theologiae,* Part I–II, Question 52, Article 3
Does every act increase a habit?

No. 6. The Decline of Habits
St. Thomas: *Summa Theologiae,* Part I–II, Question 53, Article 3
Is a habit broken or weakened by not exercising it?

SECTION A: THE POWER OF INTELLIGENCE

No. 1. Man Can Know Natural Bodies in an Intellectual Way
St. Thomas: *Summa Theologiae,* Part I, Question 84, Article 1
Does the soul know bodies by means of the intellect?

[¶ 1.] *Objection 1.* Augustine says in II, *Soliloquies:* "Bodies cannot be comprehended by intellect, nor can what is corporeal be seen except by the senses." He says also in XII, *Commentary on the Text of Genesis,*[37] that intellectual seeing is said of those things which are in the soul by their essence. But these are not bodies. Therefore, the soul cannot know bodies by means of the intellect.

[¶ 2.] *Objection 2.* The senses are related to intelligible objects, as the intellect is related to sensible objects. But the soul cannot in any way know spiritual things (which are intelligible things) by means of the senses. Therefore, in no way can the intellect know bodies, which are sensible objects.

[¶ 3.] *Objection 3.* Our intellect has as its object what is necessary and always the same. But all bodies are mobile and are not always the same. The soul, therefore, cannot know bodies by means of the intellect.

[¶ 4.] *On the contrary,* it is a fact that there is science in the intellect. But if the intellect does not know bodies, it follows that there is no science of bodies. Then all natural science, which treats of mobile bodies, will cease to be.

[¶ 5.] The first philosophers who examined the natures of things thought that the only things that existed in the world were bodies. And because they saw that all bodies are mobile, they considered them to be in constant flux, and from that concluded that we could have no true and certain knowledge about things. What is in constant flux cannot be apprehended with certitude, because it is gone before the mind can judge about it. Thus, Heraclitus said that "It is not possible to touch twice the water of a flowing river," as the Philosopher relates in IV, *Metaphysics.*

[¶ 6.] After them came Plato, who in order to preserve man's ability to reach certain and true knowledge with his intellect, posited in addition to corporeal things, another genus of beings separated from matter and movement, which he called *forms* or *ideas.* By a participation in these, every individual thing of the sense order was said to be, either a *man* or *horse* or

---

[37] *De Genesi ad Literam.*

some other thing of this kind. He held, therefore, that sciences, definitions, and anything that belongs to the act of the intellect are not to be referred to sensible bodies but to the immaterial and separated forms. Actually, then, the soul does not understand corporeal things but separated forms of these corporeal things.

[¶ 7.] But this view appears false on two counts. First, because, since these forms are immaterial and immobile, the knowledge of movement and matter (which are proper to natural science) and demonstrations through the moving cause and the material cause would be excluded from the sciences. Second, it seems very strange that when we seek knowledge of things that are clear to us, we have to bring in other beings as media, which cannot be the substances of those things because they differ from them in existence. Thus, when we have knowledge of these separated substances, we are still not able to judge about sensible objects.

[¶ 8.] On this point Plato seems to have deviated from the truth, because since he thought that all knowledge is by way of some similitude, he believed that the form of the thing known must necessarily be in the knower in the same way that it is in the known object. He realized that the form of the thing understood is in the intellect as a universal, immaterial and immobile form. This is evident from the act of the intellect which understands things as universal and as having a certain necessity, since the mode of action is determined by the mode of the agent's form. He judged, therefore, that the things which are understood immaterially and without movement must subsist in themselves without matter and without movement.

[¶ 9.] This, however, is not necessary, for even in sensible beings we can see that a form is present in a different way in one sensible object than in another, as when whiteness is brighter in one thing than in another, or when whiteness is found together with sweetness in one thing and without it in another. In this way, too, the sensible form is in a real being that exists outside the soul in a different way than it is in the sense power which receives sensible forms of things without matter, as when a sense receives the color of gold without gold. Likewise, the intellect receives the forms of bodies which are material and mobile, without matter and without movement, according to its own mode of being, since the thing received is in the recipient in the mode of being of the recipient. We must hold, therefore, that the soul through the intellect knows bodies by means of an immaterial, universal and necessary knowledge.

[¶ 10.] *Reply to Objection 1.* The words of Augustine should be understood as referring to things by which the intellect knows and not to things which the intellect knows. For it knows bodies by understanding them, but not through bodies or material and corporeal likenesses. It knows them through immaterial and intelligible forms which through the soul's essence can be present in it.

[¶ 11.] *Reply to Objection 2.* As Augustine says in XXII, *The City of God,* it is not correct to say that as the senses know only corporeal things so the intellect knows only spiritual things, for it would follow from this that God and the angels would not know corporeal things. The basis of the distinction that must be made here is that an inferior power does not extend to the objects of a higher power, but the higher power, in a more excellent way, accomplishes what belongs to the lower power.

[¶ 12.] *Reply to Objection 3.* Every movement presupposes something immobile; when there is a change of quality, for example, the substance remains immobile; and when a substantial form is changed, the matter remains immobile. There are immobile characteristics even of changeable beings. Though Socrates, for example, is not always sitting, nevertheless it remains unchangeably true that when he is sitting he remains in one place. This is the reason, we can have unchangeable scientific knowledge about changeable things.

No. 2. *The Relationship Between the Intellect and the Senses*

St. Thomas: *Summa Theologiae,* Part I, Question 84, Article 6
Is intellectual knowledge derived from sensible things?

[¶ 1.] *Objection 1.* Augustine says (*Book of Eighty-three Topics*)[38] that the fullness of truth must not be sought from the senses of the body. He proves this in two ways. First, because anything which the bodily senses reach is continually being changed, and, hence, cannot be perceived. Second, we experience all those things which we perceive through our body, even when they are not present to the senses, through images of them, as when we are asleep or angry. We cannot discern, however, through the senses whether we are perceiving the sensible objects themselves or the false images of them. But nothing can be perceived which cannot be discerned from its counterfeit. And so he concludes that we should not expect truth from the senses. But intellectual knowledge apprehends the truth. Therefore, intellectual knowledge is not to be expected from the senses.

[¶ 2.] *Objection 2.* Augustine says (*Commentary on the Text of Genesis,* Number 16): "We must not think that the body is able to make any im-

---

[38] *De Diversis Quaestionibus Octaginta-tribus.*

pression on the spirit, as though the spirit were subjected to the action of a body in place of matter; for that which acts is in every way more excellent than that which it acts upon." From this he concludes that it is not the body which causes the image of the body in the spirit, but that it is the spirit which causes it in itself. Therefore, intellectual knowledge is not derived from sensible things.

[¶ 3.] *Objection 3.* An effect does not surpass the power of its cause. But intellectual knowledge surpasses sensible things, since we know some things that the senses cannot grasp. Therefore, intellectual knowledge is not derived from sensible things.

[¶ 4.] *On the contrary,* the Philosopher proves (I, *Metaphysics,* Chapter 1; II, *Posterior Analytics,* Chapter 15) that the principle of our knowledge is in the senses.

[¶ 5.] The philosophers held three opinions in this matter. Democritus held that there is no other cause of our knowledge unless the images, which come from those bodies we are thinking about, enter into our own souls, as he is quoted by Augustine in his letter to Dioscorus. And Aristotle says (*On Sleep and Wakefulness,*[39] Chapter 2) that Democritus held that knowledge is caused by a flowing off of images. The reason for this opinion is that Democritus and the other natural philosophers did not differentiate intellect from the sense, as Aristotle says (III, *On the Soul,* Chapter 3). And because the sense is affected by the sensible, they thought that all our knowledge comes only from the impression made by sensible things. This impression was made, according to Democritus, by the flowing off of images.

[¶ 6.] Plato took an opposing view, holding that the intellect differs from the senses and is an immaterial power not employing a corporeal organ in its action. And because the incorporeal cannot be affected by the corporeal, he held that intellectual knowledge is not brought about through an alteration of the intellect by sensible things, but through a participation of the intellect in separate intelligible forms, as we have said. (*S.T.,* I, 84, 4 and 5.) He also held that the sense is a power operation of itself; hence, not even a sense power is affected by sensible things, because it is a kind of spiritual power. But the organs of sense are affected by sensible things, and by this change the soul is stimulated in some way to form within itself the species of sensible things. Augustine seems to touch on this opinion (*Commentary on the Text of Genesis,* No. 24) when he says that the body does not sense, but the soul senses through the body, using it as a kind of messenger to form in itself what is announced from without. Thus, according to Plato,

---

[39] *De Somno et Vigilantia.*

intellectual knowledge does not proceed from sensible things, and not even sensible knowledge proceeds completely from sensible things; rather, they stimulate the sensible soul to sense, and in a similar way, the senses stimulate the intellectual soul to understand.

[¶ 7.] Aristotle chose a middle path. He agreed with Plato that the intellect differs from the senses. But he held that the sense has no operation of its own except as a part of the body, so that to sense is not the act of the soul only, but of the composite. And he held the same position with respect to all the operations of the sensitive part. Since, therefore, it is not unreasonable to hold that sensible things outside the soul produce some effect on the composite, Aristotle agreed with Democritus that the operations of the sensitive part are caused through an impression by sensible things upon the sense, not by a flowing off of something from the object, as Democritus said, but by some kind of operation. Democritus held that every operation was achieved through a discharge of atoms, as we see in his book, *On Generation,* Chapter 8. Aristotle held that the intellect has an operation apart from the body, but nothing corporeal can make an impression on the incorporeal. According to Aristotle, therefore, the mere impression of sensible bodies is not sufficient to cause an intellectual operation, but something more excellent is required, since the one acting is more excellent than the one acted upon, as he says in Book III, *On the Soul.* He does not intend by this that the intellectual operation is caused by the mere impression made by some superior things, as Plato held, but that a superior and nobler agent which he calls the agent intellect, which we have already discussed (*S.T.,* I, 79, 3 and 4) causes the phantasms received from the senses to be actually intelligible by means of abstraction.

[¶ 8.] According to this opinion, then, as far as the phantasms are concerned, the intellectual operation is caused by the senses. However, because the phantasms alone cannot affect the potential intellect, but they must be made intelligible in act by the agent intellect, one cannot say that sensible knowledge is the complete and perfect cause of intellectual knowledge, but rather that it is in some way the material cause.

[¶ 9.] *Reply to Objection 1.* These words of Augustine mean that truth is not entirely from the senses. The light of an agent intellect is needed, through which we know the unchangeable truth in changeable things, and differentiate things themselves from their likenesses.

[¶ 10.] *Reply to Objection 2.* Here Augustine speaks not of intellectual knowledge, but of knowledge in the imagination. Following Plato's opinion that the imagination has an operation belonging only to the soul, Augustine, in order to show that bodies do not impress their own images upon the imagination but that the soul itself does this, uses the same argument as Aristotle does in proving that the agent intellect is something separate, namely, that "the agent is more excellent than what is acted upon." And without doubt, according to this position, there must be in the imagination not only a passive but also an active power. But if we hold with Aristotle that the act of the imagination is the act of the composite, there is no difficulty, because the sensible object is more excellent than the organ of the animal insofar as it is compared to the organ as a being in act to a being in potency, as also an object actually colored is compared to the pupil which is colored in potency. Although the first impression upon the imagination is by the movement of sensible objects, as it is stated in III, *On the Soul,* Chapter 3, we may still say that there is in man an operation of the soul which by means of division and composition forms diverse images of things, even of things not perceived by the senses. And we may take the words of Augustine to mean this.

[¶ 11.] *Reply to Objection 3.* Sensitive knowledge is not the complete cause of intellectual knowledge. Therefore, it is not strange that intellectual knowledge should surpass sensitive knowledge.

No. 3. The Intellect Abstracts Intelligible Forms from Sense Experience
   St. Thomas: *Summa Theologiae,* Part I, Question 85, Article 1
   Does our intellect know corporeal and material things by abstraction from phantasms?

[¶ 1.] *Objection 1.* The intellect is false if it understands a thing otherwise than it really is. Now the forms of material things are not abstracted from particular things, the likenesses of which are represented by phantasms. Therefore, if we understand material things through abstraction of species from phantasms, there will be falsity in our intellect.

[¶ 2.] *Objection 2.* Material things are natural things which include matter in their definition. Without that which belongs in its definition, however, nothing can be understood. Therefore, material things cannot be understood without matter. Now matter is the principle of individuation. Therefore, material things cannot be understood by abstraction of the universal from the particular, that is, by abstracting the intelligible species from the phantasms.

[¶ 3.] *Objection 3.* The Philosopher says (III, *On the Soul,* Chapter 7) that phantasms are to the intellectual soul what colors are to sight. But seeing is not achieved by abstracting species from color, but by colors impressing themselves on the power of sight. Therefore, understanding does not depend on abstraction from phantasms, but on impressions which the phantasms make upon the intellect.

[¶ 4.] *Objection 4.* The Philosopher says (III, *On the Soul,* Chapter 5) that there are two things in the intellectual soul: the possible intellect and the agent intellect. Now it is not the work of the possible intellect to abstract intelligible species from the phantasms, but to receive them when abstracted. Nor does abstraction seem to be the work of the agent intellect, which is related to the phantasms as light to colors, and light does not abstract anything from colors, but rather flows into them. Therefore, in no way do we understand by abstracting from phantasms.

[¶ 5.] *Objection 5.* Moreover, the Philosopher says (III, *On the Soul,* Chapter 7) that the intellect understands the species in the phantasm, and not, therefore, by abstraction.

[¶ 6.] *On the contrary,* the Philosopher says (III, *On the Soul,* Chapter 4) that things are intelligible only insofar as they are separable from matter. Therefore, material things must be understood as abstracted from matter and material images, that is, phantasms.

[¶ 7.] The knowable object is proportionate to the power of knowing, as was said about (*S.T.,* I, 80, 2; and I, 84, 7) Now there are three gradations of knowing powers. One cognitive power, the sense, has its act in a corporeal organ, and the object, therefore, of any sense power is a form existing in corporeal matter. And because matter of this kind is the principle of individuation, every power of the sensitive part can know only individuals. Another knowing power has an act which is not the act of a corporeal organ, nor connected with matter in any way. This is the angelic intellect, the object of whose knowing power is, therefore, form subsisting without matter. Though they know material things, the angels know them only in something immaterial, namely, in themselves or in God. The human intellect lies between the two. It is not the act of a bodily organ, yet it is a power of the soul, which is the form of the body, as we have said (*S.T.,* I, 76, 1). Therefore, its proper function is to know a form which exists individually in corporeal matter, but not insofar as it is in such matter. Now to know what is in individual matter, but not as it is in such matter, is to abstract form from individual matter, which the phantasms represent. Therefore, we must say that our intellect understands material things by abstracting from the phantasms; and through material things considered in this way, we attain some knowledge of immaterial things, as in an opposite way, angels know material things through the immaterial.

[¶ 8.] Plato, however, considering only the immateriality of the human intellect, and overlooking its being united in some way to the body, held that the objects of the intellect were separated ideas, and that we know, not by abstracting, but by participating in abstracted things, as was said above. (*S.T.,* I, 84, 1.)

[¶ 9.] *Reply to Objection 1.* Abstraction may take place in two ways. First, by way of composition and division, as when we know that something does not exist in another thing, or exists separate from it. Secondly, by way of simple and absolute consideration, as when we know one thing without considering another. Therefore, to abstract by the intellect things which in reality are not abstract, according to the first mode of abstraction, does involve falsity. But in the second mode, this does not involve falsity, as is manifest in the case of the senses. For if we understood or said that color is not in a colored body, or is separated from it, there would be falsity in our judgment or speech. But if we consider color or its properties without reference to the apple which is colored, or if we express with a word what we understand, we would not be in error, because the apple is not essential to color. Therefore, nothing prevents the color from being understood, though we know nothing of the apple. Likewise, the things which belong to the species of a material thing, such as a stone or a man or a horse, can be thought of apart from the individual principles, which do not belong to the notion of the species. And to do this is to abstract the universal from the particular, or the intelligible species from the phantasms, that is, to consider the nature of the species without considering its individual principles, which are represented by the phantasms. Therefore, if the intellect is called false when it understands something otherwise than as it is, this is true only if the word *otherwise* refers to the thing understood, for the intellect is false when it understands a thing to be otherwise than it is. Hence, the intellect would be false if it abstracted the form of a stone from matter in such a way as to suppose that the form does not exist in matter, as Plato held. But this is not so, if the word *otherwise* is taken as referring to the knower, for it involves no falsity if the mode of understanding in the one who understands differs from the mode of the thing in entitative existence. For the thing understood is in the knower immaterially, according to the mode of the intellect, and not materially, according to the mode of a material thing.

[¶ 10.] *Reply to Objection 2.* Some have thought that the essence of a natural thing is a form alone, and that matter is not a part of the essence. But according to this position, matter would not enter into the definition of natural things. Therefore, something else must be said: the matter is two-fold, common, and signate or individual; common, like *flesh* and *bone,* and individual, like *this flesh* and *these bones.* Therefore, the intellect abstracts the species of a natural thing from the individual sensible matter, not from common sensible matter. For example, it abstracts the species of man from this flesh and these bones, which do not belong to the notion of the species,[40] but are parts of the individual (III, *Metaphysics*). Therefore, the species may be thought of apart from them. The species of man, however, cannot be abstracted by the intellect from flesh and bones.

[¶ 11.] Mathematical species can be abstracted by the intellect from sensible matter, and not only from individual matter, but also from common matter; not, however, from common intelligible matter, but only from individual intelligible matter. For sensible matter is corporeal matter, as subject to sensible qualities like hot or cold, hard or soft, and so forth; but intelligible matter is substance, as the subject of quantity. Now it is evident that quantity is present in substance before other sensible qualities. Hence, quantities such as numbers, dimensions, and figures, which are the terminations of quantity, can be thought of apart from sensible qualities; this is "to abstract" them from sensible matter. They cannot be thought of, however, without understanding the substance which is subject to the quantity, for this would be to abstract them from common intelligible matter. Nevertheless, they can be considered apart from this or that substance, which is to abstract them from individual intelligible matter. Certain things can be abstracted even from common intelligible matter, such as *being, one, potency, act,* and others of this kind. All of these can exist without matter, as is clear in immaterial things. Because Plato did not consider this twofold kind of abstraction, he held that all those things we have stated to be abstracted by the intellect are abstracted according to reality.

[¶ 12.] *Reply to Objection 3.* Colors, which are individualized in corporeal matter, have the same mode of existence in the power of sight. Therefore, they can impress their own image on the power of sight. But phantasms, since they are images of individuals and exist in corporeal organs, do not have the same mode of existence as the human intellect, as is clear from what was said. (*S.T.,* I, 85, 1 and I, 84, 7.) Therefore, they cannot by their own power make an impression on the possible intellect. But through the power of the agent intellect there results a certain likeness in the possible intellect, effected by a turning of the agent intellect to the phantasms. This is the likeness of the things of which there are phantasms, but only with respect to the nature of the species. In this way, the intelligible species is said to be abstracted from phantasms, but this does not mean that the identical form which was first in the phantasm is afterward in the potential intellect, like a body is taken from one place and transferred to another.

---

[40] *Species* here is taken in the sense of essence or definition.

[¶ 13.] *Reply to Objection 4.* Not only does the agent intellect illuminate phantasms, but it also abstracts from them intelligible species. It gives light to the phantasms because, just as the sensitive part is made more powerful through its union with the intellectual part, so also the phantasms, by the power of the agent intellect, are made capable of having intelligible intentions abstracted from them. Moreover, the agent intellect abstracts the intelligible species from the phantasm inasmuch as by its power we are able to receive into our consideration the natures of species without individual conditions. Our possible intellect is informed according to the likenesses of these natures.

[¶ 14.] *Reply to Objection 5.* Our intellect abstracts the intelligible species from the phantasms, insofar as it considers the natures of things universally; nevertheless, it knows the species in phantasms, because it cannot understand the things whose species it abstracts except by turning to the phantasms, as we have said. (*S.T.,* I, 84, 6 and 7.)

No. 4. The Human Intellect Is a Passive Power
St. Thomas: *Summa Theologiae,* Part I, Question 79, Article 2
Is the intellect a passive power?

[¶ 1.] *Objection 1.* Everything is passive because of matter, but active because of form. But the intellectual power is based upon the immateriality of the knowing substance. Therefore, it seems that the intellect is not a passive power.

[¶ 2.] *Objection 2.* The intellectual power is incorruptible, as we have said. But if the intellect is passive, it is corruptible, as is said in Book III, *On the Soul.* Therefore, the intellectual power is not passive.

[¶ 3.] *Objection 3.* The agent is more excellent than what is acted upon, as Augustine (*Commentary on the Text of Genesis,* No. 16) and Aristotle (III, *On the Soul,* Chapter 5) say. But all the vegetative powers, which are the lowest powers of the soul, are active. Much more, therefore, are all the intellectual powers active, since they are the highest powers.

[¶ 4.] *On the contrary,* the Philosopher says (III, *On the Soul,* Chapter 4) that to know is in some manner to be passive.

[¶ 5.] "To be passive" may be understood in three ways. First, and most strictly, when something suitable either according to the nature or its proper inclination is taken away from a being, for example, when water loses its coolness by being heated, or when a man becomes ill or sad. Second, and less strictly, someone is said to be passive when something, either suitable or unsuitable, is taken away from a being. In this sense, not only is he who becomes ill said to be passive, but also he who is cured; not only he who is saddened, but also he who is made joyful—hence it means being changed or moved in any way whatever. Third, in a broad sense, a thing is called passive simply because it receives something it was in potency to receive, without being deprived of anything. In this sense, anything which passes from potency to act can be called *passive,* even when it is perfected. In this way, *"to know"* is to be passive. The reason for this is evident. The intellect, as has been said (*S.T.,* I, 5, 2; and I, 78, 1) has an operation extending to universal being.

[¶ 6.] We can judge, therefore, whether the intellect is in act or in potency by considering how it is related to universal being. There is an intellect which is related to universal being as the act of all beings. Such is the divine intellect, the essence of God, in which all being pre-exists originally and virtually as in its first cause. Therefore, the divine intellect is not in potency, but is pure act. But no created intellect can be in act in respect to the whole of universal being, for such an intellect would have to be an infinite being. Hence, no created intellect, by reason of its very essence, is the act of all intelligible things; rather, it is compared to those intelligible things as potency to act. Now potency has a twofold relation to act. There is a potency which is always perfectly in act, as we say the matter of heavenly bodies is. There is another potency which is not always in act, but proceeds from potency to act, as in things that are generated and corrupted. Hence, an angelic intellect, as we said (*S.T.,* I, 58, 1), is always in act with respect to its own intelligible objects, since it is so near the first intellect which is pure act. But the human intellect, lowest in the order of intellects and furthest removed from the perfection of the divine intellect, is in potency to its intelligible objects. It is in the beginning "like a tablet on which nothing is written," as the Philosopher says (III, *On the Soul,* Chapter 4). This is clear from the fact that in the beginning we are only potential knowers; afterwards, we become actual knowers. It is evident, therefore, that for us to understand is, in a way, to be passive, in the third way of being passive. Hence, the intellect is a passive power.

[¶ 7.] *Reply to Objection 1.* This objection is based on the first and second ways of being passive, which apply properly to prime matter. But the third kind of passivity belongs to anything existing in potency which is actualized.

[¶ 8.] *Reply to Objection 2.* *Passive intellect* is the name given by some to the sensitive appetite, where there are passions of the soul. This appetite is also called "rational by participation," because it obeys reason (I, *Ethics,* Chapter 13). Others give the name *passive intellect* to the cogitative power, which is called *particular reason*. In both cases *passive* can be taken in the first two senses, since this so-called "intellect" is the act of corporeal organ. But the intellect that is in potency to intelligible things, which Aristotle because of this calls the *possible intellect,* is passive only in the third sense, because it is not the act of a corporeal organ. Hence, it is incorruptible.

[¶ 9.] *Reply to Objection 3.* The agent is more excellent than that which is acted upon, if the activity and the passivity refer to the same thing, but not always if they refer to different things. Now the intellect is a passive power in respect to the whole of universal being, but the vegetative power is active in respect to a particular being, namely, the composite of body and soul. Hence, it is possible for such a passive power to be more excellent than an active one.

No. 5. *The Existence and Function of an Agent Intellect*
St. Thomas: *Summa Theologiae,* Part I, Question 79, Article 3
Is there an agent intellect?

[¶ 1.] *Objection 1.* It seems that there is no agent intellect, for just as the senses are related to sensible things, so the intellect is related to intelligible things. Now because the sense is in potency to sensible things, we do not posit an active sense, but only a passive one. Therefore, since our intellect is in potency to intelligible things, we should not posit an agent intellect, but only a possible one.

[¶ 2.] *Objection 2.* If we say that even in the sense something is active, such as light, there is the objection that light is required for sight, insofar as it makes the medium actually luminous, for color by its own nature moves what is already light. But in the operation of the intellect we do not require a medium which must be activated. Therefore, it is unnecessary to require an agent intellect.

[¶ 3.] *Objection 3.* The likeness of the agent is received into the one acted upon according to the mode of the one acted upon. But the possible intellect is an immaterial power. Therefore, its immateriality suffices to receive forms in an immaterial way. But a form is intelligible in act from the very fact that it is immaterial. Therefore, there is no need for an agent intellect to make the species intelligible in act.

[¶ 4.] *On the contrary,* the Philosopher says (III, *On the Soul,* Chapter 5) that just as in all nature, so in the soul there is something by which it becomes all things, and something by which it does all things. Therefore, we must posit an agent intellect.

[¶ 5.] According to Plato, we do not need an agent intellect to make things intelligible in act, but only, perhaps, to provide intelligible light to the knower. This we shall discuss later. (*S.T.,* I, 79, 4; and I, 84, 6.) For Plato thought that the forms of natural things subsist without matter, and consequently they are intelligible, since a thing is actually intelligible insofar as it is immaterial. Such forms he called *species* or *ideas.* He said that even corporeal matter was formed by a participation in these, so that individuals would be established naturally in their proper genera and species, and that our intellects are also formed by such participation, in order to have knowledge of the genera and species of things. But because Aristotle (III, *Metaphysics*) held that forms of natural things do not subsist without matter, and that forms existing in matter are not actually intelligible, it follows that the natures or forms of sensible things which we understand are not actually intelligible. Now nothing is brought from potency to act except by something in act; as the sense is activated by something actually sensible. We must, therefore, posit some power of the intellect which makes things actually intelligible by abstracting species from their material conditions of existence. This is why we need an agent intellect.

[¶ 6.] *Reply to Objection 1.* Sensible things exist actually outside the soul, and so there is no need of an agent sense. Thus, it is clear that in the nutritive part all powers are active; in the sensitive part all powers are passive; but in the intellectual part there is something active and something passive.

[¶ 7.] *Reply to Objection 2.* There are two opinions regarding the effect of light. Some hold that light is needed for sight, to make colors actually visible. According to this opinion, the agent intellect is needed for understanding in the same way and for the same reason that light is needed for seeing. But others say that light is needed for vision, not so that the colors may be made actually visible, but that the medium may become actually luminous, as the Commentator says (II, *On the Soul,* No. 67). According to this, Aristotle's comparison of the agent intellect to light is verified in this respect: just as light is necessary for seeing, so the agent intellect is necessary for understanding—but not for the same reason.

[¶ 8.] *Reply to Objection 3.* If the agent pre-exists, it may well happen that its likeness is received in various ways in various things, because of the recipient's diverse dispositions. But if the agent does not pre-exist, the disposition of the recipient makes no difference. Now the intelligible in act is not something existing in the nature of things, that is, in the nature of sensible things which do not subsist outside of matter. Therefore, the immateriality of the possible intellect is not sufficient for the act of understanding, unless the agent intellect is present to make things actually intelligible through abstraction.

No. 6. The Objectivity of Our Intellectual Knowledge
  St. Thomas: *Summa Theologiae,* Part I, Question 85, Article 2
  Is the intelligible species that is abstracted from the phantasm the object
  that is understood?

[¶ 1.] *Objection 1.* It seems that the intelligible species which are abstracted from phantasms are the objects which are understood, for what is actually understood is in the knower, since the thing actually understood is the same as the intellect actually understanding. But there can be nothing of the thing understood in the intellect actually knowing except the abstracted intelligible species. Therefore, a species of this kind is what is actually understood.

[¶ 2.] *Objection 2.* The object actually understood must be in something, otherwise it would not be at all. But it is not in the thing that exists outside the soul, because the thing outside the soul is material, and nothing material can be intelligible in act. Therefore, what is actually understood must be in the intellect, and this is nothing other than the intelligible species just mentioned.

[¶ 3.] *Objection 3.* The Philosopher says (I, *On Interpretation,* Chapter 1) that *words are signs of things that affect the soul.* But words signify things that are understood, for we signify by a word that we understand. Therefore, the things that affect the soul, namely, the intelligible species, are the objects which are actually understood.

[¶ 4.] *On the contrary,* intelligible species are related to the intellect as sensible species to the senses. But the sensible species is *not the thing that is sensed* but that *by which* there is sensation. Therefore, the intelligible species is not the thing that is actually understood but that by which the intellect understands.

[¶ 5.] Some held that the cognitive powers in us know nothing except their own impressions, for example, that the sense power senses only the activity upon the organ. According to this view, the intellect understands only what actually affects it, that is, the intelligible species received in itself. Thus, the species is the thing that is understood.

[¶ 7.] This opinion is evidently false for two reasons. First, because the things we understand are the same things about which we have scientific knowledge. If the things we understood were only the species that are in the soul, it would follow that no science would treat of things that exist outside the soul, but only of intelligible species that are in the soul. Following this view, the Platonists held that all science treats of ideas, which, they said, are the things that are actually understood. Second (the opinion is false) because the error of the early philosophers would follow, who said that *everything which appears true is true*. Hence, they held that contradictories could be true at the same time. It is true that if the power knows only its own impressions, it can judge only of them. Thus, a thing would appear according to the way that the power of knowing was affected. Hence, every judgment of the cognitive power would be concerned with its own impression as such, and so every judgment would be true. If taste, for example, senses only its own impression it will follow that when someone with a healthy sense of taste judges honey to be sweet, he will judge it truly, and if a person with a defective sense of taste judges honey to be bitter, this likewise will be a true judgment, for each of them judges according to the way that his sense of taste is affected. It follows, therefore, that every opinion will be equally true, and universally every impression.

[¶ 8.] We must hold, therefore, that the intelligible species is related to the intellect as that by which it understands. This is clear from the following argument. There are two kinds of activity, as was stated in IX, *Metaphysics,* one of which remains in the agent, for example, seeing and understanding, and another which passes into an external thing, for example, heating or cutting. Each of these kinds of action is effected according to a form. Just as the form by which an action tends to an external thing is the likeness of the object of the action, (as the heat in the thing which causes heat is the likeness of the thing heated), so, the form by which immanent activity is caused is the likeness of the object. Hence, the likeness of the visible object is the form by which sight sees, and the likeness of the thing understood, namely, the intelligible species, is the form by which the intellect understands.

[¶ 9.] Because the intellect reflects upon itself, in one and the same act of reflection it knows its act of understanding and the species by which it understands. Secondarily, therefore, the intelligible species is that which is understood, but that which is understood first is the thing itself of which the intelligible species is a likeness.

[¶ 10.] This can be seen in the opinion of the early philosophers who said that *like was known by like*. They held that the soul knew earth which was outside it by the earth which was present in it, and so for other things. If, therefore, we take the species of earth in place of earth, following the teaching of Aristotle, who says that not the stone but the species of the stone is in the eye, it will follow that the mind knows things outside the mind by means of intelligible species.

[¶ 11.] *Reply to Objection 1.* The thing understood is in the one understanding through a likeness. It is in this way that we say the thing actually understood is the same as the intellect in act, because the likeness of the thing understood is the form of the intellect, just as the likeness of the sensible object is the form of the sense in act. It follows, therefore, not that the abstracted intelligible species is the thing that is understood, but rather that it is the likeness of what is understood.

[¶ 12.] *Reply to Objection 2.* When we say *the thing actually understood* two things are implied, namely, the thing that is understood, and also the understanding itself. Likewise, when we say *an abstracted universal,* two things are understood, namely, the nature of the thing itself, and also the abstraction or the universality. The nature itself, which can be understood or can be abstracted, or can have the intention of universality, exists only in the singular, but to be understood or to be abstracted or considered as universal is in the intellect. We can see something similar to this in the senses. Sight sees the color of the apple but not its odor. If we ask where does that color exist which is seen without odor, it is clear that it is in the apple, but that it be seen without odor takes place in the sight itself, because in sight there is a likeness of color but not of odor. In the same way, the *humanity* which is understood exists only in this or that man, but when humanity is apprehended without its conditions of individuation, that is, when it is abstracted and considered as a universal, this is humanity as it is understood by the intellect, in which there is a likeness of the specific nature but not of the individual principles.

[¶ 13.] *Reply to Objection 3.* There are two operations in the sensitive part. One of these is the change alone, by which sensation takes place, when the sense is impressed by the sensible object. The other operation is the formation by the imagination of a representation of an absent thing or of something never seen. Both of these operations are united in the intellect. First of all there is the passivity of the possible intellect when it is informed by an intelligible species. But after it is thus formed, it then forms a definition, a division or a composition, which is signified by language. So the notion which a name signifies is the *definition,* while an enunciation signifies composition or division by the intellect. Words do not signify the intelligible species themselves but rather that which the intellect forms for itself in order to judge of external things.

No. 7. The Possibility of Error in the Human Intellect
   St. Thomas: *Summa Theologiae,* Part I, Question 85, Article 6
   Can the intellect be false?

[¶ 1.] *Objection 1.* The Philosopher says in VI, *Metaphysics* that truth and falsity are in the mind. Since the intellect and mind are the same, as we said before (*S.T.,* I, 79, 1), falsity is in the intellect.

[¶ 2.] *Objection 2.* Opinion and reasoning are in the intellect. But falsity is found in both; therefore, falsity can be in the intellect.

[¶ 3.] *Objection 3.* Sin is in the intellectual part. But sin entails falsity for "they err who do evil," as *Proverbs* 14 says. Therefore, falsity can be in the intellect.

[¶ 4.] *On the contrary,* Augustine in his *Book of Eighty-three Topics* says, "every one who is in error, in that respect in which he is in error, does not understand." The Philosopher says in III, *On the Soul* that the intellect is always true.

[¶ 5.] On this point the Philosopher in III, *On the Soul* compares the intellect to the senses, for a sense is not deceived about its proper object, for example, sight in grasping color—except, perhaps, accidentally because of an impediment in the organ. For example, a person with a fever judges something sweet to be bitter, because his tongue is full of bad humors. The sense can be deceived in regard to common sensibles, as in judging size and shape. For example, it judges the sun to be only a foot in diameter although it is larger than the earth. It is deceived even more about the accidental sensible objects, as when it judges gall to be honey, because of sameness in color. The reason that it is not deceived about its proper object is evident. Every power as such is essentially disposed to its proper object, since things of this kind are always related in the same way, as long as the power remains, it does not fail in its judgment of its proper object.

[¶ 6.] The proper object of the intellect is the essence of a thing, and, hence, strictly speaking, the intellect cannot be in error concerning the essence of a thing. But about those things which accompany the essence or quiddity, the intellect can err, when it refers one thing to another, either in composing or dividing, or even in reasoning. For this reason, it cannot be wrong about those propositions which are immediately known once the meaning of the terms is known, as in first principles, from which we arrive at the infallibility of truth in the certitude of science as regards its conclusions.

[¶ 7.] Accidentally, the intellect may be deceived about the essence of composite things, not because of the organ, since the intellect is not a power which uses an organ, but because of the composition entering into the definition; either when the definition of one thing is false when applied to something else, for example, if the definition of a circle is applied to triangles; or when some definition is false in itself, since it involves an impossible composition, as if we were to define something as "a rational animal with wings." Hence, in simple things, in whose definition there is no intervening composition, we cannot be deceived; but if we err, we grasp nothing about them at all, as is said in IX, *Metaphysics*.

[¶ 8.] *Reply to Objection 1.* The Philosopher says that falsity is in the mind in composition and division (that is, when it makes a judgment).

[¶ 9.] *Reply to Objection 2.* In the same way, there is falsity in regard to opinion and reasoning.

[¶ 10.] *Reply to Objection 3.* As for the error of sinners, it consists in a wrong practical judgment with respect to an appetible object. But in an absolute consideration of the essence of a thing, and of those things we know through it, the intellect is never deceived. This is what those authorities, who were quoted to the contrary, meant.

Section B: The Power of Free Will
  No. 1. *How the Intellect and Will Are Mutual Causes*
    St. Thomas: *Summa Theologiae,* Part I, Question 82, Article 4
    Does the will move the intellect?

[¶ 1.] *Objection 1.* The mover is more excellent and comes before what is moved; for the mover is the agent, and the agent is more excellent than what is acted upon as both Augustine (XII, *Commentary on the Text of Genesis*) and the Philosopher (III, *On the Soul*) say. But the intellect is more excellent and comes before the will, as was said above. (*S.T.,* I, 82, 3.) Therefore, the will does not move the intellect.

[¶ 2.] *Objection 2.* The mover is not moved by what is itself moved, except perhaps accidentally, but the intellect moves the will because the thing apprehended as desirable moves without being moved; but the appetite moves only when it is moved. Therefore, the intellect is not moved by the will.

[¶ 3.] *Objection 3.* We can will nothing but what we know; if therefore, in order to understand, the will wills to understand, then that act of willing must be preceded by another act of understanding, and that act of understanding must be preceded by another act of willing, and so on indefinitely, which is impossible. Therefore, the will does not move the intellect.

[¶ 4.] *On the contrary,* Damascene says that it is in our power to learn or not to learn any art that we desire (II, *On the True Faith.*[41]) Now a thing is in our power by our will, but we apprehend the arts by our intellect. Therefore, the will does move the intellect.

[¶ 5.] A thing moves another in two ways: first, by way of an end, as when we say that the end moves the agent. The intellect moves the will in this way, for the good as known is the object of the will and so moves it as an end. Second, a thing moves another as an agent, as that which alters moves what is altered, and that which pushes moves what is pushed. In this way, the will moves the intellect and all the powers of the soul, as Anselm says (II, *On Spiritual Topics*).[42] The reason is that wherever there is order among several active powers, the power related to the universal end moves the powers which are related to particular ends. We can see this in nature as well as in government. For the heavens, which strive for the preservation of all generable and corruptible things, move all the inferior bodies. Each of these inferior bodies strives for the preservation of its proper species or of the individual. A king too, in whose keeping is the common good of his whole realm, moves by his command the individual governors who rule over their own cities. Now the object of the will is the good, and the end in general. But each power is directed toward some proper good suitable to it, as sight to the sensing of color and the intellect to the knowledge of truth. Therefore, the will as an agent moves all the powers of the soul to their proper acts except the natural vegetative powers which are not subject to free choice.

[¶ 6.] *Reply to Objection 1.* We can think of the intellect in two ways. First, as knowing universal being and truth. Second, as it is a certain thing and a particular power which has a definite act. We can also think of the will in two ways. First, according to the common nature of its object, that is, insofar as it desires the common good. Second, as a particular power of the soul having a definite act. Therefore, if we compare the intellect and the will according to the universality of their objects, as we have said (*S.T.,* I, 82, 3), then the intellect is, absolutely speaking, higher and more excellent than the will. And if we think of the intellect according to the universal nature of its object, and the will as a particular kind of power, again the intellect is superior and prior to the will, because the will itself, its

---

[41] *De Fide Orthodoxa.*
[42] *De Similitudinibus.*

act, and its object are contained under the notion of *being* and *truth* which the intellect grasps. Therefore, the intellect understands the will, its act, and its object, as it understands other things, such as wood or stone which come under the universal idea of *being* and *truth*. But if we think of the will in relation to the universal nature of its object, which is goodness, and the intellect as a particular thing and a special power, then the intellect, its act, and its object, that is, truth, fall under the common idea of good, since each of these is a particular type of good. In this respect the will is higher than the intellect and can move it. We can see from this why these powers include one another in their acts, because the intellect knows that the will wills, and the will wills the intellect to understand. Likewise, the good is contained under the true, inasmuch as it is a kind of truth understood, and truth is contained under the idea of good inasmuch as it is a desired good.

[¶ 7.] *Reply to Objection 2.* The intellect moves the will in a different way than the will moves the intellect, as we have already said. (*S.T.,* I, 82, 3.)

[¶ 8.] *Reply to Objection 3.* We must not go on indefinitely, but we must stop at the intellect as the beginning, for knowledge must come before every act of the will, but an act of the will does not come before every act of knowledge. The principle of counseling and understanding is an intellectual principle higher than our intellect, namely, God, as Aristotle also says, and in this way he shows that it is not necessary to go on indefinitely (VII, *Eudemonian Ethics*).

No. 2. Comparison of the Intellect and the Will

St. Thomas: *Summa Theologiae,* Part I, Question 82, Article 3

Is the will a higher power than the intellect?

[¶ 1.] *Objection 1.* It seems that the will is a higher power than the intellect for the object of the will is the good and the end. But, the end or goal is the first and highest cause. Therefore, the will is the first and highest power.

[¶ 2.] *Objection 2.* Natural things progress from the imperfect to the perfect. This is true also of the powers of the soul, for there is a progression from the senses to the intellect which is a higher power. But there is a natural progression from the act of the intellect to the act of the will. Therefore, the will is the more perfect and higher power.

[¶ 3.] *Objection 3.* Habits are related to the powers in which they exist as the perfect thing is to the perfectible. But the habit which perfects the will, namely charity, is more excellent than the habits which perfect the intellect, for it is written (I, *Corinthians,* Chapter XIII, Verse 2) "If I should know all mysteries and if I should have all faith and have no charity, I am nothing." Therefore, the will is a higher power than the intellect.

[¶ 4.] *On the contrary,* the Philosopher holds (X, *Ethics*) that the intellect is the highest power of the soul.

[¶ 5.] We can consider the superiority of one thing over another in two ways: absolutely and relatively. We consider a thing *absolutely* when we consider it in itself, but *relatively* when we consider it in relation to something else. If, therefore, we consider the intellect and the will absolutely, the intellect is the superior power. We can see this if we compare their respective objects, for the object of the intellect is more simple and more absolute than the object of the will, since the object of the intellect is the very essence of the desirable good, but the object of the will is the concrete desired good, the essence of which is in the intellect. Now, the more simple and more abstract a thing is, the more excellent and superior it is in itself, and, therefore, the object of the intellect is higher than that of the will. Since, therefore, the proper nature of a power is in its relationship to its object, it follows that in itself and absolutely the intellect is higher and more excellent than the will.

[¶ 6.] But relatively and in relation to something else, the will is sometimes higher than the intellect, since the object of the will may reside in something higher than the object of the intellect. For instance, I might say that what I hear is relatively more excellent than what I see, because a thing in which there is sound is more excellent than the thing in which I see color, although color is more excellent and simpler than sound. For, as we stated above (*S.T.,* I, 16, 1; and I, 27, 4), the action of the intellect consists in the essence of the thing understood being present in the knower, but the act of the will is completed when the will is inclined to the thing as it exists in itself. So the Philosopher says (IV, *Metaphysics*) that good and evil, which are objects of the will, are in things; but true and false, which are objects of the intellect, are in the mind. When therefore, a thing in which there is goodness is more excellent than the soul itself in which the essence of the thing understood is present, in respect to such a thing, the will is more excellent than the intellect. But when the thing in which the good exists is inferior to the soul, then in respect to such a thing, the intellect is higher than the will. From this we see that love of God is better than knowledge of Him, but that the knowledge of corporeal things is better than love of them. Absolutely, however, the intellect is more excellent than the will.

[¶ 7.] *Reply to Objection 1.* We get the notion of a cause by comparing one thing with another. In such a comparison, we see the superiority of the notion of goodness. But truth is something more absolute and signifies the idea of goodness itself. Thus, the good is something true; but again the true is something good, for the intellect is a being and truth is its end. Among other ends this is the most excellent, just as among other powers the intellect is the most excellent.

[¶ 8.] *Reply to Objection 2.* What is first in the order of generation and time is less perfect: for in one and the same being potency is prior in time to act, and the imperfect is prior to the perfect. But what is first absolutely, and according to the order of nature, is more perfect; for thus act comes before potency. And in this way the intellect comes before the will as the motive power before the movable and the agent before that which is acted upon; for it is the known good that makes the will act.

[¶ 9.] *Reply to Objection 3.* This argument holds true if the will tends to something which is superior to the soul, for charity is the virtue by which we love God.

No. 3. The Different Kinds of Necessity
     St. Thomas: *Summa Theologiae,* Part I, Question 82, Article 1
     Does the will necessarily desire anything?

[¶ 1.] *Objection 1.* Augustine says (V, *The City of God*) that if something is necessary, it is not voluntary, but everything that the will seeks is voluntary; therefore, nothing that the will seeks is desired of necessity.

[¶ 2.] *Objection 2.* The Philosopher says in IX, *Metaphysics* that the rational powers have a relationship to contraries. But the will is a rational power, since, as is said in III, *On the Soul,* the will is in the reason. Therefore, the will has a relationship to contraries, and, thus, it is not determined by necessity to anything.

[¶ 3.] *Objection 3.* We are masters of our acts because of our will. But we are not the masters of what is necessitated. Therefore, an act of the will cannot be necessitated.

[¶ 4.] *On the contrary,* Augustine says (XIII, *On the Trinity*) [43] that everyone seeks happiness with an unaltering will. If this were not necessary but contingent, there would be at least a few exceptions. Therefore, the will of necessity wills something.

[¶ 5.] Necessity has more than one meaning. *Necessary,* in general, is

---

[43] *De Trinitate.*

defined as that which must be. Now necessity may belong to something from one of the intrinsic principles: either from the material principle, as when we say that everything composed of contraries must necessarily be corruptible; or from the formal principle, as when we say that a triangle must have its three angles equal to two right angles. This is called *a natural and absolute necessity*. Secondly, necessity may belong to something from an extrinsic principle: either because of the end or the agent. There is necessity because of the end when something cannot be achieved without what is needed, or cannot be suitably achieved; as food, for example, is necessary for life, and a horse for a journey. We call this a "necessity imposed by an end," and sometimes even call it "utility." There is necessity because of the agent, when someone is forced by an agent in such a way that he cannot do the opposite. We call this the "necessity by coercion."

[¶ 6.] This necessity by coercion is contrary to the will. For we consider violent whatever is contrary to the inclination of a thing. Now the very motion of the will is an inclination toward something. Hence, as something is said to be natural because it follows the inclination of nature, so something is voluntary when it follows the inclination of the will. Just as it is impossible that something be simultaneously violent and natural, so it is impossible that something be absolutely coerced or violent, and at the same time voluntary.

[¶ 7.] Necessity of the end, however, is not contrary to the will, even when we can attain the end in only one way; for example, a desire of crossing the ocean makes it necessary to desire a ship. Likewise, natural necessity is not contrary to the will. For example, just as the intellect adheres of necessity to first principles, so the will of necessity adheres to its final end, which is happiness, for the end in practical matters is like a principle in speculative matters, as is stated in II, *Physics*. For whatever belongs to a thing naturally and unchangeably must be the foundation and principle of everything else, since the nature of a thing is what is primary in each thing, and every motion comes from something immobile.

[¶ 8.] *Reply to Objection 1*. We should interpret the words of Augustine as referring to the necessity of coercion; natural necessity does not take away free will, as he says himself in the same work.

[¶ 9.] *Reply to Objection 2*. Insofar as the will naturally desires something, it corresponds more to the understanding of natural principles than reason, which is related to opposites. Hence, the will is more an intellectual than a rational power.

[¶ 10.] *Reply to Objection 3*. We are masters of our acts to the extent that we can choose this or that, but there is no choice of the end. Choice is not concerned with the end but with things for the end, as is said in III, *Ethics*. Therefore, the desire for our final end is not among those things of which we are masters.

No. 4. Man Has Freedom of Will
St. Thomas: *Disputed Question on Evil,* Question 6, Article 1

[¶ 1.] Some taught that man's will is moved by necessity to choose something, though they did not say that man is coerced. For not everything done by necessity implies violence, but only that which comes from an extrinsic principle. Hence, there are some natural movements which are necessary but not thereby violent. Violence, in fact, is contrary both to what is natural and to what is voluntary, since the principle of nature and freedom is intrinsic but the principle of violence is extrinsic.

[¶ 2.] Now the opinion of these men is heretical, for it takes away the concept of merit and demerit in human actions. There is no merit or demerit if someone acts out of necessity and cannot avoid doing what he does. This opinion is included among the false philosophical opinions, not only because it is contrary to faith, but because it overthrows every principle of moral philosophy, for if there is no liberty in us, but we must choose out of necessity, then deliberation, exhortation, command, and punishment, praise and blame are worth nothing—and all of these belong to the field of moral philosophy. Opinions which destroy the principles of a part of philosophy are outside the pale of true philosophy, just as it would destroy the principles of natural science were we to say that nothing moves. Some men held these opinions because of impudence, others because of sophistical arguments which they could not solve as the Philosopher says in the *Metaphysics*.

[¶ 3.] As evidence of the truth on this question we must consider that there is a principle proper to the actions of men, just as there are such principles proper to other things in nature. The motive or agent principle in men is the intellect and the will, as is said in III, *On the Soul*. Now this principle is in some ways like the active principle in natural beings, and in some ways unlike it. It is like it in this, that just as in natural beings there is a form which is a principle of action, and there is an inclination or appetite consequent upon the form, called a natural appetite, from which action naturally follows, likewise in man there is an intellectual form, and an inclination of the will consequent upon the apprehended form, from which proceeds the external action. Bu there is this difference, namely, the form of the natural being is an individuated form because of the matter. Consequently, its inclination is determined towards one particular goal, while the intellectual form is universal, so that many individual goals can be included under it. Hence, since actions are always individual, no one of which is equal to the potency of the universal, the inclination of the will remains indeterminately directed to many different objects. If, for example, an artisan conceives the form of a house universally, under which are included the various shapes of houses, it would be up to him to determine what kind of house he would make—a round one, or square one, or a house of a different shape.

[¶ 4.] Now the active principle in brute animals holds an intermediary position. For the form apprehended by the sense is individual, just like the form of a natural object. Therefore, the inclination of the animal like that of natural bodies is towards one determinate goal. But it is not always the same form that is received in the sense, as it is in natural things. For example, fire is always hot, but in one case it is perceived in one way, and at another time differently, namely, at one time, as a pleasant form, and at another time as an unpleasant one. The result is that the animal sometimes pursues the object, and at other times flees from it. In this way the animal acts something like man.

[¶ 5.] Second, we note that a potency is moved in two ways: in one way on the part of its subject, in another on the part of its object. On the part of the subject, for example, sight is moved to see well or poorly by a change in the disposition of the organ; on the part of the object, the eye at one time sees white and another time black. The first change pertains to the very exercise of the act, namely, whether there will be activity or not, or whether the activity will be strong or weak, but the second change belongs to the specifications of the act, since the act is specified by the object. Now in natural beings the specification of the act comes from the form, while the exercise of the act comes from the agent that causes the very motion. An agent always acts for an end. It follows that the first principle of motion, in regard to the exercise of the act, comes from the end. But if we consider the objects of the intellect and of the will, we find that the object of the intellect is a first principle in the genus of formal cause, since its object is *being* and *truth*. But the object of the will is a first principle in the genus of final cause, since its object is *goodness* under which are included all ends— just as under the concept of truth all apprehended forms are included. Hence, the concept of *goodness,* insofar as it is an apprehended form, is contained under *goodness,* since it is a particular kind of good. If we consider the motion of the powers of the soul from the viewpoint of the object specifying the act, the first principle of motion comes from the intellect.

In this way, the good that is understood moves the will. If we consider the motion of the powers of the soul from the viewpoint of the exercises of the act, the first principle of motion comes from the will. For the potency to which the principle end belongs will move the other potencies to which belong the means to the end. Thus, the soldier moves the leathermaker to fashion bridles. In this way the will moves itself and other powers, for I understand because I want to understand, and I use all my other power and capacities because I want to. Hence, the Commentator defines a habit as that which a man uses when he wants to.

[¶ 6.] In order to show that the will is not moved of necessity, we must consider the movement of the will both in the exercise of its act of willing and in the specification of its act, which comes from the object. In regard to the exercise of the act, it is clear, first of all, that the will is moved by itself; for just as it moves other powers, so it moves itself. It does not follow because of this that the will is at one and the same time in act and in potency with respect to the same things. Just as man moves his intellect to acquire science by the method of invention, insofar as he goes from one thing known to another not known, the intellect being in potency to the new knowledge, so because man wills something in act he moves himself to will something else in act. For example, if he wills health, he moves himself to will to take medicine to give health. Once the will desires health, there is a deliberation about the things that bring health, and from this comes the will to take the medicine. So the deliberation precedes the desire to take medicine. The deliberation comes from the will's desire to take counsel. The will moves itself through its counsel, and the counsel is a kind of search which is not a demonstration, but a search with the way open to opposites. Consequently, the will does not move itself of necessity. And since the will does not always choose deliberately to take counsel, it is necessary that it be moved by some cause which makes it will to take counsel. Now if you were to say that in this matter it is moved by itself, it is again necessary that a movement of the will precede counsel and that counsel precede the act of the will, and so we would go on *ad infinitum* in our search for the first cause that moves the will. Since this is not possible, we must say in regard to the very first act of the will, the will of any being that is not always in act, that it most be moved by some extrinsic cause. Under the impulse of this thing the will begins to will.

[¶ 7.] As Aristotle concluded in VII, *Eudemonian Ethics,* Chapter 18, that which first moves the will and the intellect is something above these powers, namely, God. God moves all things according to their principle of mobility. He moves light things up and heavy things down, and moves the will according to its own nature, not as of necessity but as indeterminately related to many different objects. It is clear, therefore, that the movement of the will, with respect to the exercise of its act, is not one of necessity. But if the motion of will is considered in relation to the object determining the act of the will to this or that object, the object that moves the will is a good apprehended as suitable to the particular individual. Hence, if some good is apprehended, but not as suitable for the individual, it will not move the will. Since, however, deliberation and choice are concerned with particular objects, it is necessary that the suitable good which is apprehended be apprehended as a particular suitable good, and not merely as good and suitable in general. If it is apprehended as a good, suitable to this individual, in all particulars (insofar as they can be known), it will of necessity move the will. For this reason, man must desire happiness which according to Boethius is the state of being in which the perfection of all goods is united. I mean that there is necessity from the point of view of the determination of the act, since he cannot will the contrary. But there is no necessity in regard to the exercise of the act, since man is still able to think of happiness or not to think of it, for the acts of the intellect and of the will are individual and particular. If there is a good which is such that it is not found to be good in all its particulars, there is no necessity even from the point of determination of the act (specification of the act). For a person can will the opposite, even while thinking of this good, since the thing is considered as good or suitable for him only in some particular way, for example, good as far as health is concerned, but not as pleasure, and so on.

[¶ 8.] The will is inclined towards what is offered to it more by one particular aspect than another in three ways. In one way insofar as one object is to be preferred and thus man's will is moved according to reason; for example, a man prefers what is useful to his health, because it is useful for his will. In another way, a person thinks of one particular circumstance and not about others. It happens many times that such a thought occurs through some chance happening, the cause of which may be intrinsic or extrinsic. Thirdly, the inclination can result from the disposition of the man, because, as Aristotle points out that (III, *Ethics,* Chapter 5) "according to a man's dispositions so does the end appear to him." Hence, the will of a person given to anger will be moved in a different way from that of a peaceful man, because the same object is not suitable to both. Likewise, food does not have the same appeal for a sick man as it does for a person in health. If the disposition, by which an object appears good and suitable, were a natural disposition and not subject to the will, the will would choose that of necessity, just as all men naturally desire to be, to live, and to understand. If the disposition is not natural, but under the domination of the will, as when a person is disposed through force of habit or passion to consider a thing good or bad in this particular circumstance, the will is not necessarily moved, because it can remove this kind of disposition, so that the object does not appear to him thus. For example, a person calms his anger, so that he will not judge like an angry man. However, movement of passion is more easily removed than a habit.

[¶ 9.] Thus, to conclude, the will is necessarily moved by some things on the part of the object, but not by all things; and on the part of the exercise of the will, it is in no way moved necessarily.

No. 5. *The Will Can Desire Only What Appears Good*
    St. Thomas: *Summa Theologiae,* Part I–II, Question 8, Article 1
    Does the will desire only the good?

[¶ 1.] *Objection 1.* The same power is related to opposites, as sight, for example, is related to white and to black. Since good and evil are opposites, the will wills not only what is good, but also what is evil.

[¶ 2.] *Objection 2.* The rational powers are related to opposites, according to the Philosopher (IX, *Metaphysics*); but the will is a rational power, for it is "in the reason," as is stated in Book III, *On the Soul.* Therefore, the will is related to opposites, and so not only to willing the good, but also to willing evil.

[¶ 3.] *Objection 3.* Good and being are convertible. But the will wills non-being as well as being, as for example, when we will sometimes not to walk or not to speak and sometimes even future things which are not actual beings. Therefore, we do not will only the good.

[¶ 4.] *On the contrary,* Dionysius says (IV, *On the Divine Names*)[44] that "evil is outside the will," and that "everything desires what is good."

[¶ 5.] The will is a rational appetite. There is no appetite except of the good, since appetite is nothing other than the inclination of a being toward something. But nothing is inclined to something unless it is similar and suitable. Since, therefore, everything by the very fact that it is a being or a substance is a kind of good, every inclination must necessarily be toward good. This is why the Philosopher says (I, *Ethics*) that good is "that which all things seek."

[¶ 6.] We should note that since every inclination tends to some form, the natural appetite tends to a form existing in nature, and the sensitive appetite

---

[44] *De Divinis Nominibus.*

and the intellectual or rational appetite (called the will) tend toward an apprehended form. Just as that to which the natural appetite tends is a good existing in reality, so that to which the animal appetite or the voluntary appetite tends is an apprehended good. In order that the will tend to something it is not necessary that it be truly good, but that it be apprehended as good. Thus, the Philosopher says (II, *Physics*) that "the end is a good or an apparent good."

[¶ 7.] *Reply to Objection 1.* The same power is related to opposites but not to each in the same manner. The will is related to both good and evil, but to the good, by desiring it, to the evil, by avoiding it. The actual desire for the good is called "volition," and this designates the act of the will, which is the way we are discussing the will. Flight from evil is better termed "aversion." Thus, as volition is of good, aversion is of evil.

[¶ 8.] *Reply to Objection 2.* The rational power does not pursue every opposite but only those which are suitable as an object, since a power moves only to an object that is suitable. Since the object of the will is good, the will pursues those opposites which are apprehended as good; for example, to move and rest, to speak or to remain silent, and the like, for the will tends to both of these under the aspect of good.

[¶ 9.] *Reply to Objection 3.* That which is not a being in reality is considered as a being in the mind; thus, negation and privation are called beings of the mind. In this way, future things, insofar as they are apprehended, are beings. Inasmuch as they are beings of this kind, they are apprehended as good and so the will tends toward them. Thus, the Philosopher says in V, *Ethics* that "to lack evil has the nature of a good."

No. 6. The Will Is Not Moved With Necessity by Particular Objects
St. Thomas: *Summa Theologiae,* Part I–II, Question 10, Article 2
Is the will moved with necessity by its objects?

[¶ 1.] *Objection 1.* It seems that the will is necessarily moved by its object, for the object is related to the will as the mover to the moveable, as is evident in III, *On the Soul.* Because any motive force (if it is sufficient) necessarily moves a mobile being, the will can necessarily be moved by its object.

[¶ 2.] *Objection 2.* The will like the intellect is an immaterial power, and both powers are ordered to a universal object, as was said above (*S.T.,* I–II, 10, 1, *ad* 3). Since the intellect is necessarily moved by its object, the will also is necessarily moved by its object.

[¶ 3.] *Objection 3.* Anything that is desired is either an end or something directed to an end. We see that everyone must necessarily will his final end, because it is like a principle in speculative matters to which we necessarily assent. The end, moreover, is the reason for our willing the means to the end. So it seems that we must necessarily will even the means to the end. Thus, the will is necessarily moved by its object.

[¶ 4.] *On the contrary,* the rational powers, according to the Philosopher (IX, *Metaphysics*) are related to opposites. The will is a rational power, since it is "in the reason," as is said in III, *On the Soul.* Since the will is related to opposites, it is not necessarily moved to either one of them.

[¶ 5.] The will is moved in two ways: first, in the exercise of its act; and second, in the specification of its act, which is from the object. In the first way, the will is not moved necessarily by any object, for a person can refuse to think of any object and consequently not actually will it.

[¶ 6.] Regarding the specification, the will is necessarily moved by one kind of object but not by another. In the movement of any power by its object, we must consider the formal reason why the object moves the power. The visible object activates the power of sight through color which is actually visible. Hence, if color is placed before the power of sight, it necessarily moves sight unless a person turns his eyes away. Now this refers to the exercise of the act. If something which is not completely colored, that is colored in one part and not in another, were placed before our vision, our power of sight would not necessarily see such an object, since it might look upon the part that is not colored and so not see it. Just as the actually colored thing is the object of sight, so goodness is the object of the will. Hence, if some object which is universally good, according to every consideration, is placed before it, the will of necessity tends to it, if it wills at all, for it cannot will the opposite. If, however, some object which is not good in every respect is placed before the will, the will does not necessarily tend toward it. A defect in something good has the character of "not-good," and therefore, only the perfect good which has no defect is beyond refusal by the will, that is, happiness. Any particular good insofar as it lacks some element of goodness, can be regarded as "not-good." Accordingly, such a good can be either rejected or approved by the will, because the will can tend toward the object according to its different aspects.

[¶ 7.] *Reply to Objection 1.* The only sufficient mover of any power is an object, which in every respect has the nature of a mover. If the mover is deficient in some respect, it will not necessarily move the power, as was said above. (*S.T.,* I–II, 10, 2.)

[¶ 8.] *Reply to Objection 2.* The intellect is necessarily moved by an object which is always and necessarily true but not by one which can be either true or false, that is, by a contingent object. The same thing has been said of a contingent good.

[¶ 9.] *Reply to Objection 3.* The final end necessarily moves the will, because the final end is the perfect good; so also, those things which are ordered to the final end and without which that end cannot be attained necessarily move the will, such as existence, life, and the like. However, it is not necessary for a person who wills the end to will those things which are not needed for the end; just as, for example, a person may accept the principles of an argumentation and not necessarily accept the conclusions, without which the principles can remain true.

No. 7. Man Has the Power of Free Choice
St. Thomas: *Summa Theologiae,* Part I–II, Question 13, Article 6
Does man choose freely or by necessity?

[¶ 1.] *Objection 1.* The end has the same relation to objects that can be chosen, as principles to what follows from them, as is evident in VII, *Ethics.* But conclusions are necessarily deduced from their principles. Therefore, the end *necessarily* moves the man to choose.

[¶ 2.] *Objection 2.* As was said above (*S.T.,* I–II, 13, 1), choice follows the judgment of reason about things to be done. But reason judges necessarily about some things because of the necessity of the premises. Therefore, it seems that choice too, follows of necessity.

[¶ 3.] *Objection 3.* If two things are absolutely equal, a person is not moved more to the one than the other. If, for example, a hungry man, as Plato says, has food equally appetizing and at equal distances on both sides of him, he is no more drawn to the one than to the other. Plato gives as the reason the fact that the earth is immoveable in the center. If we cannot choose between two things which are equal, much less can we choose something which is less good. If two or three or more things are presented to us and one of them appears better, it is impossible to choose any of the others. Therefore, we necessarily choose whatever appears more worth while. But every choice is always of what seems in some way better. Therefore, every choice is one of necessity.

[¶ 4.] *On the contrary,* the Philosopher says (IX, *Metaphysics*) that choice is an act of a rational power which is related to opposites.

[¶ 5.] Man does not choose of necessity, because what can possibly not exist, does not necessarily exist. The reason for the possibility of choosing or not choosing is understood from a twofold power of man. Man can will or not will, act or not act; he can will this or that and do this or that. The explanation is found in the very power of reason. The will can tend toward whatever the reason can apprehend as good. But the reason can see as good not only willing and acting, but even not willing and not acting. Again, in every particular good the mind can consider the goodness as well as the lack of goodness, which implies the idea of evil. In this way the mind can apprehend any one of these goods as one to be chosen or rejected. The only good which the mind cannot apprehend as evil or as defective in any way, is the perfect good, which is happiness. For this reason man of necessity wills happiness and he cannot will not to be happy, that is, to be unhappy. Now since choice is not concerned with the end but with the means to the end, as we said above (*S.T.,* I–II, 13, 3) it is not concerned with the perfect good, which is happiness, but with other particular goods. Therefore, man does not choose of necessity but freely.

[¶ 6.] *Reply to Objection 1.* Conclusions do not of necessity always proceed from the principles, but only when the principles cannot be true if the conclusion is not true. Likewise, the end does not always necessitate in man the choosing of the means to the end; because not every means is of such a nature that without it the end is impossible, or if it is of such a nature, it is not always thought of in that way.

[¶ 7.] *Reply to Objection 2.* The decision or judgment of reason about what ought to be done refers to contingent things which we can do. In these matters the conclusions do not follow from necessary principles with an absolute necessity, but only with conditional necessity as, in the example, "If he runs, he moves."

[¶ 8.] *Reply to Objection 3.* If we are presented with two things which from one point of view appear equal, nothing prevents us from considering one of them from another point of view and seeing it as superior, and so the will would be drawn to that one thing rather than to the other.

No. 8. *Choice Is an Act of Both Will and Reason*
St. Thomas: *Summa Theologiae,* Part I–II, Question 13, Article 1
Is choice an act of the will or of reason?

[¶ 1.] *Objection 1.* It seems that choice is an act of the reason and not of the will, for choice implies a comparison by which we prefer one thing to another. But to compare is a work of reason. Therefore, choice is an act of reason.

[¶ 2.] *Objection 2.* The same power that makes the syllogism draws the conclusion. But to syllogize about practical matters is the function of reason. Since choice in practical matters is like a conclusion, as is stated in VII, *Ethics,* it seems that choice is an act of reason.

[¶ 3.] *Objection 3.* Ignorance is found in the cognitive power, not in the will. Now there is a kind of ignorance in choice, as was said in III, *Ethics.* Therefore, it seems that choice does not belong to the will but to reason.

[¶ 4.] *On the contrary,* the Philosopher says in III, *Ethics* that choice is the desire for things which are in our power to achieve. But desire is an act of the will, therefore, choice is also an act of the will.

[¶ 5.] The name *choice* implies something belonging to reason or the intellect, and something also belonging to the will, for the Philosopher says in VI, *Ethics* that choice is either an appetitive intellect or an intellectual appetite. Now whenever two things come together to form one, one of these is as form in respect to the other. Hence, Gregory of Nyssa says that choice is neither appetite alone nor deliberation alone, but a composite of both, for just as we say that an animal is composed of both body and soul and not of body alone nor of soul alone but of both, so it is with choice. But when considering the acts of the soul, we must keep in mind that the act which belongs essentially to one power or habit receives its form and species from a higher power or habit according as the inferior power is directed by the superior power. If a man performs an act of courage for the love of God, materially, this is an act of fortitude, but formally, an act of charity. Now we can see that reason, in a certain way, acts before the will and specifies its act, insofar as the will tends towards its object according to the direction of reason, because an apprehensive power represents the object to the appetite. Therefore, that act by which the will tends to a thing presented to it as a good, though being ordered to an end by reason, is materially an act of the will, but formally an act of the reason. Now in acts of this kind the substance of the act is a matter in relation to the order which the higher power imposes. Therefore, choice is substantially an act of the will and not of reason, for choice is completed in a movement of the soul toward the good which is chosen. Hence, it is evidently the act of an appetite.

[¶ 6.] *Reply to Objection 1.* Choice implies a previous comparison, but it is not essentially the comparison itself.

[¶ 7.] *Reply to Objection 2.* Reason draws the conclusion in a practical syllogism, and this conclusion, which choice follows, is called a *decision* or *judgment.* Hence the conclusion seems to belong to the act of choice as to a consequence.

[¶ 8.] *Reply to Objection 3.* When we say that there is ignorance in choice, we do not mean that choice itself is a kind of knowledge, but that there is ignorance about what ought to be chosen.

Section C: The Psychology of Habits
No. 1. *The Necessity of Habits*
St. Thomas: *Summa Theologiae,* Part I–II, Question 49, Article 4
Are habits necessary?

[¶ 1.] *Objection 1.* It is by habits that we are well disposed or ill disposed toward something, as has been said (*S.T.,* I–II, 49, 2). But a thing is well disposed or ill disposed by its form, for a thing is good, just as it is being, in virtue of its form. Therefore, there is no need for habits.

[¶ 2.] *Objection 2.* Habit implies a relationship to act. But a *power* sufficiently implies the principle of act, for powers are principles of acts even without habits. Therefore, there is not a need for habits.

[¶ 3.] *Objection 3.* A habit like a power is related to good and evil. But a power does not always act; neither does a habit. Therefore, as long as powers exist, habits are superfluous.

[¶ 4.] *On the contrary,* a habit is a kind of perfection, as is said in the VII, *Physics.* And perfection is most necessary to a thing, since perfection has the nature of an end. Therefore, habits are necessary.

[¶ 5.] As was said above (*S.T.,* I–II, 49, 2 and 3), a habit implies a certain disposition relative to the nature of a thing, and to its operation or end. By means of this disposition a nature becomes well or ill disposed to its operation or end. To have to be disposed towards another thing, there are three requirements. The first requirement is that the thing to be disposed must differ from that to which it is to be disposed, and must be related to it as potency to act. It follows then that if there is a being whose nature is not composed of potency and act, whose substance is its very operation, and whose existence is self contained, such a being has no need of habit or disposition. This is evidently the case in God.

[¶ 6.] The second requirement is that whatever is in potency to something else can be determined in various ways and towards various things. Therefore, if something is in potency to something else and to that only, there is no need of a disposition or habit, because such a subject by its very nature already has the required relationship to its act. So if a heavenly body is composed of matter and form, and the matter is not in potency toward another form, as was said in the first part (*S.T.*, I, 66, 2), it does not need a disposition or habit either in relation to form or even to operation, since the nature of a heavenly body is in potency to only one specific motion.

[¶ 7.] Finally it is required that several things concur in order to dispose the subject to one of those things to which it is in potency. And these things can be adjusted in several ways so as to dispose the subject well or badly to a form or operation. Therefore, the simple qualities of the elements which belong in one determined way to the nature of the elements are not called *dispositions* or *habits,* but *simple qualities.* But we apply the name *disposition* or *habit* to health, beauty, and the like, because they imply an adjustment of various things which can be adjusted in different ways. Because of this, the Philosopher says in V, *Metaphysics* that habit is a disposition, and that a disposition is an order of a thing having parts, according to place, or potentiality, or species, as was said above (*S.T.*, I–II, 49, 1, *ad* 3). Habits are necessary in those many types of beings whose natures and operations require the concurrence of several things which are capable of being adjusted in different ways.

[¶ 8.] *Reply to Objection 1.* Form perfects the nature of a thing, but the subject must receive some disposition relative to the form itself. Form itself is further ordered to operation which is either an end or the means to an end. If the form has only one fixed operation, no other disposition than the form itself is necessary for its operation. But if the form is of such a kind that it can operate in different ways, like the soul, for example, some habits must dispose it to its operations.

[¶ 9.] *Reply to Objection 2.* A power is sometimes in potency to many different objects and therefore must be determined by something else. If there is a power not in potency to many things, it does not require a habit for its determination, as was said before (*S.T.*, I–II, 49, 4). For this reason, natural powers do not perform their operations through the medium of habits, because of themselves, they are determined to one operation.

[¶ 10.] *Reply to Objection 3.* One and the same *habit* is not related to good and evil, as will appear later (*S.T.*, I–II, 54, 3). However, one and the same *power* is related to good or evil. Therefore, habits are necessary in order that these powers be directed toward what is good.

No. 2. The Subject of Habits

St. Thomas: *Summa Theologiae,* Part I–II, Question 50, Article 2

Is the soul the subject of habits by reason of its essence or by reason of its powers?

[¶ 1.] *Objection 1.* We speak of dispositions and habits in relation to a nature, as has been said (*S.T.,* I–II, 49, 3). But nature is identified more with the essence of the soul than with its powers, for according to its essence the soul is the nature of such a body and also its form. Therefore, habits are in the soul according to its essence, not its powers.

[¶ 2.] *Objection 2.* There is not an accident of an accident. Now a habit is a certain kind of accident. But the powers of the soul, too, belong to the genus of accident, as was said in the first part (*S.T.,* I, 77, 1). Therefore, habit is not in the soul by reason of its powers.

[¶ 3.] *Objection 3.* The subject is prior to what is in the subject. Since habit is in the first species of quality, it is prior to the powers which are in the second species. Therefore, powers of the soul are not the subjects of habits.

[¶ 4.] *On the contrary,* the Philosopher in I, *Ethics* maintains that there are different habits in different parts of the soul.

[¶ 5.] As is said above (*S.T.,* I–II, 49, 2 and 3), habit entails a certain disposition in relation to nature or to operation. If we take habit in relation to nature, it cannot exist in the soul, that is, if we are speaking of human nature, for the soul itself is the form which perfects human nature. Therefore, according to this conception a habit or disposition can exist more readily in a body because of its ordering to the soul, than in the soul because of its ordering to the body. But relative to some higher nature of which man may be a participator, as is said in II, *Peter,* Chapter 1, "That we may become partakers of the divine nature," it is possible for some habit, namely grace, to exist in the soul according to its essence, as we shall show later. (*S.T.,* I–II, 110, 4.)

[¶ 6.] But a habit which is concerned with operation particularly belongs to the soul because the soul is not predetermined to one operation but to many. This is a condition for habit, as we have said above (*S.T.,* I–II, 49, 4). Therefore, since the soul, as a principle, operates through its powers, habits belong to the soul according to its powers.

[¶ 7.] *Reply to Objection 1.* The essence of the soul belongs to human nature not as a subject to be disposed to something else, but as a form and nature to which another is disposed.

[¶ 8.] *Reply to Objection 2.* In itself an accident cannot directly be the subject of another accident. But since among the accidents themselves there is a certain order, a subject by the fact that it has one accident is understood to be the subject of another accident. In this way, we say that one accident is the subject of another, for example, surface is the subject of color. Thus, also a power can be a subject of habit.

[¶ 9.] *Reply to Objection 3.* A habit is prior to a power as it implies a disposition to the nature, whereas a power always implies a relation to operation which is posterior, since nature is the principle of operation. But a habit whose subject is a power does not imply a relation to the nature but to its operation. Therefore, it is posterior to the power. Or we may hold that a habit is prior to a power as the complete is to the incomplete, or as act to potency. This is because actuality is by nature prior to potentiality, although potentiality is prior in the order of generation and time, as is said in VII and IX, *Metaphysics.*

No. 3. How Habits Can Be in the Sensory Powers of the Soul
St. Thomas: *Summa Theologiae*, Part I–II, Question 50, Article 3
Can there be habits in the powers of the sensory part of the soul?

[¶ 1.] *Objection 1.* The sensory powers like the power of nutrition are irrational. But no habit can be formed in the power of nutrition. Therefore, there are no habits in the powers of the sensory part of the soul.

[¶ 2.] *Objection 2.* Sensory powers are common to us and to brute animals. But there are no habits in brute animals, because they have no will, which enters into the definition of habit, as was said above (*S.T.*, I–II, 49, 3). Therefore, there are no habits in the sensory powers.

[¶ 3.] *Objection 3.* The habits of the soul are the sciences and the virtues; and as science is related to the apprehensive power, so virtue is related to the appetitive power. But there are no sciences in the sensory powers, because science deals with universals, which the sense powers cannot apprehend. Therefore, there cannot be habits of virtue in the sensory parts of the soul.

[¶ 4.] *On the contrary,* the Philosopher says in III, *Ethics* that some virtues, namely temperance and fortitude, are in the irrational parts of the soul.

[¶ 5.] We can look at the sense powers in two ways. First, as they act from natural impulse, and second, as they act under the rule of reason. Insofar as they act by natural impulse, they are ordered to one thing just as nature is. Therefore, just as there are no habits in natural powers, so there are none in the sense powers insofar as they operate from natural impulse. Insofar as they operate under the rule of reason, they can be ordered to diverse things. In this way, there can be habits in them by which they are well or ill disposed towards something.

[¶ 6.] *Reply to Objection 1.* The powers of nutrition do not have the innate capacity to obey the command of reason, and, therefore, there are no habits in them. But the sensitive powers do have the innate capacity to obey the rule of reason. Therefore, there can be habits in them, for insofar as they obey reason, we may call them to that extent *rational,* as is said in I, *Ethics.*

[¶ 7.] *Reply to Objection 2.* The sensitive powers of brute animals do not act under the command of reason. If brute animals are left to themselves, they act from natural impulse. Thus, in brute animals there are no habits ordered to operations, although they do have some dispositions relative to nature, such as health and beauty. But because man through his reason can dispose brute animals by a certain kind of conditioning to do something in this or that way, we can attribute habits to them in this sense. This is why Augustine says *(Book of Eighty-three Topics):* "We observe the wildest beasts abstaining from their greatest pleasures because of fear of pain. And if they become accustomed to this, we call them tame and gentle." But the essence of habit is lacking, as to the use of the will, because they do not have the control of use or nonuse, which belongs to the notion of habit. Therefore, properly speaking, they cannot have habits.

[¶ 8.] *Reply to Objection 3.* The sense appetite has a natural tendency to be moved by the rational appetite, as we said in Book III, *On the Soul;* but the rational powers of apprehension have a natural capacity to receive from the sense powers. Therefore, habits belong more to the sensitive appetitive powers than to the sensitive powers of apprehension, since, there are no habits in the sensitive appetitive powers except insofar as they operate under the rule of reason. We can even say that in the internal sensitive apprehensive powers there are habits, by which man remembers well, cogitates well, or imagines well. Hence, the Philosopher says in a chapter of the book, *On Memory and Recall,*[45] that repetition develops a good memory. This is because even these powers are set in operation by the command of reason. On the other hand, the external powers of apprehension, such as sight, hearing, and the rest, are not receptive of any habits, but are ordered to their own determined acts according to the disposition of their nature.

---

[45] *De Memoria et Reminiscentia.*

Nor do the members of a body have habits, but rather the powers which command their movements.

No. 4. *The Formation of Habits*
St. Thomas: *Summa Theologiae,* Part I–II, Question 51, Article 3
Can a habit be caused by one act?

[¶ 1.] *Objection 1.* Demonstration is an act of reason; but one demonstration causes science, which is a habit through one conclusion. Therefore, a habit can be caused by one act.

[¶ 2.] *Objection 2.* Just as acts can increase by multiplication, so they can increase by intensity. But the multiplication of an act generates a habit; therefore, if one act has great intensity, it too will be able to generate a habit.

[¶ 3.] *Objection 3.* Health and sickness are habits. But it is possible that one act may either heal a man or make him sick. Therefore, one act can cause a habit.

[¶ 4.] *On the contrary,* the Philosopher in I, *Ethics* says that just as one swallow or one day does not make spring, so neither does one day nor a short time make a man blessed or happy. But happiness is an operation according to a habit of perfect virtue, as is said in I, *Ethics.* Therefore, one act does not cause a habit of virtue, nor, for the same reason, any other habit.

[¶ 5.] As we have already mentioned (*S.T.,* I–II, 51, 2), a habit is caused by act insofar as a passive power is moved by some active principle. Now to have some quality generated in a passive power the active principle must entirely gain control of the passive principle. For example, we see that a fire which cannot consume what is combustible immediately does not cause it to burst into flames immediately, but by getting rid of the contrary dispositions little by little, thus totally gaining control over it, it imposes its likeness on it.

[¶ 6.] It is evident that the active principle which is reason cannot entirely gain control of the appetitive power in one act, for the appetitive power is inclined in different ways and to many things, whereas reason in one act judges that something is desirable according to particular conditions and circumstances. Therefore, the appetitive power is not totally overcome to such an extent that it is effectively directed to the same thing in most cases, after the fashion of nature. This belongs to a habit of virtue. For this reason a habit of virtue cannot be caused by one act but requires many.

[¶ 7.] In the powers of apprehension we must consider two passive principles. One, the possible intellect; the other, the intellect which Aristotle calls *passive,* that is, the *particular reason* or the cogitative power along with memory and imagination. In regard to this first passivity, some active principle can in one act entirely overcome the potentiality of this passive principle. Thus, one self-evident proposition forces the intellect to assent firmly to a conclusion. A probable proposition, however, does not do this. Therefore, many acts of reason are necessary to cause a habit of opinion, even with regard to the possible intellect. One act of reason, however, can bring about a habit of science, as far as the possible intellect is concerned. But with respect to the lower apprehensive powers the same acts must be repeated many times in order that something be firmly imprinted on the memory. For this reason the Philosopher says in his book *On Memory and Recall,* that meditation strengthens the memory. One act, too, can bring about bodily habits, if the active principle has great strength. For example, a strong medicine often restores health at once.

[¶ 8.] Therefore, the solutions to the objections are evident.

No. 5. The Increase of Habits
St. Thomas: *Summa Theologiae,* Part I–II, Question 52, Article 3
Does every act increase a habit?

[¶ 1.] *Objection 1.* If a cause is repeated, so are its effects. Now acts are the cause of some habits, as has been said above (*S.T.,* I–II, 51, 2). Therefore, habit increases by the repetition of its acts.

[¶ 2.] *Objection 2.* About like things there is a like judgment. But all acts proceeding from the same habit are alike, as is said in II, *Ethics.* Therefore, if some acts increase a habit, any act will increase it.

[¶ 3.] *Objection 3.* Like is increased by its like. But any act is similar to the habit from which it proceeds. Therefore, any act increases habit.

[¶ 4.] *On the contrary,* one and the same thing is not the cause of contraries. But, as is said in II, *Ethics,* some acts diminish the habit from which they proceed, namely, if they are performed carelessly. Therefore, not every act increases habit.

[¶ 5.] It is true that like acts cause like habits, as is said in II, *Ethics.* Likeness and unlikeness come not only from the sameness or difference of quality, but also from sameness or difference in their mode of participation, for not only is black different from white but also the less white is different from the more white, since there is movement from the less white to the more white, as from one opposite to another, as is said in V, *Physics*.

[¶ 6.] But the use of habit is dependent upon the will, as was shown before (*S.T.*, I–II, 49, 3; and I–II, 50, 5). And just as one who has a habit may not use it, or may perform an act contrary to it, so he may use the habit for an act which is not in proportion to the intensity of the habit. Therefore, if the intensity of an act is in proportion to the intensity of a habit or else exceeds it, such an act either increases the habit or disposes it to growth, if we may use an analogy here and compare the growth of a habit to the growth of an animal. For not every bit of food makes the animal actually grow, nor does each drop of water make a hole in stone, but repeated eating finally results in growth. Likewise, if acts are repeated, a habit grows. If, however, the intensity of the act is not proportionate to the intensity of the habit, such an act does not dispose the habit to growth, but rather to weakening.

[¶ 6.] From these remarks the responses to the objections are evident.

No. 6. *The Decline of Habits*
St. Thomas: *Summa Theologiae*, Part I–II, Question 53, Article 3
Is a habit broken or weakened by not exercising it?

[¶ 1.] *Objection 1.* Habits are not broken or weakened merely by not using them, because habits are more permanent than changeable qualities, as is evident from what has been said (*S.T.*, I–II, 49, 3). But changeable qualities are not destroyed or weakened merely by discontinuance of an act. For example, whiteness is not lessened if it does not act upon the power of sight, nor is heat lessened if it does not warm anything. Therefore, neither are habits broken or weakened by not exercising them.

[¶ 2.] *Objection 2.* The breaking and weakening of habits are kinds of change. But nothing is changed without some moving cause. Since, therefore, not using the habit does not imply any moving cause, it does not seem that ceasing to perform the act can weaken or break a habit.

[¶ 3.] *Objection 3.* The habits of science and virtue belong to the intellectual soul which is above time. The passage of time does not weaken or destroy what is above time. Therefore, neither does the passage of time weaken or break such habits, if they are not exercised for a rather long time.

[¶ 4.] *On the contrary,* the Philosopher says (*On the Length and Shortness of Life,*[46] Chapter 2) that not only is deception a corruption of science, but so is forgetfulness. And in VIII, *Ethics* he says that lack of communication destroys many friendships. For the same reason some habits of virtue are weakened or destroyed by not exercising them.

[¶ 5.] As was stated in VIII, *Physics,* a thing may be a cause of movement in two ways. First, *per se,* as an agent causes motion by means of its own form; in this way fire causes heat. Second, *per accidens,* as an agent removes an obstacle. It is in this latter way that ceasing to perform the act causes the destruction or weakening of habits, for this removes the act which offsets those causes that destroy or weaken a habit. For we said (*S.T.,* I–II, 53, 2) that habits are *per se* destroyed or weakened by contrary agents. Consequently, since the contrary of any habit is gradually undermining that habit, it must be counteracted by an act proceeding from the habit. Failure to exercise this act over a long period of time may weaken or totally destroy habits of this kind, as we see in the case of both science and virtue. It is evident that a habit of moral virtue disposes man to a prompt choice of the mean in his moral acts and the use of his passions. When, however, someone does not use the habit of virtue to moderate his passions or his actions, many of those acts and passions elude the control of virtue because of the inclinations of the sensitive appetites and other external causes. Therefore, failure to exercise a virtue weakens or destroys it.

[¶ 6.] The same thing is true of intellectual habits, which dispose man to make a prompt and correct judgment of the forms in his imagination. Hence, when someone ceases to use his intellectual habits, extraneous forms arise in the imagination and sometimes lead him to acts opposed to the habit. So that unless frequent use of his intellectual habits destroy or suppress these extraneous imaginings, a man becomes less capable of making right judgments and sometimes is totally disposed to the contrary. Thus, ceasing to perform the acts weakens or even destroys an intellectual habit.

[¶ 7.] *Reply to Objection 1.* Even heat would be destroyed by ceasing to emit heat, if through this, cold, which is destructive of heat, should increase.

[¶ 8.] *Reply to Objection 2.* Cessation from act is the agent cause of the corruption or weakening of habits, by removing the act that offsets the causes that destroy or weaken a habit, as we said above.

[¶ 9.] *Reply to Objection 3.* The intellectual part of the soul is itself above time but the sensitive part is subject to time. Therefore, by the passage of time there is a change in the passions of the appetitive part of the soul and also in the powers of apprehension. Hence, in IV, *Physics* the Philosopher says that time is the cause of forgetfulness.

---

[46] *De Longitudine et Brevitate Vitae.*

PART IV

THE NATURE OF THE HUMAN SOUL
AND THE ORIGIN OF MAN

Though his universal *methodological doubt** might incline the reader of the *Discourse on Method* to feel that at the beginning of his philosophy Descartes was a skeptic, he was really an optimist all along. He thought that anyone could, by employing a correct method and common sense, attain immediately to a clear and distinct knowledge about the nature of the human soul. From this supposedly clear intuitive knowledge of the nature of the soul, other truths about the nature of man could follow with the same clarity and distinctness. When Aristotle, on the contrary, defined the soul in his introductory work, *On the Soul*, he said that the soul was one of the most difficult things in the world to have any assurance about.

In the preceding parts of this work, we have tried to clarify the general definition of the soul given by Aristotle, but we should recognize the limitations of the knowledge that can be achieved purely on the grounds of reason. Not only should we be aware of the limitations of our philosophic investigation, but we should also keep that knowledge distinct from what we know about the soul on grounds of religious faith. Ultimately, this knowledge of the nature of the soul will remain obscure, in spite of the certainty of the premises of our science and the necessity of the conclusions drawn from them. Nevertheless, we feel that we are able to say something from the preceding study to infer some truths about the essential nature of the human soul.

In the following pages, we shall undertake, first of all, to state the philosophical proofs for the *spirituality*,* the *subsistence*,* the *simplicity*,* and the *immortality** of the human soul. After that, we shall take up the origin of the human soul. Finally, we shall discuss some of the philosophical principles involved in the theory of evolution, especially as it touches on the origin of the human body.

The Spirituality of the Human Soul (Readings: IV, No. 1)

The most direct and forceful proof for the spirituality of the human soul is the one that argues from the existence of spiritual operations and powers to the existence of a spiritual substantial principle.

We argue, first, to the spiritual operation of the soul from the fact that the intellect and will have as their objects universal truth and good. We have seen that these objects are spiritual because they are beyond the conditions of time and space that characterize all material entities. Since these objects are spiritual, the powers capable of apprehending them must also be spiritual. It would be no easier to grasp a spiritual entity like *honesty* with a mind constituted of matter, and no more foolish to seek it with a will constituted of matter, than it would be to pursue and catch *honesty* with a butterfly net. Spiritual forms and goals are not attained by corporeal powers.

The next step in the argument consists in showing the need of a spiritual substantial principle in which these powers reside as in their natural subject. Since the powers are properties of the soul, as we have seen in one of the introductory parts, they are not independent substances, but exist in the soul which operates by means of them. As properties of the soul, the intellect and will act only in virtue of the first principle of their being. Either the spiritual powers themselves are substantial principles, and, therefore, are originative sources of activity, or they belong to a more fundamental substantial principle which operates through them. But the powers of the soul are not individual substances because man is one substance, not many. Hence, his spiritual powers, as well as the other powers of the soul, belong to one substantial principle. Because the substantial principle must be equal in perfection to what proceeds from it as a property, it follows that the rational soul is a spiritual substantial principle.

Whatever can operate as a spiritual principle must also exist as a spiritual principle—for the operations of any nature follow upon its being. To operate as a spirit means to exist as a spirit; hence, the human soul has the nature of a spiritual substance and can exist apart from matter. St. Thomas draws this conclusion:

> Therefore, the intellectual principle, called mind or intellect, operates of itself, an operation in which the body does not share. However,

nothing can operate by itself unless it subsists in itself, for there is no operation except of a being in act. Hence, the mode of being determines the way it operates. This is why we do not say that heat gives heat, but that what is hot gives heat. We conclude, therefore, that the human soul, called intellect or mind, is incorporeal and subsistent.[1]

The Subsistence of the Human Soul (Readings: IV, No. 2)

Subsistence, according to the statement of St. Thomas, follows as a corollary of the soul's spiritual nature. Therefore, the human soul can exist without the body.

Since, however, the human soul is not a complete essence without the body, neither is it a completely subsistent being without the body, at least not in the same sense that subsistence is attributed to a human person. For in the complete meaning of subsistence, the existent being is autonomous and complete. Therefore, in speaking of the human soul, we should say that it is a substantial principle which has subsistence, rather than a substance which is a subsistent being.

In the order of definition as well as in the order of natural activity, the soul depends on the body; thus, the relationship to body is established in terms of substance. The use which the soul makes of the body, however, does not prove that the soul's activities must remain within the limits of matter. The soul, for example, makes use of sensory knowledge in all intellectual knowledge, but the activity of understanding, although it begins in sensory experience, does not remain there. A bird uses the earth, a house top, or a branch to begin its flight, but does not use them in actual flight; neither does the soul, which begins its act of understanding in sensory experience, employ the sensory experience as an essential instrument in the process of understanding.

The Simplicity of the Human Soul

From the subsistent nature of the human soul, we can infer its simplicity. By *simplicity* of substance, we understand the absence of any composition in essence of matter and form, and the absence of all integral and quantitative parts. That the human soul does not have physical composition follows from its subsistent spiritual nature. To inquire whether there is a matter-form union in the substance of the soul is to revive the question of whether the soul has a soul, and so

---

[1] St. Thomas: *Summa Theologiae*, I, 75, 2, Body of the Article.

on *ad infinitum*. Once we are sure that the soul can operate independently of matter, we can be sure that matter is not included in its existence and, therefore, is not included in its definition specifically as soul.

It can be shown also, even though this conclusion follows from what has already been said, that there is no composition in the soul of integral or quantitative parts. The act of self-consciousness excludes composition of this kind. It is the nature of integral and quantitative parts to be extended in space, like the organs of the body. These parts cannot by means of consciousness turn back completely upon themselves and upon their acts, as the human intellect evidently does. The intellect can know itself, can know that it knows, can know the act of knowing by which it knows itself. This is precisely the act of consciousness. Therefore, the spiritual soul in which the intellect resides is a simple, spiritual, substantial principle and does not include matter in its definition, either as a matter-form composition, or as integral or quantitative parts. It includes matter only obliquely, that is, insofar as the soul is the substantial form of the organic body having life in potency.

St. Thomas argues to the simplicity of the soul also from the fact that in the act of knowing it does not receive forms as matter receives them, namely, as individualized. He says:

It is evident that whatever is received in something else is received there according to the manner of being of the recipient. Thus, each and every thing is known in the way that form is present in the knower. Now the intellectual soul knows a thing in its nature in an absolute sense; for example, it knows a stone as stone taken absolutely. The form of stone, therefore, is in the intellectual soul in an absolute sense, that is, according to its formal notion as stone. The intellectual soul itself, consequently, is an absolute form and not a composite of matter and form. For if it were composed of matter and form, the intellectual soul would receive forms of things into itself as individualized. It would know, therefore, only individuals, as do the sensory powers, which receive the forms of things into a corporeal organ, for matter is the principle by which forms are individuated. It follows, then, that the intellectual soul and every intellectual substance which knows form absolutely must be without a composition of matter and form.[2]

_____

[2] St. Thomas: *Summa Theologiae*, I, 75, 5, Body of the Article.

The Immortality of the Human Soul (Readings: IV, No. 3)

After demonstrating that the human soul is spiritual, subsistent, and simple, we come to the question of whether the soul is immortal. We define immortality as the property of an individual, living, substantial form to persevere in unending existence without corruption. Thus, immortality is more than preservation of the species by natural reproduction; and it is more than a pantheistic absorption, of which some poets and philosophers speak, of man's spirit into an unending existence in the power of nature. By immortality we understand that the soul of each person, as an individualized form, will survive in an unending and incorruptible existence after the corruption of the body. This is the definition of *personal immortality,* which is proved by the following argument:

It remains, therefore, that the human soul is incorruptible. There are two signs of this: first, on the part of the intellect, for we see that things which are in themselves corruptible, according as they are apprehended by the intellect, are incorruptible, for the intellect apprehends things in a universal concept, and in this mode they are not subject to corruption; second, on the part of the natural appetite, which cannot be frustrated. For we see in man a desire for eternal existence. This is reasonable, for existence of itself is desirable, and an intelligent being who apprehends existence in an absolute sense and not merely the here and now, must desire existence absolutely and for all time. Hence it is clear that this desire is not in vain, but that man according to his intellectual soul, is incorruptible.[3]

By returning to the same argument which he used to prove the spirituality, subsistence, and simplicity of the human soul, St. Thomas can show that the soul is immortal because it must have the same mode of existence that it confers upon its objects, that is, an incorruptible existence, like that which is given to universal ideas. For natural forms, insofar as they exist in matter as individuals, are corruptible. By being received into the soul they are given a mode of permanence, because they are removed from the conditions of matter which make them corruptible. Since a nature operates in the measure of its own being, and since the soul is the principle of the incorruptibility of intellectual operations, it, too, must be incorruptible.

---

[3] St. Thomas: *Disputed Question On the Soul,* Article 14, Body of the Article.

The second of the two arguments, namely, the desire for eternal existence, is, under one aspect, more pertinent to ethics than to psychology. The argument proceeds from the natural desire for happiness to the existence of the object of the desire. From another point of view, however, the argument belongs properly to psychology, because the weight of the argument rests on the relationship of the will to universal knowledge in the intellect. St. Thomas says that existence can be apprehended by the intellect in an absolute sense. Existence is the kind of good that is absolute, for it is another name for being. And since being and good are different aspects of the same thing, it follows that absolute existence is an absolute good. Absolute existence, then, will attract the will as infallibly as the absolute or universal good. This is basically the same argument that St. Thomas used to prove the immortality of the soul, with this difference, that a new relationship in the will is added to the universal knowledge by the intellect.

AN INCOMPLETE ARGUMENT FOR IMMORTALITY

Some authors give an argument for the immortality of soul based upon its simplicity. It proceeds in this way: A substantial change presupposes a composition of matter and form and terminates in the corruption of the original substance. Now if the human soul is a simple substance, it evidently cannot undergo substantial change and, therefore, cannot corrupt. Since it cannot corrupt, it will necessarily continue in existence, once it has existence. This argument, however, has only partial validity apart from the proof of immortality based upon the spirituality of the soul. Any complete proof for immortality depends positively upon the possibility of subsistence of the soul apart from matter. Simplicity of itself gives a basis only for saying that the soul cannot undergo substantial change and corruption, but not that it cannot pass out of existence instantaneously. In other words, the argument from simplicity is fully valid only if it is joined to the argument from the soul's spirituality and subsistence.

The Origin of the Human Soul

One of the problems that philosophers have always been interested in is that of the origin of the human soul. It is, indeed, not one single problem but a complexity of problems. It includes, for example, the problem of whether the soul came into existence through direct creation from nothing; it touches upon the problem of the soul's *pre-existence* * as well as the possibility of its *reincarnation* * and *transmigration;* * and it also poses the very involved problem of *evolution.* *

THE HUMAN SOUL IS NOT GENERATED, BUT CREATED
(READINGS: IV, NO. 4)

Because it is a spiritual principle, the human soul cannot be generated the way natural forms are. As St. Thomas shows, a substance comes into existence in a way that corresponds to the kind of existence that it will have, since *coming to be* terminates in *existence*. A spiritual substance does not have parts; there is no matter-form union in it. Consequently, the conditions for origin through generation are not present; the soul, therefore, must come into existence instantaneously.

The cogency of the argument for a direct creation of the human soul depends upon the validity of the proof of the essential superiority of the human soul over the soul of brute animals. Unless it is shown that the soul acts as a spiritual principle, it is impossible to prove by philosophic argument that the soul of man does not evolve from some other animal soul. An evolutionary development of the human soul would be, indeed, very plausible if there were only an accidental difference between the kind of a soul that brute animals have and the kind that man has.

To deny the essential superiority of intellectual soul over the sensory soul means that we shall have to accept one or another of the following statements: either man is in the same category as irrational animals, (with the qualification that he is accidentally superior); or all animals are rational (with the qualification that they are not as intelligent as man). But we have already shown that neither of these statements is acceptable, for man is not merely the most skilled of animals, nor are other animals simply less rational than man. The human soul, therefore, has no essential continuity with the soul of the irrational animal and cannot be generated.

St. Thomas' argument in the *Summa Theologiae,* for creation of the human soul proceeds as follows:

The rational soul cannot come to be except by creation, which is not true of other forms. The reason for this is that "becoming" is the way to existence, and hence the way that a thing comes to be must correspond to the way in which it exists. Most properly a thing is said to exist which itself has being, as if subsisting in its own being. Therefore, only substances are properly and truly beings. Forms which do not subsist do not properly come to be, but they are said to come to be when the subsistent composite comes to be. Now the rational soul is a subsistent form. Therefore, it has its own proper *to be* and *coming to be*. And since it cannot come to be from pre-existing matter, neither from corporeal matter, because thus it would be a corporeal nature, nor from spiritual matter, because this would entail transferring one spiritual substance into another, we must conclude that it cannot come into existence except by creation.[4]

PRE-EXISTENCE IS INCOMPATIBLE WITH THE NATURE OF THE SOUL (READINGS: IV, NO. 5)

The pre-existence of the soul was held by some early philosophers, not only by Platonists but also by some early Christian writers. St. Augustine, for example, held the opinion that man's soul was created at the same time as the angels, but that his body was produced much later, when the *seminal causes* * implanted in the original creation had developed sufficiently to sustain the human soul. In St. Augustine's view, it is true, the human soul could not have been constituted from a seminal principle as corporeal things were, but must have been created immediately by God at the moment other spiritual substances were created. However, in his opinion, the soul existed separately until it was substantially united to the human body at a later time. This was a view which St. Augustine qualified as a probable opinion.

This doctrine of pre-existence is incompatible with the Aristotelian matter-form conception of human nature. If the human soul were a complete essence and acted in the body only as an administrator, there would be no intrinsic reason why the soul could not pre-exist. But the soul is only a co-principle with the body. Together with the body, it forms one substance and has one existence. Therefore, the soul begins to exist when it is joined to the body which is its subject. The body, made of signate matter, is its principle of individuation. Since only individuals have real existence, the soul as the natural form of the human body begins to exist when it informs a particular organic body having life in potency.

The fact of the soul's survival after death does not vitiate this position, because once the soul has existence as a subsistent form, it cannot corrupt or pass out of existence. Once the function of the body as a principle of individuation has been carried out, the body is not needed for subsistence.

---

[4] St. Thomas: *Summa Theologiae,* I, 90, 2, Body of the Article.

The Origin of the Human Body (Readings: IV, No. 6)

Though the human soul cannot come into existence by an evolutionary process, there remains the question of the origin of the human body. In trying to answer this question the philosopher should set down two qualifications for any philosophical point of view: first, the discussion is not a historical one, since it is not in his province to say what actually took place (this is the task of the theologian, and perhaps, in another respect, of the anthropologist); second, the question of the origin of the soul must be kept distinct from that of the origin of the human body, because distinct philosophical principles are to be applied in each case.

For the philosopher, the problem of the evolution of the human body is essentially one of causality: Is there in nature a causality capable of developing an organism from a lower to a higher species until the kind of body is produced that it can be inhabited by the human soul? In its usual form, it is a question of efficient causality only. Thus, many philosophers deny the possibility of the origin of the human body through evolution, because they hold that it is impossible for a lower species to be the efficient cause of a higher one. These philosophers do not envisage movement in nature as a process which involves above all, final causality. They limit their discussion to the question of efficient causality, and they do so within a static conception of nature.

THE DOCTRINE OF EVOLUTION AND THOMISTIC PHILOSOPHY

It is a mistake to suppose that the philosophy of St. Thomas is uncongenial to the theory of organic evolution. To some philosophers, the doctrine of "forms" appears as an obstacle to the theory of evolution, because they cannot see how the lower form can develop into a higher, nor can they overlook what would appear to be a kind of suicidal tendency of forms, that is, a tendency to self destruction in an evolutionary process. This view does not take into account the fertile possibilities of explanation in the doctrine of prime matter. The concept of prime matter is an ideal situation for the passage from one kind of form to another, not only within the same species but within the whole order of corporeal substantial forms. The continuity of prime matter throughout the physical order makes plausible the continuity of one species with another.

Thus, the doctrine of evolution can be easily related to the doctrine of generation and corruption. As we know from the study of the general principles of the philosophy of nature, generation and corruption occur because all natural beings are composed of matter and form. Prime matter, as indeterminate potency, is of itself ordered to all kinds of natural corporeal forms and does not tend to a permanent union with any specific type of natural form. Since prime matter is in potency to all these forms, it is not necessary to introduce *a creative act in the strict sense* at each stage of substantial change, for the corruption of one substantial form brings forth a new substantial form from the potency of matter. Until the point where a spiritual substantial form exists, the movement from one type of substantial form to another might possibly be explained within the framework of the potentialities of this principle of nature and of final causality.

MAN: THE GOAL OF ALL NATURAL STRIVING

The process of generation and corruption is not for the sake of itself; change simply for the sake of change is not reasonable. Every movement of a potency tends towards something other than itself, as we know from an analysis of change. The generation of mobile beings, therefore, is ordered towards something else. All movement must begin from something immobile and tend towards something immobile. But the only immobile form in nature is the spiritual soul of man. Consequently, the whole movement of the potency of prime matter, through the series of substantial changes, seems ultimately to point to the existence of man within nature. The natural appetite of prime matter cannot be satisfied with anything less.

THE PRIMACY OF THE FINAL CAUSE

In the building of a house, the final cause, the goal at which the architect aims, is the cause which determines all other causes that enter into the building process and the finished product. Is the house to be built of stone or bricks or wood? Is it to be ranch style or chalet? Will the builders be carpenters, bricklayers, or stone masons? The plan in the mind of the architect will determine all these. Likewise, in nature, there is a plan which corresponds to that of the architect. In this plan the final cause of the material universe is the existence of man, because nature has no meaning except as ordered to man. Stones, stars, roses, spiders, and horses, and all things of the physical universe have no meaning without man, because they are ordered to the existence of man as knowing and loving his Creator naturally and supernaturally. Of all the beings in the physical universe only man can contemplate the world and direct his will to its First Cause. Man is, therefore, the goal of all natural striving. All animate and inanimate things fulfill their purpose in creation only when man has taken his place among them.

Since man is the end toward which nature is directed, the philosopher should not examine the various causes in nature as though they operate as isolated and independent units, repeating over and over again, without any higher purpose than themselves, a kind of activity that tends to go nowhere. Nature is not like a stream of water which turns a water wheel in a monotonous motion, as though that is all that it can do and as if that were its only goal. On the contrary, nature is like water that turns a turbine, to make electricity, which eventually lights up and heats the homes of men.

EVOLUTION AS A WORK OF DIVINE WISDOM

The evolutionary conception of the origin of the human body need not prescind from the direction of a Supreme Architect. To deny evolution simply because it "seems" to support agnostic and atheistic doctrine is really to accept the position of the adversaries, namely, to suppose that there is no inner harmony and dependence, no common striving to a predetermined goal. In the broad view of St. Thomas, a universe in which all beings are hierarchically ordained to a common end, and one in which divine wisdom uses all beings in accordance with their natures as instruments in a common work of divine art, is a greater work of creation than one in which there is no such plan. It is the mark of greater wisdom and power to use a series of intermediary causes to accomplish a work than to do the work in a single act, for in the employment of subordinate causes the wisdom and power and goodness of the superior agent are diffused.

The objection is raised that essential forms are inexorably fixed, since they are like numbers that cannot be converted into any other number. This objection would hold if forms were to be thought of in isolation, as abstracted ideas, without respect to the subject in which they must exist. But natural forms are not complete substances. Hence, a form cannot be isolated from the matter with which it constitutes one substance. Since matter is the principle of mobility, then forms, too, participate in the mobility of their subject.

Left to itself, human reason could never prove positively that the human body is evolved from less perfect natural beings, but reason can offer a plausible theory of the development of organic bodies through evolution. It seems reasonable that man should not appear on earth without a continuity with the past, without attachment to his environment, and without causal relationships with other beings which, like man himself, help make up the changing physical universe. The problem is not one of the origin of something spiritual in a world of matter, but of whether the highest form in nature was inserted suddenly and abruptly without any visible preparation. It is not a question of whether man's appearance on earth is the proper effect of the material causes operating in nature, for material nature is not capable of lifting itself up to the level of thought. It is a question only of the continuity of man's physical nature with the past and with his environment.

THE ROLE OF CONTINGENCY IN EVOLUTION

In stating the philosophical theory of evolution, we should not think that matter always seeks determinately this or that form at every stage of development. There is in the physical universe a *contingency* * that excludes a wholly necessary and predetermined evolution in its proximate causes. Chance cannot be excluded from nature without destroying nature as we know it, that is, as a principle that attains its goal *ut in pluribus* (for the most part). Due account must be taken of chance. Chance, however, does not destroy an over-all direction in nature, since the First Cause is the cause of contingent causes and events as well as of necessary causes and events. The investigation of this contingent process demands the methods of the experimental sciences in cooperation with the methods of philosophy. On this point only the general lines of the theory of evolution fall within the scope of what we usually call philosophy.

One author who is favorably inclined towards this philosophical theory of evolution, A. D. Sertillanges, O.P.,[5] says that we do not give the statement, "Matter was made for mind," the depth of meaning it should have. Many understand it simply in the sense that matter is made to serve mind, as the fruit of the garden is made for our use. But the service of matter to mind has another vitally important function, for it serves our "makeup" and conditions our being. The conditioning of our being by matter affects even the level of our spiritual personality, since what in us lives, feels, and thinks is the human composite in its entirety, and not merely one of its elements alone, whether that be matter or spirit. The condition of our spirit is so bound up with that of matter that we must view them as con-

---

[5] Antonin Gilbert Sertillanges: *L'Idée de Création,* Aubier, Editions Mongaigne, Paris, 1945.

stituting one single whole in the essential order, and should perhaps
in the genetic order constitute one single history.

Conclusion: Made to God's Image

Once we are inclined to accept the relationship of matter to spirit,
we are better able to understand that spirit can enter the world without altering the course of phenomena, since the course of nature tends
to the appearance of man and has no *raison d'être* without him.   This
conception procures for man his true place in the general harmony
of the universe and its history.   Conditioned by the evolution of nature,
man finds in it, biologically speaking, the explanation of his existence.
Because nature is made for him, it is man who in the last analysis
explains nature.   Genesis must not be confused with finality, nor the
order inverted.   In the genetic order, efficient cause is first; but in
the order of causes, the final cause is the first cause.   If nature is our
mother insofar as our biological nature is concerned, nature is, nevertheless, dependent on the idea of man's coming to be.   God would
not have created heaven and earth if He had not first thought, "Let
us make man to our own image and likeness."

Bibliography for Part IV

Dufault, Lucien: "The Philosophical and Biological Implications of Evolution."
  Proceedings of the American Catholic Philosophical Association, Volume XXVI, 66–80.

Gruender, Hubert: *Psychology Without a Soul.*
  St. Louis: B. Herder, 1912.

Luyten, Norbert: "Philosophical Implications of Evolution."
  The New Scholasticism, Volume XXV, 290–312.

Reany, William: *The Creation of the Human Soul.*
  New York: Benziger Brothers, 1932.

READINGS FOR PART IV

No. 1. The Spirituality of the Human Soul
St. Thomas: *Summa Contra Gentiles,* Book II, Chapter 49
An intellectual substance is not a body.

[¶ 1.] A body contains something only according to the measure of quantity. Consequently, if a body contains some whole entirely, it will contain a part in a part, the greater in the greater, the smaller in the smaller. Now the intellect does not comprehend its object through some measure of quantity, since in the whole itself it understands and comprehends the whole and the part, the greater and smaller in quantity. Therefore, no intellectual substance is a body.

[¶ 2.] Moreover, no body can receive the substantial form of another body without losing its own form through corruption. But the intellect is perfected rather than corrupted when it receives the forms of all bodies, for to understand, which means having the forms of things understood in the intellect, is to be perfected. Therefore, no intellectual substance is a body.

[¶ 3.] Likewise, the principle of the diversity of individuals within a species is the division of matter according to quantity; one form of fire differs from another only because they are in the diverse parts into which matter is divided. For matter can only be divided by division of quantity; otherwise, substance is indivisible. But that which is received in a body is received in it according to the division of quantity. Therefore, a form is received in a body only as individuated. If, then, the intellect were a body, any intelligible form received by the intellect would be individuated. The intellect, then, would not understand universals, but only particulars since it understands things through their forms which it has in itself. This is evidently false; hence, it follows that no intellect is a body.

[¶ 4.] Again, everything acts according to its species, for in each thing form is the principle of its acting. Now if the intellect were a body, its action would not rise above the limit of bodies. The intellect, then, would understand only bodies. This is clearly false, for we understand many things that are not bodies. Therefore, the intellect is not a body.

[¶ 5.] If an intelligent substance is a body, it is either infinite or finite. But that a body be infinite in act is impossible, as is proved in III, *Physics* and in I, *On the Heavens.* If, therefore, it is a body, it is finite. But this, too, is impossible, since no finite body can have an infinite potency, as has already been shown. The potency of the intellect, however, is in a certain respect infinite in understanding. It can know an infinitely progressive series of numbers, of geometrical figures, and of proportions. It also knows the universal, which is virtually infinite according to extension, for the individuals which it contains are potentially infinite. Therefore, the intellect is not a body.

[¶ 6.] It is impossible, too, that bodies mutually contain each other, since the containing body is always larger than the one it contains. But two intellects can contain and comprehend each other by understanding each other. Therefore, the intellect is not a body.

[¶ 7.] No body is capable of reflective activity, for it was shown in VII and VIII, *Physics* that a body moves itself only according to a part, one part being the mover and the other the moved. But the intellect does have reflective activity, since it knows itself, not merely according to a part, but according to the whole. Therefore, it is not a body.

[¶ 8.] The act of a body does not terminate in action, nor does motion terminate in the thing moved, as was shown in V, *Physics*. But the act of an intellectual substance terminates in action, for the intellect understands a thing, and understands its act of understanding, and so on to infinity. Therefore, an intellectual substance is not a body.

[¶ 9.] Hence, it is that Sacred Scripture calls intellectual substances spirits. In the same way, God Himself is called incorporeal in *John,* Chapter IV, Verse 24, "God is a Spirit." It is said also in *Wisdom,* Chapter VII, Verse 22, "There is in it," namely, divine wisdom, "the spirit of understanding," which comprehends all intelligible Spirits.

[¶ 10.] Through this we avoid the error of those early philosophers of nature, of whom Aristotle spoke (I, *On the Soul,* Chapter 2). They said that the only substances are corporeal ones, and consequently held that the soul is a body, composed of fire, or air, or water, or some other thing of this kind. Some tried to introduce this opinion into Christian faith, saying that the soul is a "body thinned out," like the outline alone of a body.

No. 2. The Subsistence of the Human Soul
St. Thomas: *Summa Theologiae,* Part I, Question 75, Article 2
Is the human soul subsistent?

[¶ 1.] *Objection 1.* That which is subsistent is said to be a particular thing. The soul is not a particular thing, but the composite of body and soul is. Therefore, the soul is not subsistent.

[¶ 2.] *Objection 2.* Every subsistent thing can be said to operate. But the soul is not said to operate, for in Book I, *On the Soul,* the Philosopher states that to say *the soul feels or understands* is like saying that it *weaves or builds*. Therefore, the soul is not a subsistent thing.

[¶ 3.] *Objection 3.* If the soul were a subsistent thing, it would have some operation without the body. But there are no operations without the body, not even understanding, for there is no understanding without a phantasm, and there is no phantasm apart from the body. Therefore, the human soul is not a subsistent thing.

[¶ 4.] *On the contrary,* in Book X, *On the Trinity,* Augustine holds: "Whoever realizes that it is the nature of the mind to be a substance, and not corporeal, sees that those who attribute a corporeal nature to it go astray, because they join to it the things without which they can know no nature, that is, bodily phantasms." Therefore, the nature of the human mind is not only incorporeal but is even substantial, that is, subsistent.

[¶ 5.] The principle of intellectual operation, which we call the *soul* of man, must necessarily be an incorporeal and subsistent principle, for it is evident that through his intellect man can know the natures of all bodies. But that which is able to know some things must have nothing of them in its nature, because that which would be present to it naturally would hinder knowledge of other things. For example, the tongue of a sick man, which is infected by fever and bitterness, cannot taste any thing sweet, but everything seems bitter to it. If, therefore, the intellectual principle had in it the nature of some body, it could not know all bodies, for every body has a limited nature. It is impossible, therefore, for the intellectual principle to be a body.

[¶ 6.] It is also impossible for the soul to understand by means of a corporeal organ, for the particular nature of that corporeal organ would prevent knowledge of all bodies, as when a particular color is both in the eye and in the glass of a vase, the liquid in the vase seems to be of the same color.

[¶ 7.] Therefore, the intellectual principle, called mind or intellect, has an operation of its own in which the body does not share. However, nothing can operate by itself unless it subsists in itself, for there is no operation except of a being in act. Hence, the mode of being determines the way it operates. This is why we do not say that heat heats, but what is hot heats. We can conclude, therefore, that the human soul, called intellect or mind, is incorporeal and subsistent.

[¶ 8.] *Reply to Objection 1.* "A particular thing," can be understood in two ways. First, it can mean any subsistent thing; second, it can mean a subsistent thing which is complete in the nature of some species. The first way excludes the inherence of an accident and of a material form. The second excludes also the imperfection of the part. Hence, we can call a hand *a particular thing* in the first sense, but not in the second.   Accordingly, since the human soul is a part of the human species, we can call it a *particular thing* in the first sense, as a subsistent thing, but not in the second sense.   In the second sense we call the composite of soul and body *a particular thing*.

[¶ 9.] *Reply to Objection 2.*   These words do not express Aristotle's own opinion, but the opinion of those who say that to understand is to be moved, as is evident from context.

Or we may answer the objection in this way:

Self-operation is characteristic of that which exists of itself.   But sometimes we can say that a thing exists of itself if it does not inhere as accident or as a material form, even though it is a part.   But in the proper sense a thing is called self-subsistent which neither inheres in the way mentioned nor exists simply as a part.   In this sense neither the eye nor the hand can be called self-subsistent and consequently not self-operating.   Hence, the operation of parts belongs to the whole by virtue of its parts, for the way a man sees with the eye and feels with the hand is different from the way a hot thing heats by its heat, because, strictly speaking, heat does not heat.   Therefore, we can say that the soul understands as the eye sees, but it is more precise to say that man understands through his soul.

[¶ 10.] *Reply to Objection 3.*   The action of understanding needs the body, not as an organ by which it performs such an act, but because of the nature of its object, for the phantasm is to the intellect as color is to sight.   The need of the body for understanding does not prove that the intellect is not subsistent; otherwise, an animal would not be subsistent, because it needs exterior sensibles for sensation.

No. 3. The Immortality of the Human Soul
      St. Thomas: *Disputed Question On the Soul,* Article 14
      Is the human soul immortal?

[¶ 1.] In the *Book of Wisdom* (Chapter II, Verse 23) it is said: "God made man indestructible, and He made him to the image of His likeness."   It can be taken from this that man is indestructible, that is, incorruptible, according as he is made to the image of God.   But he is made to the image of God according to his soul, as Augustine says in Book X, *On the Trinity.*   Therefore, the human soul is incorruptible.

[¶ 2.] Everything which is corrupted has contraries or is composed of contraries.   But the human soul is entirely without contrariety, since even those things which are contraries in themselves are not contraries in the soul, for the concepts of contraries in the soul are not contraries. Therefore, the human soul is incorruptible.

[¶ 3.] The heavenly bodies are said to be incorruptible because they do not have matter of the sort found in generable and corruptible things. But the human soul is entirely immaterial, which is evident from the fact that it receives the species of things in an immaterial way. Therefore, the human soul is incorruptible.

[¶ 4.] In Book III, *On the Soul,* the Philosopher says that the intellect is separated as the eternal from the corruptible. But the intellect is part of the soul, as he himself says. Therefore, the human soul is incorruptible.

[¶ 5.] The human soul must be completely incorruptible. In proof of this it should be noted that whatever by its very nature follows upon a thing cannot be taken away from it. For example, *animal* cannot be taken away from what man is, nor even or odd from number. Now, it is evident that by its very nature existence follows upon form, for each thing has existence according to its proper form. This is why existence can in no way be separated from form. Therefore, composites of matter and form are corrupted when they lose the form which gives existence. Now the form cannot be corrupted essentially, but it is corrupted in an accidental way when the composite is corrupted, inasmuch as the composite which exists by virtue of the form, ceases to exist. This happens if the form is such that it does not have existence but is only that by which a composite exists.

[¶ 6.] Therefore, if there is any form which has existence, that form must be incorruptible. For existence is taken from something having existence only if its form is separated from it. This is why, if that which has existence is the form itself, it is impossible that existence be separated from it. Now it is clear that the principle by which man understands is a form having existence in itself, and not merely a form by which something exists. For, as the Philosopher proves in Book III, *On the Soul,* understanding is not an act performed through a bodily organ, for a bodily organ capable of receiving all sensible natures cannot be found, especially since the recipient would have to be without the nature of things received, as the eye is without color. Now every bodily organ has some sensible nature. But the intellect by which we understand is capable of knowing all sensible natures. This is why it is impossible that its operation, namely understanding, be exercised by a bodily organ. Hence, it is apparent that the intellect has an operation of its own, in which the body does not share. Now each thing operates according to its nature, for things which have existence of themselves operate of themselves, but what does not have existence of itself does not operate of itself. For example, heat in itself does not produce warmth, but something hot does. Therefore, it is clear that the intellectual principle by which man understands has an existence elevated above the body, and not dependent upon it.

[¶ 7.] It is also clear that an intellectual principle of this kind is not something composed of matter and form since species are received in it in a completely immaterial way. This is shown from the fact that the intellect knows universals which are considered in abstraction from matter and from material conditions. We must conclude, therefore, that the intellectual principle by which man understands is a form having existence. Hence, it must be incorruptible. This is also what the Philosopher says in Book III, *On the Soul,* namely, that the intellect is in a certain way divine and eternal. It was shown in the preceding questions that the intellectual principle by which man understands is not a separated substance, but something formally inhering in man, since it is the soul or part of the soul. Hence, it follows from the preceding argument that the human soul is incorruptible.

[¶ 8.] All those who held that the human soul is corrupted missed some of the preceding points, for some, who held the soul to be a body, argued that it is not a form but something composed of matter and form. Others holding that the intellect does not differ from the senses argued, consequently, that it operates only through bodily organs and so does not have an existence superior to the body; hence, it is not a form having existence. Others held that the intellect by which man understands is a separated substance. But in the preceding arguments the falsity of all these opinions has been pointed out. We must conclude, therefore, that the human soul is incorruptible.

[¶ 9.] There are two signs of the incorruptibility of the soul. First, on the part of the intellect, for we see that things which are in themselves corruptible, according as they are apprehended by the intellect, are incorruptible. For the intellect apprehends things universally, and in this mode they are not subject to corruption. Second, on the part of natural appetite, which cannot be frustrated. For we see in man a desire for eternal existence. This is reasonable, for existence of itself is desirable, and an intelligent being who apprehends existence in an absolute sense, and not merely the here and now, must desire existence absolutely and for all time. Hence, we see that this desire is not in vain, but that man, according to his intellectual soul, is incorruptible.

No. 4. The Human Soul Must Be Created

St. Thomas: *Summa Theologiae,* Part I, Question 90, Article 2
Is the human soul produced by creation?

[¶ 1.] *Objection 1.* It seems that the soul is not the product of creation, for what has in itself something material is made from matter. But the soul has in itself something material, since it is not pure act. Therefore, the soul is made from matter and is not created.

[¶ 2.] *Objection 2.* Every act of matter seems to come from the potency of the matter, for since matter is in potency to act, any act pre-exists in matter potentially. But the soul is an act of corporeal matter, as is evident from its definition. Therefore, the soul comes from the potencies of matter.

[¶ 3.] *Objection 3.* The soul is one kind of form. If, therefore, the soul is created for the same reason, all other forms are created. Thus, no form would come into existence by generation, which is incorrect.

[¶ 4.] *On the contrary,* it is said in Genesis, Chapter I, Verse 27: "God created man to His own image." Now man is the image of God because of his soul. Therefore, the soul is produced in being through creation.

[¶ 5.] The rational soul cannot come to be except by creation, which is not true of other forms. The reason for this is that "becoming" is the way to existence, and, hence, the way in which a thing comes to be must be suitable to the way in which it exists. Most properly a thing is said to exist which has its being as if subsisting in its own being. Therefore, only substances are properly and truly beings. An accident does not have being but by it something is, and because of this it is called being. For example, whiteness is called being because by it something is white. This is why in VII, *Metaphysics* it is said that accident is more of a being than a being. The same holds for all other forms which are not subsistent. And, therefore, forms which do not subsist do not properly come to be, but they are said to come to be when the subsistent composites come to be. Now the rational soul is subsistent form as was explained above (*S.T.,* I, 75, 2). Therefore, it belongs to it properly to be and to come to be. And since it cannot come to be from pre-existing matter, neither from corporeal matter because thus it would be a corporeal nature, nor from spiritual matter, because this would entail changing one spiritual substance into another, therefore, we must conclude that it cannot come into existence except by creation.

[¶ 6.] *Reply to Objection 1.* In the soul, there is as a material principle the simple essence itself, and as the formal principle, the participated existence. This participated existence is necessarily simultaneous with the essence of the soul since being follows upon form. There would be the same reasoning if it were held that the soul is composed of some kind of spiritual matter, as some do maintain. This kind of matter, like the matter of the heavenly bodies, is not in potency to another form, otherwise, the soul would be corruptible. Therefore, in no way can the soul come to be from pre-existing matter.

[¶ 7.] *Reply to Objection 2.* The eduction of act from the potency of matter is nothing else but the coming to be in act of something which was previously in potency. But since the rational soul does not have its being dependent on corporeal matter but has subsistent being and exceeds the capacity of corporeal matter, as was said above (*S.T.,* I, 75, 2) it is not educed from the potency of matter.

[¶ 8.] *Reply to Objection 3.* There is no parallel between the rational soul and other forms, as we have said. (*S.T.,* I, 90, 2, Body of Article.)

No. 5. *The Human Soul Was Not Made Before Its Existence in the Body*
St. Thomas: *Summa Theologiae,* Part I, Question 90, Article 4
Was the human soul made before the body?

[¶ 1.] *Objection 1.* It seems that the human soul was produced before the body, for the work of creation came before the work of perfection and adornment, as we explained above (*S.T.,* I, 66 and 70). But the soul was brought into existence by creation, while the body was made at the end of the work of adornment. Therefore, the soul of man was produced before the body.

[¶ 2.] *Objection 2.* The rational soul is associated more with the angels than with the brute animals. But angels were created before bodies or, at least, in the beginning along with corporeal matter. The body of man, however, was formed on the sixth day after the brute animals had already been made. Therefore, the soul of man was created before the body.

[¶ 3.] *Objection 3.* The end of something is proportionate to the beginning. But in the end, the soul remains after the body. Therefore, in the beginning it was created before the body.

[¶ 4.] *On the contrary,* the proper act is joined to its proper potency. Since, therefore, the soul is the proper act of the body, the soul is produced in the body.

[¶ 5.] Origen held that not only the soul of the first man but the souls of all men were created before their bodies along with the angels. For this reason he believed that all spiritual substances, souls as well as angels, were equal in their natural conditions, and differed only in merit. The result was that some of them, namely, the souls of men or of heavenly bodies, were joined to bodies, whereas others, according to their different orders, remained in their original purity. We spoke about this opinion before (*S.T.*, I, 47, 2), so we will not say anything about it now.

[¶ 6.] Augustine (VII, *Commentary on the Text of Genesis,* Chapter 24) says that the soul of the first man was created along with the angels before the body, but he employs a different reason. He holds that the body of man was not actually made in the work of the six days, but only in its causal principles. This cannot be said of the soul, because neither was it made from any corporeal or spiritual pre-existent matter, nor could it be produced by any created power. Therefore, it seems that the soul was created along with the angels in the work of the six days when all things were made, and afterwards by its proper will was inclined to administer to the body. But he does not assert this as his words show, for he says "it may be believed, if neither the authority of scripture or truth prevent it, that man was made on the sixth day in such a way that the causal principle of the human body was in the elements of the world, but that the soul itself was already created."

[¶ 7.] This opinion would also be held by those who argue that the soul is in itself a species and a complete nature and that it is united to the body not as a form but only as an administrator. But if the soul is united to the body as a form and is naturally part of human nature, this is entirely impossible. For it is evident that God created the first things in a complete state of their nature, as each species required. The soul, however, since it is part of human nature, has its natural perfection only when united to the body. Therefore, it would have been unfitting for the soul to have been created without a body.

[¶ 8.] Therefore, in order to agree with Augustine on the work of the six days we can say that in the work of the six days the human soul came first according to a certain generic likeness, since it has an intellectual nature in common with the angels. But it was itself created along with the body. According to other holy men, both the body and the soul of the first man were created in the work of the six days.

[¶ 9.] *Reply to Objection 1.* If, by its nature, the soul were an integral species, so that it could be created by itself, we could then show that it was created by itself in the beginning of time. But since it is naturally the form of the body, it had to be created not separately but in a body.

[¶ 10.] *Reply to Objection 2.* The second reply is similar to the first. If the soul were in itself a species, it would be more like the angels. But since it is the form of the body, it belongs to the genus animal as a formal principle.

[¶ 11.] *Reply to Objection 3.* That the soul remains after the body is because of the defect of the body which is death. This defect did not have to be present when the soul was first created.

No. 6. Man's Body Must Be Suitably Disposed for the Soul
St. Thomas: *Summa Theologiae,* Part I, Question 91, Article 3
Does man's body have a suitable disposition?

[¶ 1.] *Objection 1.* It seems that the body of man does not have a suitable disposition for this reason: since man is the highest animal, his body should be most perfectly equipped for those things which are proper to an animal, namely, sensation and motion. But some animals have better senses and quicker movements than man. For example, dogs have a better sense of smell and birds move faster. Therefore, the body of man is not properly disposed.

[¶ 2.] *Objection 2.* A thing is perfect if it lacks nothing. But the human body lacks more things than the bodies of other animals, since they have covering and natural means for their own defense, which man lacks. Therefore, the body of man is least perfectly equipped.

[¶ 3.] *Objection 3.* Man is more distant from plants than from brute animals. But plants have an erect stature, while brutes are stooped in stature. Therefore, man should not be of an erect stature.

[¶ 4.] *On the contrary,* in VII, *Book of Ecclesiastes* (Chapter 30) it is said; "God made man correctly."

[¶ 5.] All of nature is a product of divine art, so in a certain way it may be called the artifact of God Himself. Every artist gives his work the best disposition possible, not in an absolute sense, but the best in relation to an end. If a certain disposition involves some defect, the artist does not care. For example, when an artisan makes a saw, he makes it out of iron because this is suitable for cutting. He does not want to make it from glass, though it might be a more beautiful material, because the beauty would be an obstacle in attaining the end. Therefore, God gives to each natural thing the best disposition, not absolutely the best, but the best in reference to its proper end. The Philosopher also says this in II, *Physics,* "and because it is better thus, not, however, absolutely, but in regard to the essence of each one."

[¶ 6.] The proximate end of the human body is the rational soul and its operations, for matter exists for form, and instruments for the actions of the agent. I say, therefore, that God gave the human body the disposition which was most in accord with such a form and with such operations. And if any defect seems to exist in the dispositions of the human body, we must realize that such a defect follows from the necessity of matter in relation to those things which are required in a body, in order to make it correctly proportioned to the soul and to its operations.

[¶ 7.] *Reply to Objection 1.* Touch, which is the basis of all the other senses, is more perfect in man than in any other animal, and, because of this, man had to have the most balanced construction of all animals. The interior sense powers of man are superior to those of all the other animals, as is apparent from what was said before (*S.T.,* I, 78, 4). But by a kind of necessity some of the exterior senses of man are inferior to those of other animals. For example, among all animals, man's sense of smell is the weakest. This is so because of all animals man needed the largest brain in relation to his body, so that his interior sense powers, which the intellect needs in order to operate, might have more freedom in their operation, as was said above (*S.T.,* I, 84, 7); and, also, so that the low temperature of the brain might temper the warmth of his heart, for this must be very warm in order that man be erect. This large size of his brain, because of its dampness, is what hinders the sense of smell which requires dryness. A similar reason can be given to explain why certain animals have keener vision and a more delicate sense of hearing than man, namely, the hindrance of these senses, which is a necessary consequence of man's perfect balance of construction. The same reason is used to explain why certain animals are quicker than man, since this excellence of speed is repugnant to the balance of his construction.

[¶ 8.] *Reply to Objection 2.* Horns and claws, the defense of some animals, toughness of hide, and abundance of hair or feathers, the covering of animals, testifies to the variety of earthly elements which are repugnant to the balance and delicacy of human structure. Therefore, they are not suitable for man. But in place of these he has reason and hands, and these enable him to make arms, clothing, and other vital necessities of infinite variety. This is why in III, *On the Soul* it is said that the hands are the "organ of organs." This was also more fitting for a rational nature capable of conceiving an infinite number of things, that it have the ability to devise for itself a limitless amount of instruments.

[¶ 9.] *Reply to Objection 3.* Four reasons can be given why an erect stature is suitable for man. First, because man was given senses not only to procure vital necessities, as is true for the other animals, but also for knowledge. Hence, while the other animals are gratified by sensible things only as related to food or sex, man alone delights in the beauty itself of sensible things for its own sake. For this reason, since the senses are for the most part located in the head, other animals have a head which is turned toward the earth, as if to seek food and provide a means of nourishment for themselves. But man's head is erect, in order that by his senses, especially sight which is more delicate and makes known many differences in things, he can easily observe sensible objects in every direction, both the things of the heavens and of earth, and from all of them gather intelligible truth. Second, he is erect so that his interior powers may operate more freely. Hence, the brain, in which, in a certain respect, they operate, is not situated at a low point but is above all the other parts of the body. Third, if man were stooped over he would have to use his hands as forefeet. Thus, the utility of the hands for making other things would cease. Fourth, if he were stooped over and if he used his hands as forefeet, he would have to take food with his mouth. If this were so, his mouth would protrude, his lips would be hard and thick, and his tongue would also be hard so that exterior things would not hurt it, as is the case among the other animals. Such a disposition would prevent speech which is a proper work of reason.

[¶ 10.] And though having an erect stature, he is far above the plants, for the superior part of man, his head, is turned toward the superior part of the world, and his inferior parts toward the inferior part of the world. Therefore, he is best disposed in view of his total structure. But the superior parts of plants are turned toward the inferior part of the world, for roots are like the mouth, whereas their inferior parts face the superior part of the world. Brute animals have a middle position, for the superior part of an animal takes food, while the inferior part disposes of the surplus.

GLOSSARY OF TERMS AND PROPER NAMES

Abstraction: The process of intellectual knowledge proper to man; the act by which the intellect grasps an intelligible universal form in sensible things; for example, it understands the universal nature of animal after the sensing of individual animals like men, cats, dogs, and the like.

Accident: That which does not exist in itself and is not essential to the subject in which it exists; any specification of a subject after it has its first act of substantial existence, such as the color, size, position, and so on, of a substance. *Cf. Proper Accident.*

Act: In general, any perfection of being; actuality, as opposed to potentiality.

First Act: Substantial act; the act of existence which is presupposed for the existence of any other act; for example, the existence of soul as presupposed for the existence of vital activity.

Second Act: Any form or perfection after substantial existence, such as walking or thinking in man.

Activity: The exercise of a power; the second act of an operative potency, such as the use of the power of imagination.

Immanent Activity: Activity that begins and ends in the power that produces the activity and whose purpose is the perfection of the power itself, such as the act of understanding.

Transitive Activity: Activity that begins in one subject and has its effect in another, and whose purpose is primarily the perfection of the work produced, such as the building of a house.

Actual: Something that exists in the present, as opposed to what can exist (the potential) or what does not exist at all (the non-existent).

Adler, Alfred: (1807–1937) Viennese psychiatrist, disciple of Freud; he later broke away from the Freudian school of pan-sexuality and stressed the desire for power as the predominant motivation in man.

Affection: A synonym for the sensory appetite, especially the concupiscible appetite which deals with pleasurable goods of the sensory order.

Agent: The active principle which produces an effect; the efficient cause; for example, the carpenter who builds a house; *cf. Cause: Efficient.*

Analogous: The signification of a word as it refers to two or more things—not with the same meaning, as with *univocal,* nor with diverse meaning, as with *equivocal*—but as signifying one primarily and the other secondarily and with reference to the first; for example, "religious" as it signifies a quality of man and a quality of music.

A Posteriori Reasoning: An argument which proceeds from accepted facts or propositions to the knowledge of the principles in which the facts or propositions have their explanation; for example, the proof of God's existence which can be known from the presence of order in nature.

Appetite: In general, a tendency toward a natural goal, or a movement toward an end, presupposing some kind of direction either from the being itself that is to be perfected, or from an extrinsic agent directing the movement toward an end.

> *Elicited Appetite:* The appetite proper to cognitive beings, following upon knowledge of the good to be sought for; for example, the movement of the human will, following upon knowledge by the intellect.

A Priori Reasoning: As opposed to *A Posteriori* reasoning, an argument which proceeds from a knowledge of principles to the knowledge of the propositions which follow with necessity or probability from such principles; for example, the proof that the human soul is immortal is based on *a priori* reasoning from the intellectual nature of the human soul.

Aquinas, St. Thomas: (1225–1274) Dominican monk, philosopher, and theologian; born at Roccasecca, near Naples. More than any other person he is responsible for the synthesis of Aristotelian and Christian thought.

Argument: A process of reasoning by which a conclusion is proved from better known propositions.

Aristotle: (384–322 B.C.) Greek philosopher born in the Greek colony of Stagira, one of the world's great philosophers.

Atomism: The philosophical theory that all substances are constituted of combinations of tiny, indivisible, elements called atoms; substances thus differ only by physical arrangements of the atoms.

Atomistic: Adjective referring to atomism.

Augustine, St.: (354–430) one of the world's great philosophers and theologians; his philosophical inquiry centered about the problems of the nature of God, of the soul, and of human knowledge.

Avicebron: (1020–1070) Jewish philosopher and theologian born in Malaga, Spain.

Avicenna: (980–1037) Persian philosopher and interpreter of Aristotle.

Averroës: (1126–1198) Mohammedan philosopher and interpreter of Aristotle, called the *Commentator.*

Bergson, Henri: (1859–1941) French philosopher, proponent of dynamic evolutionism and opponent of mechanistic materialism.

Brentano, Franz: (1838–1907) Philosopher and psychologist; though belonging to an Aristotelian tradition, he exercised great influence on German phenomenology of the early 20th century.

Cajetan, Cardinal De Vio: (1468–1534) Philosopher, theologian, and commentator on St. Thomas.

Categories: According to Aristotle, the 10 supreme genera of real beings; for example, substance, quantity, quality, *etc.;* also called the *predicaments.*

Cartesian: Adjective derived from *Cartesius,* the Latin name for Descartes.

Cause: That which is productive of an effect; that upon which something depends for its coming to be or its being.

> *Efficient:* The agent by whose power and activity something is produced; for example, the activity of a carpenter in making a house.

> *Final:* The end or that for the sake of which something is done; for example, the purpose or plan in the mind of the builder.

> *Formal:* The perfection of form which is produced in the material by means of efficient causality; for example, the kind of house built.

> *Material:* That out of which something is made; that which is formed; for example, the wood or stone out of which the house is made.

Central Sense (Sensus Communis): One of the internal senses whose function it is to correlate the various objects of the external senses and to make the knower aware of his act of sensation.

Certitude: A state of mind in which evidence is such that a proposition can be affirmed or denied without reasonable fear of error in judgment.

Choice: (Election) the free, deliberate selection of means to attain a goal; for example, the selection of meat instead of eggs to satisfy hunger.

Circular Argumentation: An invalid type of demonstration in which the proposition to be proved is assumed to be true in one of the premises.

Coercion: Compulsion which arises from the application of irresistible force by an extrinsic agent, contrary to the natural tendency of a free agent.

Cogitative Sense (Vis Cogitativa): The estimative power in man; one of the internal senses in man whose function it is to know what is beneficial or harmful in the sensible order; it is also called *particular reason.*

Common Sense: Cf. either *Central Sense* or *Sensible Object: Common.*

Commentator: A name applied to Averroës by mediaeval writers.

Composite: A compound made up of several substantial co-principles such as matter and form, body and soul; a complete substance made up of integral parts.

Conation: A term referring to the sensory appetite; an urging or movement of the sensory appetite.

Concept: An intentional form produced by the intellect in simple apprehension, in which the intellect knows an intelligible object. *Cf. Mental Word, Idea.*

Concupiscible Appetite: That division of the sensory appetite which deals with pleasurable goods of the sensory order.

Conditioned Reflex: The developed automatic response to a stimulus in an organ or in a power even when a substitute stimulus is employed.

Consciousness: A state of mind in which the knower is aware of his psychic experiences; an awareness of one's self as acting or being acted upon.

Creation: In the broad sense, the production of anything by an efficient cause; in the strict sense, the total production of something by an agent with no previous material or form presupposed; thus the making of the total substance.

Democritus: (460–360 B.C.) Greek philosopher of nature, disciple of Leucippus, who was the founder of Greek atomism.

Demonstration: Certain proof of a proposition by means of deduction from previously known principles, causes or more evident propositions.

Descartes, René: (1596–1650) French philosopher and mathematician, sometimes called the father of modern philosophy, particularly in its epistemological aspects.

Determinism: The philosophical view that all effects are infallibly accounted for in their antecedents; with respect to the human will, this view affirms that choice is wholly determined by the conditions in which the so-called free agent operates.

Dewey, John: (1859–1952) American philosopher and educator, exponent of a pragmatic philosophy and that philosophy of education known as *Instrumentalism* or *Functionalism.*

Dialectical: A method of discovery by debate; in another context, a type of knowledge that approximates certitude, and is capable of further approximation; lacking strictly scientific certitude; probable or hypothetical knowledge.

Discourse: A method of argumentation in which one proceeds in orderly fashion from principles to conclusions, as opposed to intuitive knowledge.

Disposition: The first division of the category of quality; an easily changeable characteristic of a subject, such as a tendency to anger in man.

Driesch, Hans: (1867–1941), Biologist and philosopher, opponent of mechanistic biology and exponent of a principle of biological *entelechy.*

Dualism: In Aristotelian psychology, the view that a living being is made up of two distinct substantial principles: the body as a potential principle, and the soul as the active and specifying principle.

> *Extreme Dualism:* The view that the body and the soul are two distinct and irreducible substances, joined in the composite by an accidental union.

Eddington, Sir Arthur: (1882–1944) English physicist and philosopher of nature.

Efficient Cause: Cf. Agent or *Cause: Efficient.*

Eidola: The species by which, according to the atomists, knowledge is effected; the minute surface images that rise from bodies and are joined to the knower.

Election: Cf. Choice.

Emotion: A term referring to the sensory appetite; it has the connotation of a strong tendency toward a sensible good or away from a sensible evil.

Empedocles: (490–430 B.C.) Greek philosopher of nature who, like Heraclitus, emphasized the conflict of natural principles.

Empiriological: A term coined by Maritain to define the essential characteristics of the natural sciences in our day: from *empeiria,* experiment or experience and *logos,* theory or understanding.

End: The goal or purpose of an action; for example, the good to be attained in a moral action. *Cf. Cause: Final.*

Engels, Friedrich: (1820–1895) German political philosopher, collaborator of Karl Marx; he is responsible for much of the formulation of the theoretical principles of communism as a philosophy of nature.

Entelechy: A directive and unifying principle of an organism. In the psychology of Aristotle the soul is the substantial principle of entelechy; in the psychology of Driesch, the principle of entelechy is not substantial but operational.

Entitative: Referring to the objective existence of being as opposed to intentional existence in the mind.

Epicurus: (341–270 B.C.) Ethical and natural philosopher influenced by the atomism of Democritus.

Epistemology: That part of philosophy which treats of the problem of the validity of human knowledge.

   Realistic Epistemology: The view that the intellect attains objective reality in its acts of knowing. *Cf. Realism.*

Error: Lack of conformity between the judgment of intellect and reality; in a broader sense, the lack of conformity between a power of knowledge and its object.

Estimative Sense: One of the internal sense powers of animals; it has the function of recognizing what is harmful or beneficial among objects of sense with respect to the individual animal or the species.

Experimental: Scientific experiment as opposed to common experience; designating the method of the physical sciences in which a situation capable of being controlled is set up for observation and verification.

Expressed Species: Cf. Species: Expressed.

External Sense: Cf. Sense: External.

Evolution: In biology or philosophy, a theory that living beings have developed through a series of essential changes from lower to higher orders of biological species.

Faculty: A synonym for a power or potency of the soul.

Faculty Theory: (Extreme)—a view that overemphasizes the independence of the different powers of the soul, setting them apart from each other as though there were distinct compartments in the soul each with its own principle of being and operation.

Fechner, Gustav: (1801–1887) German physicist and psychologist.

Final Cause: Cf. Cause: Final; End.

First Philosophy: The name given by Aristotelians to metaphysics; the *first* refers to the quality of being the basic science rather than to a chronological order of study; hence the study of the first principles, causes and essential attributes of being as such.

Form: The principle of specification of a subject, either in the substantial or accidental order; as distinguished from matter. *Cf. Act* and *Cause: Formal.*

Formal Object: Cf. Object: Formal.

Formal Sign: Cf. Sign: Formal.

Freedom: In general, the power of self-determination found in intellectual beings, as opposed to determinism.

> *Of Exercise:* The power of self-determination with respect to the act itself, whether the agent chooses to act or not to act.

> *Of Specification:* The power of self-determination with respect to the kind of good which the agent selects in preference to another.

Freud, Sigmund: (1856–1940) Viennese physician and psychologist; originator of the psychoanalytic method for the treatment of mental disorders.

Functionalism: A view held by some American psychologists, particularly James, Dewey, and Ladd, who regarded the psychic processes as being fundamentally biological in nature and subject to the influences of environment.

Gestalt Psychology: A school of psychology which teaches the psychic unity of cognitive experiences, as opposed to the atomic or associationist views; from the German word *Gestalt* meaning *appearance* or *shape.* The founders of the school were Wertheimer, K. Koffka, and W. Köhler.

Habit: The first species of quality; a permanent disposition of a subject. In Thomistic psychology, a permanent disposition or "second nature" added to the rational powers to dispose them consistently and effectively toward their objects; to be distinguished from the special category referring to clothing.

Habitude: A fixed manner of acting in the presence of similar objects; the pattern of repetitious activity that follows upon habits.

Habitus: Latin term for the first species of quality; *cf. Habit.*

Hegel, George: (1770–1831) German idealist philosopher, exponent of idealist, dialectical philosophy.

Human Act: A moral act, that is, one which proceeds from specifically human principles of intelligence and will.

Hutcheson, Francis: (1694–1746) Scottish moralist and epistemologist; exponent of an extreme faculty theory.

Idea: Concept; idea has the connotation of representation or image pertaining to intentional existence as the counterpart of physical existence.

Imagination: An internal sense power by which one retains the past impressions of the external senses when the sensible objects themselves are absent.

Immanent: That which exists or has its principle of activity within a being, and terminates within the agent.

Immanent Activity: Cf. Activity: Immanent.

Immortality: Unending duration of life; the doctrine of personal immortality holds that in its unending existence the human soul remains not only specifically but also numerically the same; thus each individual soul will endure forever without essential corruption.

Impressed Species: Cf. Species: Impressed.

Instrumentalism: The pragmatic philosophy of Dewey, particularly his early view which considered the psychic processes as a function of the biological organism, as distinct from his later view on social functionalism.

Intellect: A power of knowing which grasps objects in an intelligible way; from the Latin word *intus,* within, and *legere,* to read; a power of penetrating the meaning of its objects; as contrasted with the sensory knowing of phenomena.

> *Agent:* The power which makes, through the instrumentality of sensible forms, an intelligible impressed species for the possible intellect.

> *Possible:* The power of becoming in an intentional and intelligible way the forms of other things.

Intelligence. Cf. Intellect.

Intentio Insensata: An intentional form not originating in the external senses; a cognitive form in the internal senses which originate on the occasion of external sensation but whose source as formal knowledge is more immediately in the animal nature itself, such as the recognition of harmful or beneficial sensory objects or the memory of these objects.

Intentional: The mode of existence of beings in a power of knowing; from the Latin word *intendere,* to stretch out; hence, the property of reaching out beyond the knower's individual form of existence to the forms that exist in other beings; the form of knowledge which is the counterpart of the entitative form.

Internal Sense: A sensory power of knowing which grasps its objects as conditioned by time and space but without the necessity of physical presence; for example, the imagination.

Intuition: In general, the immediate grasp of an object physically present, as opposed to abstraction, discourse, or syllogistic reasoning; the word is derived from the Latin *intueri,* to see.

Irascible: That division of the sensory appetite which deals with difficulties encountered in attaining or the avoiding of objects of the concupiscible appetite.

James, William: (1842–1910) American philosopher, psychologist, educator, exponent of pragmatism and radical empiricism.

John of St. Thomas: (1589–1644) Dominican philosopher and theologian, commentator on the writings of St. Thomas.

Judgment: A reflexive act of the intellect in which the agreement or disagreement of the subject and predicate of a proposition is seen to conform to reality.

Jung, C. G.: (1875–   ) Viennese psychologist and philosopher; formerly a disciple of Freud, he later developed his own principles and method of psycho-analysis.

Kant, Immanuel: (1724–1804) German philosopher, critical idealist whose critique of knowledge has deeply influenced all subsequent study of the problem of knowledge.

Koffka, Kurt: (1886–1941) Psychologist collaborator of Kohler and Wertheimer in founding the school of gestalt psychology.

Köhler, Wolfgang: (1887–   ) Psychologist, co-founder of gestalt psychology.

Külpe, Oswald: (1862–1915) Psychologist and philosopher; he dealt chiefly with the epistemological problems of psychology.

Leibnitz, Gottfried: (1646–1716) German philosopher, proponent of the doctrine of monads, the doctrine of continuity, and the principle of pre-established harmony.

Leucippus: (Born about 460 B.C.) Philosopher of nature; father of the Greek atomistic school of philosophy.

Locomotion: The power of moving oneself from place to place under the impulse of the appetites.

Lucretius: (98–54 B.C.) Roman poet and philosopher; exponent of the atomistic philosophy of Epicurus and author of *On the Nature of Things.*

Marx, Karl: (1818–1883) Writer and philosopher; the father of Communist social economic philosophy; collaborator with Friedrich Engels in formulating the principles of dialectical materialism.

Materialism: In general, the philosophical position which holds that the only reality is matter, and that all things have their origin and end in matter.

Materialistic: Referring to a philosophy of materialism.

Matter: In the Aristotelian philosophy of nature, matter is conceived as the potential subject which is made actual and specified by the presence of form.

    Prime Matter: The unlimited potential passive principle which is the subject of substantial form; an infinitely potential capacity for natural form.

    Signate Matter: The composite as already constituted in existence with its natural quantity; the principle of individuation of natural substances; matter as existing under quantity.

Mechanism: A philosophical theory which holds that all vital activity can be explained through the organization and movement of material elements.

Memory: In general, the power by which one is able to retain and recognize past experiences.

    Intellectual: The power of recalling intellectual objects and experiences of the past.

Recall (Reminiscientia): The power of sense memory in man which operates in conjunction with reason and employs a kind of syllogistic process.

Sense Memory (Memoria): One of the internal senses; its function is to retain the insensate intentions of the past and to recognize past sensory experiences in their situation in the past.

Mental Word: Idea, concept, expressed species; as mental word, the emphasis is on communication and expression as a property of intelligence.

Metabolism: The sum of the processes concerned with the building up of proto-plasm and its destruction incidental to life; the process contains both anabolism (the building up) and catabolism (the breaking down) of cell structure.

Methodology: The systematic investigation and analysis proper to a scientific inquiry as distinguished from common experience.

Mind: From the Latin *mens:* the conscious part of the soul; generally it has a broader meaning than simply the power of intellect.

Mobile Being: The being of nature, subject to substantial and accidental change; the object of the philosophy of nature; the changing physical universe.

Moerbeke, William of: (1215–1286) Translator of the works of Aristotle from the Greek to Latin; his translation of the *De Anima* was used by St. Thomas.

Nature: In Aristotelian philosophy, the primary and intrinsic source of move-ment and of rest; as a synonym for *substance:* definition, essence; real being as opposed to being of the mind; the cosmos or whole of the physical world; when capitalized, sometimes used as the Author of nature.

Natural Philosophy: The division of philosophy which deals with mobile being or with nature taken as the intrinsic and primary principle of movement and of rest.

Necessity: That which cannot be other than it is; that which must follow from its antecedents or from the principles of its being.

Nominalism: The philosophical view that universal ideas or concepts are simply constructs of the mind and that no objective realities correspond to them; the view that universal names are practical symbols to express a series of similar experiences.

Nominalist: One who professes a nominalistic position on intellectual knowledge.

Object: Correlative of subject; the end or goal of any power; for example, color as the object of sight.

    Formal: That aspect of the material object which corresponds to a particular function of a power; the particular manner of approach that charac-terizes a science or power of the soul, such as a second intention with respect to the science of logic or color with respect to the power of seeing.

    Material: The subject matter with which a science or power deals; thus the material object may be the same for different sciences, which have dif-ferent formal objects, such as *man* who is studied in psychology and in moral philosophy.

Ontological: Pertaining to the order of existence as distinct from the logical order, and also from a subjective order; in a more restricted sense, the metaphysical order.

Organ: An instrument; an integral part of a living body through which the substantial form operates; while differing in function and construction, various organs have the same substantial principle.

Organic: Pertaining to organs and an organic body.

Organism: A living composite, made up of diverse organs, but having the same vital substantial principle.

Orexsis: Synonym for sensory appetite, with emphasis on the striving for a pleasurable good.

Parmenides: (500–400 B.C.) Founder of the Eleatic School and philosopher of unity and permanence of being.

Particular Reason: The cogitative power in man corresponding to the estimative power in animals.

Passion: In Aristotelian psychology, a synonym for the sensory appetite; it has the connotation of strong emotion that accompanies appetites like sensual love or anger.

Perception: The awareness of the act of sensation as distinct from sensation itself; the act of the central sense is called *perception,* while the act of seeing is called *sensation.*

Phantasm (Phantasy): The power of imagination; or the object of the power of imagination.

Phenomena: Sensory appearances; forms that can be grasped by the external senses; from the Greek *phainomena* meaning *appearances.*

Philosopher, The: A title referring to Aristotle, used by medieval writers.

Philosophy of Nature: That branch of philosophy which treats of mobile being; the general study of the physical world.

Physics: In Aristotelian terminology, that part of philosophy which treats of the general principles of nature, such as time, space, motion, and so on, sometimes called *cosmology.*

Plato: (428–348 B.C.) Greek philosopher, teacher of Aristotle; one of the world's great philosophers. Founder of the Academy at Athens.

Platonic: Pertaining to those who follow the doctrine and method of Plato, even though the doctrine bears only a general resemblance to the original.

Potency: In general, the capacity to produce or to receive a form which is not actually present.

    Active: A power which determines and specifies the objects it acts upon, for example, the agent intellect or the power of nutrition.

    Passive: In general, the capacity to receive a form from some extrinsic agent. In psychology, a power of the soul which is specified by an extrinsic cause before it becomes operative; for example, the eye is acted upon before it sees color.

Potential: Referring to potency.

Power: In psychology, a potency of the soul; a property by which the soul is potentially operative; sometimes called a *faculty.*

Practical Knowledge: Knowledge ordered to action or directed to serving an end other than the perfection of the intellect itself; for example, the knowledge of engineering or of medicine.

Pre-Existence, Doctrine of: A view held by some philosophers, who thought the human soul had existence, conscious or not, before its present existence in the body.

Privative: Cf. Privation.

Privation: The absence of a quality or of a perfection that can be or ought to be (privation in the strict sense) present in a subject; for example, blindness in a human being.

Proper Accident: Cf. Property.

Property: The fourth mode of the predicables; a characteristic that follows necessarily, only, and always from the essence of something, such as the property of speech in man.

Psychophysical Parallelism: A view held by some psychologists who taught that mental activities are in direct correspondence with the body's physiological activities.

Quality: One of the nine categories of accidental modifications of substance.

    Primary Sense Quality: Terminology used by certain schools of epistemology and psychology, referring to modifications in the quantity of a substance such as size, shape, extension, *etc.,* that can be recognized by the external senses.

    Secondary Sense Quality: Referring to modifications of a substance in the order of the proper sensibles, such as color, sound, taste, *etc.*

Realism: In epistemology, the view that universal concepts are not merely constructs of the mind but correspond to objective reality; the opposite of *nominalism.*

    Extreme Realism: The view that for every universal concept existing in the mind there is an identical form existing in reality outside the mind.

    Moderate Realism: The view that universal concepts have a real foundation outside the mind but that the form in the condition of universality as such exists only in the mind.

Realist: One who holds the objectivity of universal concepts.

Reason: The intellectual power peculiar to man; the intellectual power by which man proceeds from principles to conclusions; power of learning by means of intermediary terms, as opposed to intuition.

Reasoning: The third operation of the intellect; *cf. Reason.*

Recall: The power of sense memory as found in man; sense memory that operates deliberately and in the manner of syllogistic reasoning.

Reid, Thomas: (1710–1796) Scottish philosopher, exponent of the common-sense approach to problems of epistemology and exponent of the faculty theory.

Reproduction: A vegetative power of the soul by means of which a living substance produces from its own substance another living being of the same species.

Russell, Bertrand: (1872–   ) Contemporary mathematician and logician.

St. Augustine: Cf. Augustine.

St. Thomas: Cf. Aquinas.

Science: In an Aristotelian context: universal and necessary knowledge through causes; in the context of contemporary science, a body of knowledge gathered through the use of the strictly experimental method, resulting in a synthesis of facts by means of theory and hypothesis.

Seminal Cause (Ratio Seminalis): A position attributed to St. Augustine according to which some natural objects including the body of man, were created in a seminal or potential condition and were later developed through an evolution of the original creation.

Sensation: The act by which a power receives the sensible forms of things without their matter but with their particular conditions of time and space; the reference is to external sensation unless otherwise indicated.

Sensible Object: That which is grasped by a sense power.

    Accidental: An object that is only indirectly known by a sense power, either because it is immediately the object of the intellect or primarily the object of another sense power; for example, the eyes seeing a man; or the eyes seeing tasty food.

    Common: An object that can be sensed by all or at least by several of the external senses; for example, shape or movement.

    Proper: An object which can be sensed by only one kind of external sense power; for example, color is grasped only by sight.

Sign: In general, that which represents something other than itself to a knowing power.

    Artificial (Conventional): One in which the relationship of the sign to the signified is not constituted by nature, but by free choice or chance, such as a flag is a sign of a country.

    Formal: One whose very essence it is to represent or to make something known; for example, the concept.

    Natural: One in which the relationship of the sign to the signified is constituted by nature, as tears are a sign of sorrow.

Simple Apprehension: The first operation of the intellect which consists in grasping, by means of a concept, a simple object without affirming or denying anything about it.

Simplicity: The perfection of being without parts in one's nature; for example, the human soul is simple because it has no integral or quantitative parts.

Species: In psychology, the intentional form present in the act of knowing; for example, the impressed or expressed species of knowledge. The usage is different from that of logic or biology where the connotation is one of classification. *Cf. Intentional.*

Speculative Knowledge: Knowledge for the sake of the perfection of the intellect as opposed to knowledge for the sake of acting or making, as in practical knowledge.

Spinoza, Baruch: (1632–1677) Philosopher and moralist whose aim was to seek the knowledge that would make men happy; his chief work was his *Ethica,* conceived and written in a mathematical mode.

Spiritual: A mode of being or operation without matter either in one's substance or operation; the mode of being and operation that transcends time and space.

Spirituality: Cf. Spiritual.

Structuralism: The point of view held by some psychologists who stressed the analysis of the content of sensations and of consciousness in opposition to those psychologists who stressed the biological and functional aspects.

Subsistent: The property of having one's own substantial existence; being able to exist without being a part of another.

Substance: The first category of being; being that exists in itself and not in a subject, as do accidents. For example, a man is a substance; his whiteness is an accident.

Symbol: An indirect representation of something by means of figures or signs; a kind of metaphor employing artificial signs. For example, ∞ is a symbol of infinity in mathematics, or a triangle a symbol of the Trinity.

Synthetic Sense: A name used by some psychologists for the central sense.

Teleological: Referring to purposive activity, or to activity directed to an end.

Thomas Aquinas: Cf. Aquinas.

Titchener, Edward: (1867–1927) Sensist psychologist and disciple of Wundt; he advocated an analysis of structural content of consciousness instead of functions of man.

Transitive Activity: Cf. Activity.

Transmigration: A doctrine held by some philosophers according to which the human soul passes after death from one body to another.

Understanding: Cf. Intellect.

Universal: All inclusive; in psychology a common or general concept which is abstracted from individuals; in logic, a concept that can be predicated of all individuals of the same nature; *cf. Nominalism, Realism.*

Virtue: A habit of the rational powers (thus a moral or an intellectual virtue) which disposes a person to act well with respect to particular kinds of objects of an intellectual or moral order.

Vice: The habit contrary to a virtue.

Weber, E. H.: (1795–1878) German psychologist; exponent of a physiological explanation of psychological processes; discoverer of the law for measuring the relationship of stimulus to sensitivity.

Will: The intellectual appetite; the elicited appetite which seeks a universal good; the power of self-determination proper to intellectual beings with respect to what is seen as good.

Wundt, Wilhelm: (1832–1920) German physiologist and psychologist; founder of the first psychological laboratory.

INDEXES

NAME INDEX

A

Adler, Alfred, 105
* Allers, Rudolph, 121, 207
* Andrews, Thomas G., 35
Anselm of Canterbury, Saint, 180
Augustine, Saint, 62, 64, 92, 112, 212–216, 260, 277

B

Bergson, Henri, 154
* Boulogne, Charles D., 121
* Bourke, Vernon, 207
* Brennan, Robert E., 35, 207
Brentano, Franz, 11

C

Cajetan, Cardinal, 4, 6
* Cunningham, Francis, 207

D

Democritus, 11–13, 85, 157, 184, 214–215
Descartes, René, 9–10, 13, 29, 154, 253
Dewey, John, 11
* Donceel, J. F., 35
Driesch, Hans, 11

* Dufault, Lucien, 266
* Dunne, Peter, 207

E

Eddington, Arthur, 184–185
Ellis, Havelock, 152
Engels, Friedrich, 182, 185
Epicurus, 85

F

Fechner, Gustav, 11
Fink, David, 152
* Flugel, J. C., 35
* Flynn, Thomas V., 121
* Franz, Edward, 207
Freud, Sigmund, 11, 105, 184–185

G

* Gaffney, Mark A., 121
* Gilson, Etiénne, 207
* Gruender, Hubert, 266

H

* Hart, Charles A., 35
Hegel, Georg, 29

---

* Those names preceded by an asterisk are the names of authors whose works are listed in the bibliographies.

SUBJECT INDEX

W